Translation Practice

Translation Practices Explained is a series of course books designed to help self-learners and teachers of translation. Each volume focuses on a specific aspect of professional translation practice, in many cases corresponding to actual courses available in translator-training institutions. Special volumes are devoted to well consolidated professional areas, such as legal translation or European Union texts; to areas where labour-market demands are currently undergoing considerable growth, such as screen translation in its different forms; and to specific aspects of professional practices on which little teaching and learning material is available, the case of editing and revising, or electronic tools. The authors are practising translators or translator trainers in the fields concerned. Although specialists, they explain their professional insights in a manner accessible to the wider learning public.

These books start from the recognition that professional translation practices require something more than elaborate abstraction or fixed methodologies. They are located close to work on authentic texts, and encourage learners to proceed inductively, solving problems as they arise from examples and case studies.

Each volume includes activities and exercises designed to help self-learners consolidate their knowledge; teachers may also find these useful for direct application in class, or alternatively as the basis for the design and preparation of their own material. Updated reading lists and website addresses will also help individual learners gain further insight into the realities of professional practice.

Dorothy Kelly
Sara Laviosa
Series Editors

Subtitling through Speech Recognition

Respeaking

Pablo Romero-Fresco

LONDON AND NEW YORK

First published 2011 by St. Jerome Publishing

Published 2014 by Routledge
2 Park Square, Milton Park, Abingdon, Oxon OX14 4RN
711 Third Avenue, New York, NY 10017, USA

Routledge is an imprint of the Taylor & Francis Group, an informa business

© Pablo Romero-Fresco 2011

All rights reserved. No part of this book may be reprinted or reproduced or utilised in any form or by any electronic, mechanical, or other means, now known or hereafter invented, including photocopying and recording, or in any information storage or retrieval system, without permission in writing from the publishers.

Notices
Knowledge and best practice in this field are constantly changing. As new research and experience broaden our understanding, changes in research methods, professional practices, or medical treatment may become necessary.

Practitioners and researchers must always rely on their own experience and knowledge in evaluating and using any information, methods, compounds, or experiments described herein. In using such information or methods they should be mindful of their own safety and the safety of others, including parties for whom they have a professional responsibility.

To the fullest extent of the law, neither the Publisher nor the authors, contributors, or editors, assume any liability for any injury and/or damage to persons or property as a matter of products liability, negligence or otherwise, or from any use or operation of any methods, products, instructions, or ideas contained in the material herein.

ISBN 13: 978-1-905763-28-3 (pbk)
ISSN 1470-966X (Translation Practices Explained)

Typeset by
Delta Typesetters, Cairo, Egypt

British Library Cataloguing in Publication Data
A catalogue record of this book is available from the British Library

Library of Congress Cataloging-in-Publication Data
Romero-Fresco, Pablo.
  Subtitling through speech recognition : respeaking / Pablo Romero-Fresco.
    p. cm. -- (Translation practices explained)
  Includes bibliographical references and index.
  ISBN 978-1-905763-28-3 (pbk. : alk. paper)
  1. Translating and interpreting. I. Title.
  P306.R67 2011
  418'.02--dc22
                     2010054161

Subtitling through Speech Recognition: Respeaking

Pablo Romero-Fresco

Based on sound research and first-hand experience in the field, *Subtitling through Speech Recognition: Respeaking* is the first book to present a comprehensive overview of the production of subtitles through speech recognition in Europe. Topics covered include the origins of subtitling for the deaf and hard of hearing, the different methods used to provide live subtitles and the training and professional practice of respeaking around the world. The core of the book is devoted to elaborating an in-depth respeaking course, including the skills required before, during and after the respeaking process. The volume also offers detailed analysis of the reception of respeaking, featuring information about viewers' preferences, comprehension and perception of respoken subtitles obtained with eye-tracking technology.

An accompanying DVD features a wealth of video clips and documents designed to illustrate the material in the book and to serve as a basis for the exercises included at the end of each chapter. The working language of the book is English, but the DVD also contains sample material in Dutch, French, Galician, German, Italian and Spanish.

Subtitling through Speech Recognition: Respeaking is designed for use as a coursebook for classroom practice or as a handbook for self-learning. It will be of interest to undergraduate and postgraduate students as well as freelance and in-house language professionals. It will also find a reading public among broadcasters, cinema, theatre and museum managers, as well as the deaf and members of deaf associations, who may use the volume to support future campaigns and enhance the quality of the speech-to-text accessibility they provide to their members.

Pablo Romero-Fresco is a Senior Lecturer in Audiovisual Translation at Roehampton University, London, UK. He has worked as a respeaker for the National Gallery in the UK and has provided respeaking training to different universities and companies around the world. As a member of the research group TransMedia Catalonia, he has published and carried out research on dubbing, subtitling and audio-description, and has coordinated the subtitling part of DTV4ALL, an EU-funded research project exploring the possibility of providing a common standard for subtitling for the deaf and hard of hearing in Europe.

Contents

List of abbreviations, figures and tables
Contents of Accompanying DVD
Acknowledgements

How to Use this Book and DVD

1. Introduction to Respeaking	**1**
1.1 What is respeaking?	1
1.2. The name game	2
1.3. Discussion points	5
1.3.1. Definition	5
1.3.2. Respeaking terminology in English	5
1.3.3. Respeaking terminology in other languages	5
2. Live Subtitling	**6**
2.0. Introduction	6
2.1. Origins of SDH and live subtitling	6
2.2. Legislation and developments	9
2.3. Classification and methods	11
2.3.1. Programme type: live, as-live, pre-recorded	12
2.3.2. Production approach: live, semi-live, pre-recorded	12
2.3.3. Language: intralingual or interlingual	12
2.3.4. Transcription method: QWERTY, Velotype, dual, stenotype and SR (respeaking)	13
2.3.5. Correction method: no correction, self-correction, parallel correction	16
2.3.6. Editing policy: verbatim, reduced	16
2.3.7. Display mode: blocks, scrolling	17
2.3.8. SDH features: none, character ID, sound information	17
2.4. Discussion points and exercises	18
2.4.1. Legislation	18
2.4.2. Users	18
2.4.3. Guidelines	18
2.4.4. Different approaches to live subtitling	19
2.4.5. Assessment of live subtitles	20
3. Respeaking as a Professional Practice	**22**
3.0. Introduction	22
3.1. Respeaking on TV	22
3.1.1. Respeaking in the UK	22
3.1.1.1. Companies	22
3.1.1.2. Working conditions	23
3.1.1.3. Recruitment and training	24
3.1.1.4. Respoken subtitles	25

	3.1.2. Respeaking in Spain	27
	3.1.3. Respeaking in Flanders	28
	3.1.4. Respeaking in Switzerland	30
	3.1.5. Respeaking in Denmark	34
	3.1.6. Respeaking in France	35
	3.1.7. Respeaking in Italy	36
	3.1.8. Respeaking in Canada	37
	3.1.9. Voice Writing in the US	38
	3.2. Respeaking training at University	40
	3.2.1. Universitat Autònoma de Barcelona	40
	3.2.2. Roehampton University	41
	3.2.3. Higher Institute for Translation and Interpreting of Artesis University College (Antwerp, Belgium)	41
	3.3. Respeaking training in the US	42
	3.4. Discussion points and exercises	43
	3.4.1. Respeaking in the UK	43
	3.4.2. Respeaking in Flanders	43
	3.4.3. Respeaking in Switzerland and Italy	44
	3.4.4. Respeaking in Canada, France and the US	44
	3.4.5. Respeaking at University	44
4.	**Respeaking Skills**	**45**
	4.0. Introduction	45
	4.1. Respeaking and interpreting	45
	4.2. Respeaking and subtitling	47
	4.3. The specificity of respeaking	48
	4.4. Respeaking skills summarized	50
	4.5. Discussion points and exercises	55
	4.5.1. Respeaking skills as viewed by respeakers and employers	55
	4.5.2. Research	55
5.	**Respeaking Skills Applied before the Process I:** **General Knowledge of SR**	**56**
	5.0. Introduction	56
	5.1. How it works: main components and process	57
	5.1.1. Main components	57
	5.1.2. Process	58
	5.2. How it works for respeakers	60
	5.3. The origins of SR	61
	5.4. The present: state of the art and software available	63
	5.4.1. Viascribe	63
	5.4.2. Windows Speech Recognition	64
	5.4.3. ViaVoice	65
	5.4.4. Dragon NaturallySpeaking	66
	5.4.4.1. Dragon 10	66
	5.4.4.2. Dragon 11	68
	5.4.5. Speaker-independent SR: Google, LLC and MIT	69

	5.4.6. Subtitling software to use with SR	70
	5.4.7. Screencasting software to use with SR	70
	5.5. The future of SR	71
	5.6. Discussion points and exercises	71
	5.6.1. Viascribe	71
	5.6.2. Windows Speech Recognition, ViaVoice and Dragon	72
	5.6.3. Speaker-independent SR	72
	5.6.4. Automatic punctuation in SR	73
6.	**Respeaking Skills Applied before the Process II: Preparation of the Software - Respeaking with Dragon**	**74**
	6.0. Introduction	74
	6.1. Choosing and using a microphone	74
	6.1.1. Type of microphone	74
	6.1.2. Set up	75
	6.2. Creating a user profile	75
	6.3. Dictating to SR software	76
	6.4. Improving the user profile	78
	6.4.1. Speed settings: faster display in Dragon	78
	6.4.2. Initial dictation and use of commands	80
	6.4.3. How to correct errors	84
	6.4.4. Refining the acoustic model	86
	6.4.5. Refining the language model: customisation of the vocabulary	86
	6.4.5.1. Adding new words	86
	6.4.5.2. Adding words/phrases from lists	87
	6.4.5.3. Adding words from documents & adapting to writing style	88
	6.4.5.4. Use of macros: the vocabulary editor	89
	6.4.5.5. The Dragon Vocabulary Tool (Voctool) and the middle slot	92
	6.5. Dragon 11	92
	6.6. Exercises	93
	6.6.1. Creating a user profile	93
	6.6.2. Dictating to SR software and improving the user profile	94
7.	**Respeaking Skills Applied During the Process I**	**95**
	7.0. Introduction	95
	7.1. Split attention: dealing with simultaneous but non-overlapping inputs	95
	7.1.1. Listening and speaking (and listening again)	95
	7.1.2. Watching: reading and keeping the audiovisual coherence	97
	7.1.3. Typing	99
	7.1.4. Dealing with simultaneous but non-overlapping inputs	100
	7.2. Punctuation	101
	7.2.1. Automatic vs. non-automatic punctuation	101
	7.2.2. Punctuation in respeaking	102
	7.2.3. The use of the comma in respeaking	103
	7.3. Rhythm: respeaking units and the salami technique	107
	7.3.1. *Décalage* and units of meaning in interpreting	107
	7.3.2. Unit level: respeaking units	108
	7.3.3. Sentence level: the salami technique	109
	7.4. Speed: edited vs. verbatim respeaking	112
	7.4.1. More to speed than meets the eye: the parties involved	112
	7.4.2. Speech rates	114

	7.4.3. Reading rates	114
	7.4.4. Respeaking rates	116
	7.4.5. Edited vs. verbatim respeaking	118
	7.4.6. Training respeaking speed	119
	7.5. Exercises	120
	7.5.1. Split attention	120
	7.5.2. Punctuation	121
	7.5.3. Rhythm	121
	7.5.4. Speed	122

8. Respeaking Skills Applied during the Process II: Respeaking Different Genres — 123

- 8.0. Introduction — 123
- 8.1. Sports — 123
- 8.2. News — 125
  - 8.2.1. Headlines — 126
  - 8.2.2. News reports — 128
  - 8.2.3. Weather forecasts — 129
  - 8.2.4. News summary — 130
- 8.3. Interviews, debates and chat shows — 130
- 8.4. Exercises — 132
  - 8.4.1. Sports — 132
  - 8.4.2. News — 134
    - 8.4.2.1. Headlines — 134
    - 8.4.2.2. News — 134
    - 8.4.2.3. Weather — 135
    - 8.4.2.4. News Summary — 136
  - 8.4.3. Interviews and debates — 136

9. Respeaking Skills Applied during the Process III: Respeaking in other Settings — 138

- 9.0. Introduction — 138
- 9.1. Respeaking in museums and other arts venues — 138
- 9.2. Respeaking in the classroom — 142
- 9.3. Respeaking in conferences and churches — 143
- 9.4. Respeaking in live webcasts and telephones — 144
- 9.5. Discussion points and exercises — 146
  - 9.5.1. Respeaking in museums and other arts venues — 146
  - 9.5.2. Respeaking in the classroom — 147
  - 9.5.3. Respeaking in conferences, churches, live webcasts/telephones — 148

10. Respeaking Skills Applied after the Process: Accuracy Rate - the NERD model — 150

- 10.0. Introduction — 150
- 10.1. Basic requirements — 150
- 10.2. Traditional WER methods — 151
- 10.3. The CRIM method — 152
- 10.4. The NERD model — 152

	10.5. Application of the NERD model	154
	10.6. Exercises and discussion points	161

11. The Reception of Respeaking — **162**
    11.0. Introduction — 162
    11.1. Viewers' comprehension of respoken subtitles — 162
        11.1.1. Description of the experiment — 163
        11.1.2. Findings — 164
        11.1.3. Discussion — 165
    11.2 Viewers' perception of respoken subtitles — 166
        11.2.1. Eye-tracking and subtitling — 166
        11.2.2. Description of the experiment — 168
        11.2.3. Findings — 168
        11.2.4. Discussion — 169
    11.3. Viewers' opinion about respoken subtitles — 171
        11.3.1. Introduction — 171
        11.3.2. Description of the survey — 172
        11.3.3. Results of the survey — 173
    11.4. Discussion points and exercises — 175
        11.4.1. Processing subtitles: eye-tracking — 175
        11.4.2. The viewers' opinion — 176

12. Final Thoughts — **177**

Glossary — 179
References — 183
Index — 189

List of abbreviations, figures and tables

Abbreviations

Ms: milliseconds.
IMS: Independent Media Support.
RBM: Red Bee Media.
SDH: Subtitling for the deaf and hard of hearing.
SR: Speech recognition.
WER: Word error rate.
WPM: Words per minute.
WSR: Windows Speech Recognition.

Figures and tables

Figure 2.1:	Velotype	14
Figure 2.2:	Dual keyboard	14
Figure 2.3:	Five-way keyboard	14
Table 2.1:	Comparison of live subtitling methods	15
Table 3.1:	Voice writing vs. stenography	39
Table 4.1:	Taxonomy of respeaking skills	51
Figure 5.1:	The process of SR	59
Figure 5.2:	IBM Hosted Transcription Service Engine Controller	69
Table 6.1:	Different types of dictation	76
Figure 6.1:	Speed settings I	78
Figure 6.2:	Speed settings II	78
Figure 6.3:	NaturallySpeakometer	80
Figure 6.4:	Result box I	81
Figure 6.5:	Result box II	81
Figure 6.6:	Result box III	81
Figure 6.7:	Correction I	84
Figure 6.8:	Correction II	84
Figure 6.9:	Further training	86
Figure 6.10:	Adding new words	86
Figure 6.11:	Adding words from lists	87
Figure 6.12:	Vocabulary editor	89
Figure 6.13:	Word properties	90
Figure 7.1:	Deictics in respeaking I	97
Figure 7.2:	Moving subtitles	97
Figures 7.3 and 7.4:	Deictics in respeaking II	98
Figure 7.5:	Correction	98
Figures 7.6 and 7.7:	Segmentation in respeaking	109
Figure 7.8:	Comparison of original speech rate and respeakers' speech rate	116
Figure 7.9:	Original speech rate and respeakers' speech rate including punctuation marks	116

Figure 8.1: Sports I	123
Figure 8.2: Sports II	123
Figure 8.3: News I	126
Figure 8.4: News II	126
Figure 8.5: News III	126
Figure 8.6: News IV	128
Figure 8.7: Weather I	128
Figure 8.8: Weather II	129
Figure 8.9: Debates I	130
Figure 8.10: Debates II	130
Figure 8.11: Keypad	131
Figures 8.12 and 8.13: Correcting errors	131
Figures 9.1 and 9.2: Talk at the National Gallery	138
Figures 9.3 and 9.4: Respeaking at the National Gallery	138
Table 9.1: Results of the respeaking trial at the National Gallery	139
Figure 9.5: PDA for respeaking	140
Figure 9.6: Videoguide	141
Figure 9.7: Respeaking in live webcasts	144
Figure 9.8: CapTel	145
Figure 11.1: Hearing viewers with no subtitles	163
Table 11.1: Hearing viewers with no subtitles	163
Table 11.2: Hearing, hard of hearing and deaf viewers with subtitles at 220 wpm	163
Table 11.3: Hearing, hard of hearing and deaf viewers with subtitles at 180 wpm	164
Figures 11.2 and 11.3: Viewing patterns in pre-recorded subtitling	166
Table 11.4: Fixations with subtitles in blocks and scrolling	167
Table 11.5: Time spent on images with subtitles in blocks and scrolling	167
Figures 11.4, 11.5, 11.6 and 11.7: The quicksand effect	169
Figures 11.8 and 11.9: Regressions	169
Figures 11.10 and 11.11: Viewing pattern with block subtitles	170

Contents of Accompanying DVD

Acknowledgments
Readme File

Chapter 1
    1.3.1 Respeaking at IMS 1 (video)

Chapter 2
    2.4.1 EU-Written Declaration-2008 (pdf)
    2.4.2 Hearing Loss-Decibels and Effect of Spoken Words (pdf)
    Ofcom Study (pdf)
    Table on Hearing Loss (pdf)
    2.4.3 NCRA-Realtime Captioning Guidelines (pdf)
    Ofcom Guidelines 2006 (pdf)
    2.4.4 Live Captioning with Steno (pdf)
    Live Subtitling Methods 1 (video)
    Live Subtitling Methods 2 (video)
    2.4.5 BBC News (video)
    BBC Weather (video)
    Newsnight 1 (video)
    Realtime Captions – Spanish (video)
    Realtime Captions – Teletext (video)
    Realtime Captions (video)
    Sky News (video)

Chapter 3
    3.4.1 IMS Pic 1 (picture)
    IMS Pic 2 (picture)
    Red Bee Pic 1 (picture)
    Red Bee Pic 2 (picture)
    Respeaking at IMS 2 (video)
    Respeaking at the BBC-Red Bee (video)
    3.4.2 VTM Pic 1 (picture)
    VTM Pic 2 (picture)
    VTM Pic 3 (picture)
    VTM Video 1 (video)
    VTM Video 2 (video)
    VTM Video 3 (video)
    VTM Video 4 (video)
    3.4.3 Respeaking at Colby (video)
    Respeaking at Swiss TXT-RSI-La1 (video)
    Respeaking at Swiss TXT-SF Sports (video)
    Respeaking at Swiss TXT-SF (video)
    Respeaking at Swiss TXT (video)
    Swiss TXT – Add-on Phrase Mode (video)
    Swiss TXT – Add-on Sentence Mode (video)
    3.4.4. EclipseVox with Dragon (video)
    FR3 – Respoken Subtitles (video)

Respeaking at TF1 (video)
Respeaking at VTA (video)
TF1-Live subtitling Commercial (video)
3.4.5 Respeaking in Class – UAB (video)

Chapter 4
4.5.1 Colby-Live subtitling (pdf)
Descriptif du Poste Paris (pdf)
Journée Type (pdf)
Respeakers' Account-IMS (pdf)
Respeaker's Account-Red Bee (pdf)
Respeaking Job at Red Bee 1 (pdf)
Respeaking Job at Red Bee 2 (pdf)

Chapter 5
5.6.1 Viascribe 1 (video)
Viascribe 2 (video)
5.6.2 Dragon 1 (video)
Dragon 2 (video)
Viavoice 1 (video)
Viavoice 2 (video)
ViaVoice-Vista-Install (pdf)
WSR 1 (video)
WSR 2 (video)
5.6.3 Google vs IBM – Video (video)
Google vs IBM (pdf)
5.6.4 Automatic Punctuation (video)

Chapter 6
6.6.1 Creating a User Profile (video)
Dragon 10 – End-User Workbook (pdf)
Recommended Microphones (pdf)
Saving User Profile in Dragon (video)
ViaVoice – User Guide (pdf)
Windows Speech Recogniton – User Guide (pdf)
6.6.2 Dictation 1 (video)
Dictation 2 (video)
Dictation Practice 1 (pdf)
Dictation Practice 2 (pdf)
Dragon System Administrator Guide (pdf)
Dragon Voctool (pdf)
Editing and Correcting (video)
Knowbrainer – Dragon Speed Settings (pdf)
NaturallySpeakometer (zip)
Review of Dragon 11 (pdf)
Vocabulary Editor (video)

Chapter 7
7.5.1 Adam's Rib (pdf)

    I Have a Dream (pdf)
    Obama's Election Victory Speech 1 (pdf)
    Quiz Show (pdf)
    The Great Dictator (pdf)
    To Kill a Mockingbird (pdf)
7.5.2 BBC World News – Karin Giannone – Script (pdf)
    Obama's Election Victory Speech 2 (pdf)
7.5.3 BBC News 1982 (video)
    BBC News 1982 (pdf)
    Newsnight 2 (video)
    Newsnight 2 (pdf)
7.5.4 BBC News 24 - Wrong Guy – Transcript (pdf)
    BBC News 24-Wrong Guy (video)
    Film 2008-Jonathan Ross-Transcript (pdf)
    Film 2008-Jonathan Ross (video)

Chapter 8
8.4.1 Match of the Day 1 (video)
    Match of the Day 2 (video)
    Match of the Day 3 (video)
    Respeaking – South Africa (video)
    Wimbledon (video)
8.4.2 News
    BBC News – Chris Lowe (video)
    BBC News – Intro and Headlines (video)
    BBC News – Kasia Madera (video)
    BBC News – Summary 1 (video)
    BBC News – Summary 2 (video)
    BBC World News – Karin Giannone (video)
    BBC World News – Martine Croxall (video)
    Karin Giannone – BBC World News – Wordlist (txt)
    Weather
    Weather 1 (video)
    Weather 2 (video)
    Weather 3 (video)
    Weather Reviews 1 (pdf)
    Weather Reviews 2 (pdf)
8.4.3 Interview about Regional Accents (video)
    Interview with Michael Howard (video)
    Interview with Kara Tointon – Research (pdf)
    Interview with Kara Tointon (video)
    Interview with Nicola Roberts (video)

Chapter 9
9.5.1 Airscript (pdf)
    Caption Mic -Theatre Captioning (video)
    Stagetext (video)
9.5.2 Ai Training Program (pdf)
    Ai-Live 1 (video)

Ai-Live 2 (video)
Ai-Live Skills 1 (video)
Ai-Live Skills 2 (video)
Ai-Media Release 2 (pdf)
Ai-Media Release 1 (pdf)
Ai-Radio Interview (pdf)
Caption Mic 1 (video)
Caption Mic 2 (video)
Caption Mic 3 (video)
Caption Mic – Classroom (pdf)
Captionwrap (pdf)
Translation Lecture (video)
Viascribe 3 (video)
9.5.3 CapTel (video)
Caption Mic – Church (picture)
Caption Mic – Live Webcast (pdf)
Interlingual Respeaking – Vigo (video)
Roehampton 1 – Script (word)
Roehampton 1 (video)
Roehampton 2 – Script (word)
Roehampton 2 (video)
Roehampton 3 – Script (word)
Roehampton 3 (video)
Roehampton 4 – Script (word)
Roehampton 4 (video)
Roehampton 5 – Script (word)
Roehampton 5 (video)
Sprint CapTel (video)

Chapter 10
10.6 Application of the NERD Model (pdf)

Chapter 11
11.4.1 Eye Tracker 1 (video)
Eye Tracker 2 (video)
11.4.2 Complaints about Live Subtitling (pdf)
RNID - Live subtitles – Leaflet (pdf)
SDH in the UK – The Viewers' Preferences (pdf)
The Netherlands – Interlingual Subtitling 1 (video)
The Netherlands – Interlingual Subtitling 2 (video)
11.4.3 BBC Item on Respeaking (video)

Note: The videos included in this DVD can be played with the following free software: *Media Player Classic Home Cinema* (version v1.3.1774.0 or more recent), *VLC Media Player* (version 1.0.5 Goldeneye or more recent), *Real Player* (version 1.1.4 or more recent) and *Windows Media Player* (version 11.0.5271.5268 or more recent). It may be advisable to install an updated codec pack such as *K-Lite Codec Pack*, available online for free, to make sure the different video formats are supported. For further information about some of the above videos, see the 'Readme' file on the accompanying DVD.

Acknowledgements

I would like to express my gratitude to the many people who have helped me in the writing and editing of this book and DVD, be they colleagues in academia and the subtitling profession or professionals in other fields, as well as friends and family.

For giving me permission to use clips and pictures as well as other useful material: Keith Bain (Liberated Learning Consortium), Edward Collins, Robet Dube, Keith Hicks, Diane Bray and Sabela Melchor-Couto (Roehampton University), Evan Dorrestein (Subtext Language & Media), Vicky Mitchell (BBC) and Nick Tanton (BBC Research & Development), Anthony Pym (Universitat Rovira I Virgili), Rosa Vallverdú (TV3) and the staff at www.voicerecognition.com.au.

For their invaluable help with Chapter 3: Harry Carr (IMS) and Alison Marsh (Red Bee Media) in the UK, Patricia Martínez Zapico and Diana Sánchez (Mundovisión / Red Bee) in Spain, Veerle and Reinhilde Haverhals (VTM) and Aline Remael (Artesis University College) in Flanders, Gion Linder (SWISS TXT) in Switzerland, Pia Nothlev (TV2) in Denmark, Milena Diglio and Carlo Cafarella (Colby) in Italy, Karine Déry (TVA) and Pierre Dumouchel (CRIM) in Canada and Mark Hall (MHA), Chris Ales and Ardith Spies in the US.

For their collaboration in the projects mentioned in Chapter 9 and Chapter 11, thanks to James Buchanan (RNID), Tabitha Allum and Peter Pullan (Stagetext) and particularly to Jan-Louis Kruger, Fanny Lacroix and Esté Hefer (North-West University) for their warm welcome in South Africa.

For providing useful advice and practical help, Dick Bates, Mary Carroll (Titelbild), Frederic Chaume (Universitat Jaume I), Jorge Díaz-Cintas (Imperial College London), Carlo Eugeni (Intersteno), Elena di Giovanni (University of Macerata), Lourdes Lorenzo, Ana Pereira, Luis Alonso and Marta Dahlgren (Universidade de Vigo), Stephanie Moor and Tom Wootton (IMS), Tia Muller and Marta Arumí Ribas (Universitat Autonoma de Barcelona), Godefroy Saint-Georges and Scott Jarvie (www.scottjarvie.co.uk) and Agnieszka Szarkowska (University of Warsaw).

Special thanks are due to Juaniño Martínez (SWISS TXT) and everyone at TransMedia Catalonia, particularly Anna Matamala and Pilar Orero.

At Roehampton University: Lucile Desblache, Dionysis Kapsaskis, Andy Walker, Miguel Bernal-Merino, Lourdes Melción, Isabel Santaolalla and Elvira Antón.

Back in Galicia, for their help with the practical part of the book: Ángel Chino Casado, Pablo Babe Pulido, Luis Ruso Montenegro, Fer de Vega, Emilio Bianchi, Fernando Pandiani, Jorgiño and Assumpta, Paula, Daniel and Andreas, María Verónica, Andrés Torres and especially Beatriz and Antón Lampón.

I would also like to express my gratitude to Dorothy Kelly and Sara Laviosa, the series editors, and to Ken and Mona Baker for inviting me to write this contribution to the Translation Practices Explained series.

E por enriba de todo, á miña nai, ás miñas irmás e a Melch.

Saudiña,
Pablo Romero-Fresco
London, 2011

Note: This research is supported by a grant from the Spanish Ministry of Science and Innovation FFI2009-08027, Subtitling for the Deaf and Hard of Hearing and Audio Description: objective tests and future plans, and also by the Catalan Government funds 2009SGR700.

How to Use this Book and DVD

The book

Originating from the need to provide live subtitles on TV in order to meet legal requirements regarding accessibility for deaf and hard of hearing viewers, the professional practice of respeaking has not been accompanied by extensive research or publications in the field. This multimedia project aims to fill this gap, if only partially, and is intended first of all as a textbook for trainers and students wishing to master the fundamental aspects of respeaking, both from a theoretical and a practical point of view. Professionals working in the field of respeaking, be they trainers or practitioners, may also benefit from real-life material and numerous examples about how respeaking is currently used around the world. The book is also aimed at researchers working on Audiovisual Translation, who will find suggestions and examples of research carried out in the field of respeaking, as well as at cinema, theatre and museum managers, currently embarking on the challenging task of making their live events accessible to the hearing impaired through speech recognition. Finally, this book is also addressed to members of deaf associations, who may use it to support future campaigns and enhance the quality of the accessibility they provide to their members.

The twelve chapters of the book offer a graded approach to the training of respeakers. The book starts with an introduction to respeaking, a contextualization within the bigger picture of live subtitling and a description of how respeaking is currently carried out throughout the world. Then, the focus is placed on the skills required to respeak, depending on whether they are to be implemented before, during or after the process. Finally, the last part of the book tackles the quality of respoken subtitles from the point of view of the viewers as well as the future development of respeaking and live subtitling in general. The chapters are subdivided into sections and end with discussion points and exercises. The discussion points serve as a revision of the information provided in the chapter, test the readers' comprehension of this material and offer suggestions for further research. The exercises offer real respeaking practice and are often based on the videos included in the DVD. Although the book focuses mainly on the speech recognition software Dragon NaturallySpeaking, which is currently the most common software in the industry, the exercises included here can be done with any other speech recognition programme.

Chapter 1 presents a definition of respeaking and gives an account of the different terms used so far to refer to this discipline around the world. It also includes several criteria that can be applied to find or coin a term in those cases in which it hasn't been found yet. The chapter ends with a discussion about the definition of respeaking and the terminology used in English and other languages.

Chapter 2 tracks the origin of respeaking as a live subtitling method. After describing the origin of subtitling for the deaf and hard of hearing in general and live subtitling in particular, it provides an overview of the relevant legislation around the world. Secondly, a comparative analysis is presented of the different live subtitling methods used over the years, focusing on the key issues of delay, speed, accuracy, difficulty, cost and errors. The end of the chapter is devoted to a discussion on subtitling legislation, users, guidelines and methods as well as to the assessment of live subtitles as shown in several videos included in the DVD.

Chapter 3 focuses on respeaking as a professional practice, accounting for the differences across countries with regard to the respeakers' working conditions, their recruitment and training and the respoken subtitles they produce. It includes information about respeaking companies and practices in the UK, Spain, Flanders, Switzerland, Denmark, France, Italy, Canada and the US, as well as a section on respeaking training at university level. A discussion and a series of exercises are included at the end of the chapter to compare the different respeaking practices on the basis of the information provided in this chapter and the videos and pictures included in the DVD.

Chapter 4 deals with the different skills that are required to respeak, whether they come from interpreting, subtitling or are specific to respeaking and therefore new. These skills are in turn divided into skills applied before, during or after the process, which shapes the second part of the book, devoted to a software-based explanation on "how to respeak".

Chapter 5 deals with the first set of skills that must be developed and implemented before the process, namely those devoted to familiarization with speech recognition technology. After a brief explanation of how speech recognition works and how it is applied to respeaking, an overview is provided of the origins of this technology. This is followed by a description of the present state of the art, including software currently available for respeaking, and a section devoted to the future developments of this technology. The chapter ends with a series of discussions and exercises about the samples of different speech recognition programmes contained in the DVD.

Chapter 6 introduces readers to Dragon NaturallySpeaking, one of the speech recognition programmes that can be used to do the practical respeaking exercises included in this book. Information is provided, first of all, about how to choose and use a microphone for respeaking, how to create a user profile and how to dictate to speech recognition software. The second part of the chapter is devoted to the improvement of the user profile by adjusting speed settings, correcting errors and using the different tools available in the software to refine both the acoustic and the language model. The exercises included at the end of the chapter will help readers to create and develop their voice profiles and to prepare the software for the respeaking exercises presented in the next chapters.

Chapter 7 constitutes the core of the book and covers some of the most important skills to be implemented during the process of respeaking, namely the ability to split-attention, to dictate punctuation and to respeak with appropriate rhythm and speed. As far as split attention is concerned, the focus is placed first of all on the combination of listening and speaking, followed by reading and typing. The issue of punctuation is introduced with an overview of current discussions regarding the use of automatic and manual punctuation in speech recognition, followed by a description of the main conventions and, more specifically, the use of the comma in respeaking. The next section introduces readers to the notion of rhythm in respeaking, more specifically the use of respeaking units and the application of the salami technique. Finally, the last section deals with speed in respeaking, including information about original speech rates, viewers' reading rates and conventional respeaking speeds. Exercises and explanations are provided to allow readers to understand and practise all these skills.

Chapter 8 delves into the particularities of respeaking depending on the TV genre for which it is intended. The focus is placed in this case on sports, news and interviews, debates and chat shows. The chapter includes several respeaking exercises based on the videos included in the DVD.

Chapter 9, the last chapter devoted to the respeaking skills to be implemented during the process, presents the use of this technique in other settings, such as museums and arts venues, classrooms, conferences, churches, live webcasts and telephones. The corresponding section of the DVD includes examples of the use of respeaking in these settings and further exercises.

Chapter 10 deals with the skills to be applied after the process, namely those devoted to the calculation of accuracy in respeaking. Following a review of different methods used so far for this purpose, a new model is presented. Exercises and a series of discussion points are provided at the end of the chapter to test and critique this and other models.

Chapter 11 focuses on the reception of respoken subtitles. More specifically, it provides information about how viewers in the UK comprehend these subtitles, how they perceive them and what they think about them. Some of this information can be found in the video "BBC Item on Respeaking" (DVD > Chapter 11 > Discussion points and exercises > 11.4.3), which sums up many of the contents included in this book.

Chapter 12, the final one, points to possible developments in the field of respeaking and live subtitling in general.

The book ends with a glossary of terms used in respeaking, a list of bibliographical references and an index.

The DVD

The DVD will launch automatically and is divided into chapters and sections, following the structure of the book. The contents take up about 1.70 GB of disk space and consist of over 80 videos and practical appendices with exercises and information about companies, programmes and useful references. The material of the DVD is mainly relevant to the last part of every chapter, devoted to exercises and discussion points. However, some of the videos and documents serve to illustrate points made throughout the chapters.

1. Introduction to Respeaking

1.1. What is respeaking?

In general terms, **respeaking** may be defined as the production of subtitles by means of **speech recognition**. Yet, this is too broad to give an accurate idea of what respeaking entails. The problem here is that any attempt to provide a definition of respeaking is likely to be either too simplistic (falling short of accounting for its features and variations) or too cumbersome (trying to grasp its full scope). Be that as it may, this book needs a working definition as a starting point, so at the risk of falling into either trap, here is one:

> A technique in which a respeaker listens to the original sound of a live programme or event and respeaks it, including punctuation marks and some specific features for the deaf and hard of hearing audience, to a speech recognition software, which turns the recognized utterances into subtitles displayed on the screen with the shortest possible delay.

The terms that are underlined in this definition need further explanation, as they may only be telling part of the story:

- Live: respeaking is also being used nowadays for pre-recorded subtitling, due to the fast throughput it produces.
- Programme: see "subtitles" below.
- Respeak: depending on the case, this verb could mean to repeat, to rephrase or even to translate from one language to another. To start with, respeaking is mostly carried out intralingually. Respeakers are often encouraged to repeat the original soundtrack so as to produce verbatim subtitles. Yet, the high speech rate of the source text often makes it impossible for respeakers to follow the original soundtrack literally. This means they have to edit it, thus rephrasing it rather than repeating it. Finally, respeakers in Red Bee Media Wales or VTM (Flanders), to name but two examples, respeak interlingually from Welsh into English and from English into Dutch respectively.
- Features for the deaf and hard of hearing audience: the amount of extra information provided for deaf and hard of hearing viewers depends on many factors such as the channel, the programme, the respeaker, the time available, etc. Most respeakers introduce information to identify the different speakers and sometimes other extra-linguistic elements such as clapping, booing or laughing.
- Speech recognition software: respeaking usually involves two types of software. Firstly, there is a speech recognition (**SR**) application that recognizes the respeaker's utterances and can display them, for example, on an ordinary text application such as Microsoft Word. Then, this

speech recognizer is integrated into a subtitling application that shows the recognized utterances as subtitles on the screen.
- <u>Subtitles</u>: as will be explained in Chapter 9, respeaking is not only used to subtitle programmes on TV but also to provide speech-to-text-based accessibility (real-time transcription) in live events held in different venues such as museums, theatres, conferences and even churches. In these cases, for example in a gallery talk, the screen may not display images, but only the respoken utterances, which are then not exactly subtitles.
- <u>Minimum delay</u>: the delay may vary greatly depending on a number of factors including the software, the correction method or the subtitling mode. The delay in Windows Speech Recognition (WSR) is longer than in Dragon or ViaVoice; the correction method used by the French broadcasters TF1 and France 2, involving two people, causes longer delay than in other channels where respeakers correct their own mistakes; finally, when respeaking is used for pre-recorded subtitling and thus not intended for a live audience, a longer delay is not a problem at all.

1.2. The name game

One of the consequences of the very little research carried out so far in respeaking is the lack of established terminology to refer not only to the professionals engaged in this discipline but also to the discipline itself. As far as the English language is concerned, a quick look at some of the publications available yields several long and precise labels such as **speech-based live subtitling** (Lambourne *et al.* 2004), (*real time*) **speech recognition-based subtitling** and **real-time subtitling via speech recognition** (Eugeni 2008). Shorter alternatives such as **speech captioning** (see section 9.2) or **shadow speaking** (Boulianne *et al.* 2009) may be found in Australia and Canada, while in the USA, **revoicing** (Muzii 2006), **voice-writing** (Vincent 2007) and **realtime voice writing** (Keyes 2007) refer to the use of SR not only to produce live subtitles but also transcriptions in trials, classes and different types of public events. For all these alternatives, it seems that the term *respeaking* is rapidly consolidating both in the industry (Marsh 2006) and in academia (van der Veer 2007, Romero-Fresco 2008). As a matter of fact, in the same way that the term *audio-visual translation* has become a household name in Translation Studies and no longer seems to need a hyphen, *re-speaking* (Lambourne *et al.* 2004) has lost its hyphen as it has gained visibility.

Other languages present a different situation, the respeaking technique having consolidated much earlier than the terminology. As a result, there is a significant lack of consistency to refer to what has sometimes been branded as a "tâche sans nom" (Moussadek 2008), that is, a trade without a name.

In French, for example, there are long terms such as *sous-titrage en direct via le respeaking* (Imhauser 2007) or *sous-titrage pour sourds et malentendants en direct ou en temps réel*, used by the subtitling company Subbabel in their translated website. Yet, the most common terms have so far been *respeaking*, used in the

French-speaking Swiss channels TSR1 and TSR2, *sous-titrage vocal*, used in Red Bee Media France, and *la technique du perroquet*, used in TF1 and France 2. In the first two options, the professional is referred to as *respeaker* and *sous-titreur vocal* respectively. The third option refers to a slightly different approach, where a *perroquet* (parrot) or *rédacteur oral* does the respeaking, a *souffleur* (whisperer) suggests possible corrections and a *correcteur* implements changes and has the final say over what will be displayed on the screen.

In other European languages such as German, the calque *respeaking* seems to have prevailed so far, although in this case both *Re-speaking* and *Re-speaker* are written with initial upper case as per German spelling rules. In Italian, Eugeni (2006) proposed the term *rispeakeraggio* in an attempt to "adapt as much as possible to the morpho-syntactic rules of the Italian grammar" while avoiding both "yet another integral loan" and "ambiguous labels that may already be used to refer to similar or more generic techniques, such as *repetition* or *reformulation*". However, the direct calque *respeaking* has so far proved more common in the industry than *rispeakeraggio*. This discrepancy between academia and industry is also applicable to the Dutch language, particularly in Flanders, the Dutch-speaking part of Belgium, where *respeaken* is found in academic publications (van der Veer 2007) while TV channels and subtitling companies seem to have opted for the more general *live-ondertiteling*.

In the case of Spanish, researchers, professionals and the official institution responsible for regulating the Spanish language (Real Academia Española) seem to have agreed on a specific term (*rehablado*) for respeaking following the discussion and proposals presented in Romero-Fresco (2008). It may be useful, particularly for those languages where no consistent terminology has been coined, to go over the criteria used in this article, namely brevity, flexibility, naturalness and specificity.

- *Brevity*: whereas long and expository labels such as *real-time subtitling via speech recognition* may be good by way of introduction, they are not really functional. If a similar term is chosen in a language other than English, the need to find a shorter alternative may lead users to opt for the calque *respeaking*, which is already available.
- *Flexibility*: a well as the length, a key issue to make a name functional is the possibility of declining it into an adjective, a noun for the professional doing the respeaking and a verb. This is difficult if foreign languages adopt long terms or the calque *respeaking*, which would require the use of *respeaker, respoke, respoken*, etc.
- *Naturalness*: the term chosen may be a foreign form (*respeaking* in any language other than English), an adaptation (*rehablado* in Spanish) or a natural form (*reformulació simultània* in Catalan, as proposed by Termcat, a centre for the development of terminology in the Catalan language).
- *Specificity*: the term chosen may be specific (in this case a new term for

a new reality) or generic, such as *simultaneous reformulation*, which could be or has been used for something else.
- *Transparency*: the term chosen may be more or less self-explanatory. *Speech recognition-based live subtitling* is quite transparent, although also long and non-functional. *Respeaking*, in contrast, is more opaque.

In Spanish, some of the options considered were:

* *Subtitulación (en directo) por reconocimiento de habla*
([Live] subtitling by speech recognition):
long / not flexible / natural / specific / transparent
* *Respeaking*: short / not flexible / foreign / specific / opaque
* *Subtitulación interpretada* (Interpreted subtitling):
±short / not flexible / natural / specific / ±opaque
* *Interpretación (simultánea) subtitulada*
(Subtitled / Print interpreting)
± short / not flexible / natural / specific / ± transparent
* *Reformulación simultánea*
(Simultaneous reformulation)
± short / flexible / natural / generic / opaque
* *Rehablado / Subtitulación rehablada* (Respeaking / Respoken subtitling):
short / flexible / natural / specific / opaque

Given that the term in question is not a theoretical concept or a research notion but a professional technique used on a daily basis, usability is an important issue. In other words, it makes sense to consider brevity and flexibility over the other criteria. Specificity can be considered next, as it is important to avoid terms that may be used for other techniques or activities; naturalness could follow, in the sense that it may be advisable (though not essential) to have a natural term. Finally, transparency is probably the least important criterion. After all, the term *respeaking* is not transparent in English, as is often the case with new terms coining new realities.

On the basis of this discussion, the term chosen in Romero-Fresco (2008) is *rehablado*, as usable as *reformulación simultánea* but also more specific. The Real Academia Española seems to have given its blessing to this choice:

> We accept the calque *rehablado* (as well as the family *rehablar, rehablador*) which, as compared to *reformulación simultánea* [simultaneous reformulation], is closer to the English term and therefore more recognizable.
> (in Romero-Fresco 2008:59-60; my translation)

What is interesting here beyond the purely terminological debate is the notion of respeaking underlying every label. Is respeaking closer to a repetition of the source text or to a reformulation? More importantly, in the light of proposals such as *subtitulación interpretada* or *interpretación subtitulada*, is respeaking closer to interpreting or to subtitling? Chapters 3 and 4 will provide more information on this issue, which, far from being a merely theoretical ivory-tower discussion, lies at the root of the current professional consideration of this new discipline and has important professional and financial implications. Yet, it is important first of all to trace back the origins of respeaking and contextualize it as a type of **live subtitling**, an issue which will be dealt with in the next chapter.

1.3. Discussion points

1.3.1. Definition

In the light of the information presented in this chapter and the video "Respeaking at IMS 1" (included in DVD > Chapter 1 > Discussion points > 1.3.1), can you provide a comprehensive definition of respeaking covering all the aspects involved in this technique?

1.3.2. Respeaking terminology in English

With the benefit of hindsight and given that many things may have changed regarding terminology, what terms are nowadays used in English? Is there still a noticeable difference between British and American terminology? Are different terms being used for respeaking on TV and in public events?

Assess the terms you have found using the parameters provided in this chapter (brevity, flexibility, naturalness, specificity and transparency).

1.3.3. Respeaking terminology in other languages

How has terminology evolved in the languages mentioned in this chapter? And in other languages? Assess the terms you have found using the parameters provided in this chapter and suggest alternatives in your own languages.

2. Live Subtitling

2.0. Introduction

Respeaking, as implemented firstly by VRT (Belgium) and the BBC (UK) in 2001, was conceived as a method to produce real-time subtitles, which are a specific type of subtitles for the deaf and hard of hearing (**SDH**) used for live programmes. Taking this background into consideration, this chapter offers first of all a brief account of the origins of SDH and live subtitling as well as the legislation in place in different countries. It then goes on to describe and compare different live subtitling methods, including respeaking.

2.1. Origins of SDH and live subtitling[1]

The origins of SDH were very different in the US and in Europe. In the US, after some initial experiments in the late 40s, the 50s and the 60s (Neves 2005), the real breakthrough happened in 1971, with the First National Conference on Television for the Hearing Impaired hosted in Nashville, Tennessee. In this conference, broadcasters, producers, viewers and other parties involved had the opportunity to see and discuss the potential technology for the provision of **captions** on TV. In 1971, *The French Chef* became the first television programme to be captioned in the US and in 1973 PBS rebroadcast the ABC News with captions, thus becoming the first news bulletin to be accessible for the deaf and hard of hearing viewers. In both cases, the captions were **open**, that is, burned on the images and always visible on the screen. **Closed captions**, not visible on the screen unless activated by a decoder, were first introduced on 16 March 1980 using the Telecaption Adaptor, a decoding unit that could be connected to a TV set. According to the National Captioning Institute, the first programmes to be seen with closed captions were the ABC *Sunday Night Movie*, *Semi-Tough*, the Disney feature *Son of Flubber* on NBC and *Masterpiece Theatre* on PBS.

In Europe, the beginning of SDH is inextricably linked with television, the teletext and more specifically with the BBC, which announced its Ceefax Teletext service in 1972 and started providing SDH in 1979. In the same year, France 2 subtitled a weather forecast programme with the so-called ANTIOPE system, also teletext-based. In the rest of Europe, most countries started providing SDH in the 1980s. Germany, for instance, started on 1 June 1980 with a project launched by the two public broadcasters ARD and ZDF. In Flanders, the Dutch-speaking part of Belgium, SDH was introduced by the public channel VRT in 1983, mostly for sports programmes. Italy started three years later, on 5 May 1986, when RAI 1

---

[1] This section draws heavily on Remael (2007) as well as on information obtained in personal communication with Joselia Neves (Portugal), Carlo Eugeni (Italy), Tia Muller (France) and Pilar Orero and Verónica Arnáiz (Spain).

subtitled the Italian-dubbed version of Alfred Hitchcock's *Rear Window*. Spain and Portugal joined this group in the 1990s. In Spain, the first channel to provide SDH was the Catalan TV corporation CCRTV, which was later on joined by the state-owned channel TVE and gradually by other channels. In Portugal, an agreement signed between the Portuguese government, the national broadcaster RTP and the national association for the Deaf (*Associação Portuguesa de Surdos*) led to the introduction of SDH on 15 April 1999.

As in the case of SDH, the introduction of live subtitling also varied considerably across countries. In the US, the National Captioning Institute developed its real-time captioning service in 1982. Court reporters, who used **steno** machines to transcribe speech in hearings, depositions and other official proceedings, were re-trained to caption newscasts, sports and other live programmes. As for respeaking, known in the US as voice writing or realtime voice writing, its origins may be traced back to the experiments conducted by court reporter Horace Webb, who explains (NVRA 2008) that "the system was born in a Chicago courtroom in the early forties. Its father was a pen shorthand reporter and its mother frustration". Up until then, reporters took shorthand notes of the speech in court and then dictated their notes for transcription into typewritten form: approximately two hours of dictation for every hour spent in court. Attempts were made to use microphones in the courtrooms in order to record all voices directly for later transcription, but the noise and the overlapping interventions made it impossible. Webb proposed to have the reporter repeat every word of the original speech into a microphone using a stenomask to cancel the noise. The subsequent recording of the reporter's words would then be used for transcription. Although no SR was used at the time and no live transcription was provided, the basic principle of respeaking was already applied. Webb's method is now known as stenomasking or as voice writing, and may thus be seen as the precursor of respeaking or realtime voice writing, which involves the same technique using SR software for the production of captions and transcriptions in courtrooms, classrooms, meetings and other settings. Realtime voice writing was first used in 1999 by court reporter Chris Ales, who used Dragon NaturallySpeaking to transcribe a session in the Circuit Court in Lapeer, Michigan. For TV captioning, it was introduced in the US in 2003 by Chris Ales and Mark Hall Associates in news and Home Shopping Network respectively.

In Europe, the first experiments regarding live subtitling were conducted in the UK and Flanders. In 1982, the British channel ITV began to subtitle headlines of public events such as a visit of the Pope or the football World Cup using a standard QWERTY keyboard. In 1987, given that this method was not fast enough, ITV started using the so-called **Velotype**, a syllabic keyboard developed in the Netherlands which allowed subtitlers to produce between 90 and 120 words per minute (**wpm**) after a training period of 12 months. Also in 1987, ITV set up its own live subtitling unit, focusing on news programmes. Experiments were then conducted to test a **tandem** method whereby two subtitlers would share the workload in a given programme. This approach increased speed up to somewhere in between 120 and 160 wpm, much closer to the 180-wpm standard speech rate of news presenters in the UK. In 1990, the BBC set up its own live subtitling unit, resorting firstly to keyboards and then to steno. Following what the National Captioning Institute had done in the US in 1982, the BBC hired professional stenotypists to increase the speed of the subtitles. The result was very satisfactory – live verbatim subtitles at up to 220-250 wpm, in other words, suitable for news programmes. The problem, however, was that the training required to become a stenotypist, between three and four years long, made this method particularly expensive. Looking for an alternative, Damper *et al.* proposed in 1985 the use of SR combined with keyboards to change the colour and position of live subtitles. However, SR technology was still not up to scratch, and its use for subtitling was postponed for over a decade, until 1998, when it was investigated again by Synapsys Ltd. (now Sysmedia) and University of Hertfordshire. Encouraged by the results obtained in this and other similar projects, the BBC finally decided to test respeaking in April 2001 with the World Snooker Championship. This was followed by Wimbledon, other important sports events and later on by parliament sessions, regional news and national news on BBC News 24.

Another early start is that of Flanders. Live subtitles were tested by VRT in 1981 and first broadcast in 1982. Initially, one person would dictate the text and another would type the subtitles as fast as possible. The second method tested was Velotype (1998-1999) but it never went into production. SR was introduced in 2000 and the first respoken subtitles were produced in spring 2001. Today, respeaking seems to have taken over as the preferred method not only in public channels such as VRT but also in private channels like VTM. In Germany, live subtitles were introduced by ARD for the popular news and public affairs programme *Tagesschau* in 1984. Since then, although different methods have been tested, keyboards (mostly in tandem) and now respeaking seem to be the preferred methods. France started a year later, in 1985, when the French broadcaster Antenne 2 provided live subtitles for a rugby tournament as well as for Wimbledon. Since then, at least three different methods have been tested: steno, velotype and respeaking. Used for the first time by M6 and TF1 in March and April 2007 respectively, respeaking is often approached very differently to what has been described so far (see Chapter 3).

Other countries such as Italy and Spain have been much slower in the introduction of live subtitles. Italy started in 2000, when RAI used steno to subtitle the 17.00 news, the 20.30 news and the Angelus. Respeaking was introduced much later, on 7 July 2008, in this case by RAI 3 using the Colby live subtitling unit for the gossip show *Cominciamo bene estate*. In Spain, the first subtitles for live programmes were provided by TV3 in Catalonia in 1990. Yet, these were actually **semi-live subtitles**. Although the programmes (*Trenta minuts* and *Entre línies*) were broadcast live, the subtitles were prepared in advance (since the scripts were available beforehand) and released in real-time. The national broadcaster RTVE also adopted this semi-live approach for many of its news programmes, such as

Telediario Primera Edición and *Telediario Fin de Semana*. In 2000, TV3 developed its own technology to provide live subtitles. As explained by Orero (2006),

> The system allows multiplexing of five operators with QWERTY keyboards, and uses a sort of 'traffic light' to organize their workflow: when the screen shows the green light, the operator types what he hears through the headphones; when the red light appears, he stops writing.

Given that no effective SR software has been developed in Catalan to date, respeaking is still not an option. In TVE, however, respeaking was first tested in Spanish in 2004 and used only for non-scripted parts of the news such as certain items delivered by foreign correspondents. Regular provision of live subtitles was not a reality until 2008, when Mundovisión, a Red Bee Media company, set up a respeaking unit to provide subtitles for programmes such as *Gente* or *59 Segundos*.

2.2. Legislation and developments

According to Remael (2007:25), the speed with which developments in SDH in general and live subtitling in particular are taking place has usually tied in with "new legislation or other forms of agreement brokered between governments and, for instance, public broadcasting channels, following constant pressure from the deaf and hard of hearing organisations". These developments are also boosted by hard data, such as the fact that in the US, nearly 10 million people are hard of hearing and close to 1 million are functionally deaf, that is, unable to hear a normal conversation even with the use of a hearing aid. In Europe, people with disabilities constitute about 15% of the European population and whereas 18% of the European population was aged over 60 in 1990, this is expected to rise to 30% by 2030.[2] In the light of this situation, different types of legislation have been passed.

In the US, the Television Decoder Circuitry Act in 1990 required all television receivers with screens 13 inches or larger to be capable of displaying closed captions. Since this act failed to provide a substantial increase in captioning, the Congress intervened again with the Telecommunications Act of 1996, which directed the Federal Commmunications Commission to develop a timetable for phasing in mandatory captioning. The result is that from 2006, and with very few exceptions, all television programming, whether in English or Spanish, must be captioned. Also relevant in this sense is the Americans with Disabilities Act (1990), which gives deaf and hard of hearing people the right to request access to real-time transcription in classrooms and public events by viewing text on computer monitors or large display screens.

---

[2] Communication from the Commission to the Council, the European Parliament and the European Economic and Social Committee and the Committee of the Regions: eAccessibility [SEC(2005)1095] Brussels, 13.9.2005 COM(2005) 425 final.

In Europe, two important pieces of legislation are Television Without Frontiers (1989, updated in 1997) and the written declaration issued by the European Parliament on 26 February 2008[3] calling on the Commission to put forward "a legislative proposal requiring public-service television broadcasters in the EU to subtitle all of their programmes". Specific mention is made in this declaration of the potential of subtitles to "help with foreign-language learning". Indeed, independent user research conducted for the Office of Communications (Ofcom) in the UK in 2006[4] shows that out of 7.5 million people using subtitles to watch television, 6 million do not have a hearing impairment.

As well as European directives, there is also national legislation requiring SDH on television. In the UK, the 1990 Broadcasting Act stated that all major television companies had to increase their subtitle output to 90% by 2010. This has been followed by a series of Acts of Parliament which have extended the scope of the initial act to non-terrestrial broadcasters. According to these acts, Ofcom is to be the independent regulator to ensure that the provision of access services is met as stipulated in the Code on Television Access Services. The first report for 2011 shows that most broadcasters are exceeding their quotas for subtitling as well as for audiodescription and signing. Since April 2008, the BBC subtitles all its programmes (50,000-60,000 hours a year), which includes some 20,000-25,000 hours of live subtitles, one third with steno and two thirds with respeaking.

In Flanders, developments in relation with SDH are being facilitated by local pressure from interest groups, the very positive attitude of the Flemish public television's Teletext subtitling team, the interest taken in media accessibility by some politicians and the training programmes and research developed at institutions such as Artesis University College. Until recently, media accessibility legislation in Flanders applied only to the public channel VRT. A management contract (Media Decree) between VRT and the Flemish government from 2006 stated that VRT should aim at providing SDH for 95% of all Flemish programmes by 2010. On 18 March 2009, however, an amendment was passed during the plenary vote in Flemish Parliament thanks to the pressure put by the MP's Helga Stevens (N-VA, who is deaf) and Bart Caron. According to this amendment, private or commercial television broadcasters are also required to provide SDH. From 1 January 2010 or from the moment that private television broadcasters achieve a market share of 2% during a period of 6 consecutive months, they must meet the following requirements: complete subtitling of the main newscast within 12 months and complete subtitling of all news broadcasts and 90% of all news programmes or current affairs programmes within 36 months. Needless to say, most of these programmes require live subtitling.

In Germany, the situation is different. To date, no legislation has been passed requiring broadcasters to meet specific SDH quotas. Yet, an Act known as Gesetz

---

[3] Written declaration pursuant to Rule 116 of the Rules of Procedure by Lidia Joanna Geringer de Oedenberg on the subtitling of all public-service television programmes in the EU.
[4] http://stakeholders.ofcom.org.uk/consultations/accessservs/summary

zur Gleichstellung behinderter Menschen und zur Änderung anderer Gesetze (1 May 2002) grants deaf associations the right to negotiate with enterprises and other bodies the possibility of drawing up "target agreements" and improving access. Resulting from this, regional public broadcasters are under pressure to increase their provision of SDH and some of them have even set self-imposed agreements to increase their accessibility services.

In Italy, the so-called Stanca law (9 January 2004), although focused mainly on IT accessibility, requires national broadcasters to increase their volume of subtitled programmes and to make most of their services accessible. Moreover, every two or three years, an agreement is signed between the government and RAI (the main state-owned **public service broadcaster** in Italy) stipulating the SDH quota to be met in the following years. According to their 2006 agreement, RAI was to subtitle 60% of their programmes by the end of 2009. As far as live subtitling is concerned, although steno is still used, most national broadcasters are now resorting to respeaking.

In Spain, SDH was provided on a voluntary basis until 2001, when the Ley de Fomento y Promoción de la Cinematografía y el Sector Audiovisual (10 July 2001) was passed offering subsidies for films with SDH and audiodescription. However, proper SDH quotas were not set until 16 October 2009, when the Ley General Audiovisual required public channels and other national broadcasters to subtitle 90% and 75% of their programmes respectively by 2013.

In France, the first law regarding SDH was passed in 2000. It was an amendment of a 1986 law on communications liberties and it set obligations for public and commercial broadcasters to start making their programmes accessible (7% of their annual broadcasting from 2002). In 2005, a new law was passed requiring that TV broadcasters with a minimum audience share of 2.5% make accessible 100% of their programmes for the deaf and hard of hearing by 2010 either via subtitles or sign language (Muller 2009). With a similar role to Ofcom in the UK, the Conseil Supérieur de l'Audiovisuel (CSA) is the regulatory authority in charge of publishing the amount of hours subtitled by every channel throughout the year. According to 2008 figures, broadcasters subtitled 59% of their programmes (25,789 hours). This is a considerable increase in comparison to the 10% subtitled in 2002 but it is still far from the 100% requirement for 2010.

2.3. Classification and methods

As seen in the previous two sections, there are different approaches to live subtitling. Although this book is mainly concerned with respeaking, it is important to have a look at these methods, not least to determine where respeaking fits in the bigger (live) subtitling picture and how it compares to other approaches. Drawing on Lambourne (2007), this section includes a set of criteria to classify live subtitling not only on the basis of the production method (Velotype, stenotype, SR, etc.) but also other relevant criteria.

2.3.1. Programme type: live, as-live, pre-recorded

Live television refers to television broadcast in real time. Although it was more common in the early years of television, when video recording was not prevalent, it is still used for news, sports, awards programmes, etc.

As-live programmes are those which feature a broadcast delay, also known as tape delay. This is used to prevent material deemed undesirable from making it to air, namely technical malfunctions, coughing or profanity. The latter is known as seven-second delay or profanity delay. Shows broadcast in this as-live mode include the Academy Awards in the US and *Big Brother* in the UK, which has been broadcast on E4 with a 10-15 minute delay since 2001.

Finally, not much needs to be said about pre-recorded programmes, which constitute the majority of the content shown on TV and are edited before going on air.

2.3.2. Production approach: live, semi-live, pre-recorded

Live subtitling is, according to the European Broadcasting Union (EBU) (2004:10), the most ambitious type of subtitling, where "the live subtitler seeks to understand the context of the programme in advance" and then, on transmission, "creates the subtitles in real-time". This is the case in news programmes, sports, live discussions and parliamentary proceedings. The EBU highlights the similarity between a simultaneous interpreter and a live subtitler, and adds that the latter may be "a stenographer who writes phonetic shorthand at a special keyboard, a velotypist who types words at a special keyboard" or "a respeaker who uses speech recognition to generate subtitles" (*ibid.*).

Semi-live or as-live subtitling is often used for live programmes which are heavily scripted and include pre-edited segments such as interviews, archive footage or items from previous bulletins. In this case, "the subtitler creates a list of subtitles, without time-codes, and during transmission **cues** these manually in sync with the programme" (EBU 2004:10). Semi-live subtitling is often used in news programmes (when the scripts are available in advance), but also in other contexts such as the theatre and the opera.

Finally, pre-recorded subtitling, also known as off-line or pre-prepared subtitling, is the standard mode of subtitling as defined and explained by Díaz Cintas and Remael (2007). In this case, subtitles are prepared beforehand "with precise in and out timecodes, based on the speech in each time period" (EBU 2004:10).

2.3.3. Language: intralingual or interlingual

As explained in Chapter 1, live subtitling has so far been done mostly **intralingually**, in other words, not involving language transfer in the traditional sense. Yet, over the past years, instances of **interlingual** live subtitling have become more and more common. In some cases, this is due to the particular (multi)linguistic reality of a given area, such as Wales, where live programmes in Welsh are often subtitled into English. In other cases, interlingual live subtitling is used as a means to access important events conducted in a foreign country/language. Broadcasters in countries such as Denmark, Belgium and the Netherlands often provide their viewers with live subtitles in Danish and Dutch for relevant events such as campaign debates or important speeches. President Obama's inauguration speech, delivered on 20 January 2009, was respoken live into Danish by TV2 and into Dutch by VRT and VTM. In the Netherlands, channels are on these occasions allowed to broadcast their signal with a 10-second delay, which enables them to provide perfectly synchronized subtitles without errors. This use of the antenna delay (the only way found so far to produce error-free, perfectly cued subtitles for live programmes) is very sensitive and not popular at all among broadcasters and producers, as it brings about issues of competition among channels and even censorship. Be that as it may, many of these issues could be solved if the decision to have or not have the signal delayed was taken at the viewers' end (see Chapter 12).

2.3.4. Transcription method: QWERTY, Velotype, dual, stenotype and SR (respeaking)

Used by ITV in the UK in 1982 to subtitle headlines of a visit of the Pope and the football World Cup, standard QWERTY keyboards were quickly dismissed as too slow. Although some expert typists may work at speeds above 120 wpm, average professional typists are expected to reach 50 to 70 wpm and advanced typists between 80 and 100 wpm. These figures are always far from the average speech rate of TV presenters, in the region of 180 wpm.

With a view to increasing the typists' speed, Nico Berkelmans and Marius den Outer invented the Velotype, currently known as Veyboard. This is a syllabic chord keyboard which allows the user to press several keys simultaneously, producing syllables and words rather than letters. Although speeds of 200 wpm have been recorded using Velotype, the average sustained speed for live subtitling using this method after a 12-month training period seems to be around 90-120 wpm (Lambourne et al. 2004).

Another method is the so-called tandem or **dual keyboard**, where two operators take turns to transcribe alternate utterances, for instance subtitling a sentence each or even completing each other's sentences. Used by ITV in 1987 and later on by Titelbild in Germany, this approach can yield high quality edited real-time subtitling (Lambourne *et al.* 2004) at up to 150 wpm after 6 months training. As explained above, the Catalan broadcaster TV3 has modified this tandem method to allow multiplexing of five subtitlers using QWERTY keyboards.

Before describing the next method, the stenotype, a brief comment is in order regarding terminology. In the literature on live subtitling, the terms *stenography*

Figure 2.1: Velotype

Figure 2.2: Dual keyboard

Figure 2.3: Five-way keyboard

(Marsh 2006) and *stenotypy* (Lambourne 2006) are often used interchangeably. Yet, they are not synonyms. Coming from the Greek *stenos* (narrow) and *graphein* (to write), stenography is defined by the *Merriam-Webster's Online Dictionary* as "the art or process of writing in shorthand". Stenotypy is, according to the *Encyclopaedia Britannica*, "a system of machine shorthand in which letters or groups of letters phonetically represent syllables, words, phrases, and punctuation marks". In other words, stenotypy is effectively a machine-based type of stenography.

The direct ancestor of today's stenotype was created by Ward Stone Ireland in the early 20th century (dates vary between 1906 and 1911) but the first stenotype-like machine was built by Karl Drais as early as 1830. Like the Velotype, the stenotype is a chording system, that is, the operator can press multiple keys simultaneously to spell out whole syllables, words and phrases with a single hand motion. Unlike the Velotype, though, the stenotype does not feature all the letters in the English alphabet and so letter combinations are substituted for the missing letters.

The use of the stenotype is particularly frequent in court reporting, where high transcription speed is of the essence. Trained court reporters are expected to reach speeds of 200-250 wpm and it is not unusual to find advanced users who can go over 300 wpm. This is what has led many broadcasters (not only the BBC in the UK, but also others in countries such as Italy and Spain) to use this technique in live subtitling. The main advantage is clear: it allows accurate subtitling of just about any audiovisual genre, including fast-paced interviews and debates. The results obtained with stenotype are yet to be matched by those obtained with respeaking or any other transcription method. The downside, however, is the 2-to-4-year training required to master the technique, which makes it particularly expensive. More information about how steno-based subtitling works can be found in the document "Live Captioning with Steno" (DVD > Chapter 2 > Discussion points and exercises > 2.4.4).

The last method, SR-based subtitling or respeaking, has been defined in Chapter 1 and will be further characterized throughout the book, so no more needs to be added at this stage. Before moving on to the next criteria, though, it may be interesting to have a look at Lambourne's (2007) table comparing the above-described methods not only on the basis of their speed, but also other relevant factors such as delay, accuracy, training required, cost and seriousness of errors. Standard QWERTY keyboard is not included, as it is no longer commonly used in live subtitling:

	Delay	Speed (wpm)	Accuracy	Training	Cost	Seriousness of errors
Velotype	Medium	Medium (90-120)	95%	12 months	Medium	High
Dual keyb	Medium	Medium/ High 140-150	95-98%	6 months	Medium	Low
Stenotype	Low	Very high 220 - up to 300	97-98%	3 years	High	Medium
Respeaking	Low	High 160-190	97-98%	2-3 months	Low	Medium-High

Table 2.1: Comparison of live subtitling methods

2.3.5. Correction method: no correction, self-correction, parallel correction

Corrections in live subtitling and more specifically in respeaking will be covered throughout this book from many different angles: how they are done and displayed (Chapter 3), what they entail for the respeakers (Chapter 7) and how they are received by the viewers (Chapter 11).

For now, suffice it to say that there are three main methods (no correction, self-correction, parallel correction), the choice of which depends on whether the priority is to provide correct subtitles or to reduce the delay of the subtitles with regard to the images and the audio. The first method, no correction, is not very common, but it is the approach chosen by TVA in Canada. The stress is placed in this case on reducing the delay even at the expense of having more errors in the subtitles.

The most common approach is self-correction. Subtitlers correct their own mistakes live after they have been displayed on the screen. Although the way to go about this varies across companies and countries, the most common practice is to introduce the correct word after the error followed by a hyphen. Once the correction is complete, subtitlers carry on with the programme. Although there is some delay involved, it is always smaller than in parallel correction. On the downside, self-correction places extra strain on the already challenging task performed by the live subtitler.

Finally, parallel correction clearly favours the correctness of the final subtitles over their speed of display. Corrections may be done by a one person (VTM in Flanders) or even two people (France 2 and TF1 in France) before the subtitles are released on air. This leads to error-free subtitles with delays of up to 15 seconds in the case of the French broadcasters.

2.3.6. Editing policy: verbatim, reduced

Live subtitles may be verbatim (conveying 100% of the original soundtrack) or reduced (offering a version that has been summarized to some extent). Far from being a mere technical issue, this is one of the long-standing bones of contention in SDH, where it has political, ideological and financial connotations (see Chapter 7).

For now, it may be useful to make a distinction between what is preferred and what is possible. As for preferences, broadcasters, companies and deaf associations seem to choose verbatim (and therefore faster) subtitles, whereas academics and researchers usually prefer edited (and slower) subtitles (Romero-Fresco 2009). An explanation for this is provided in section 7.4.1. Yet, a closer look at what is actually possible in terms of subtitling speed reveals that only stenotyping can cope with the current speech rates of 180-220 wpm found in many live programmes. This explains why the most common type of live subtitling as far as editing policy is concerned is near-verbatim subtitling, that is, as verbatim as possible but often failing to convey 100% of the original soundtrack.

2.3.7. Display mode: blocks, scrolling

Although the main distinction is made here between live subtitles displayed in blocks and scrolling, each mode allows for further variation. Thus, subtitles may be displayed in blocks of one, two or three lines, or even in phrases or sentences (see 3.1.4). In turn, scrolling subtitles may be displayed letter by letter, syllable by syllable or word by word, as is often the case in respeaking. The choice depends, from a strictly technical point of view, on the SR software used. ViaVoice, for example, features a word-for-word display mode, whereas Dragon NaturallySpeaking displays utterances in blocks. Very often, the subtitling software used along with the speech recognizer allows users to change the display mode to suit their needs.

Yet, it is the subtitling companies or often the broadcasters who have the final say regarding the display mode of live subtitles. This is decided on the basis of different factors such as delay, accuracy, ease of reading and the viewers' preferences and habits. More information about the different display modes and what they entail for the viewers may be found in chapters 3 and 11.

2.3.8. SDH features: none, character ID, sound information

Pre-recorded SDH often includes a series of features that may not be found in subtitles for hearing viewers (Neves 2005). This is usually information about the tone or volume of the speakers' utterances (angry, sad, low, loud), sound effects (steps, gunfire, explosion), music (rock music, funky beats) and character identification, which can be done by means of name tags, colours or displacement, that is, positioning the subtitle under the speaker. The time constraints involved in live subtitling make it virtually impossible to include all this information. Subtitlers must thus choose what is essential and what is not. Typically, live subtitles provide some information about sound (crowd cheering, applause, etc.) and speaker identification (with colours or labels, as displacement is difficult in a live environment). Yet, as may be seen in Chapter 3, this is not always the case.

Having described the eight proposed criteria to classify live subtitles, the next step is to apply this taxonomy to the subtitles currently produced in different countries. This will be done in Chapter 3 as follows: (2) (6) (3) (4) subtitles with (5) correction displayed in (7) mode with (8) for a (1) programme. Thus, to name but one example, the subtitles currently shown in the BBC News in the UK are live near-verbatim intralingual respoken subtitles with self correction, displayed in scrolling mode[5] with character identification and sound information for live and as-live programmes.

---

[5] As explained in Chapter 3, plans are afoot to replace ViaVoice, the speech recognition software currently used by RBM in the UK, with Dragon NaturallySpeaking, which may result in live subtitles being displayed in blocks.

2.4. Discussion points and exercises

2.4.1. Legislation

Have a look at the written declaration issued by the European Parliament in 2008 (DVD > Chapter 2 > Discussion points and exercises > 2.4.1 > EU-Written Declaration-2008). Particularly important here are the number of people affected by partial or complete loss of hearing in the EU (page 2, section B), the inclusion of foreign language viewers with no hearing impairment as potential subtitle users (page 2, section 1) and the requirement for the Commission to put forward a legislative proposal urging public-service television broadcasters in the EU to subtitle all of their programmes (page 2, section 2). Has any other written declaration or even legislation at European level been passed since this document was issued in 2008? What is the current number of people affected by partial or complete loss of hearing in Europe? And in your country?

2.4.2. Users

"Provision of Access Services" (2006) is a study carried out by Ofcom to measure the size of the market using access services in the UK and to understand the needs and preferences of users of these services across the hearing and visually impaired communities. You can access this study in DVD > Chapter 2 > Discussion points and exercises > 2.4.2. > Ofcom Study.

Although subtitle viewers are often categorized as deaf or hard of hearing, another common criterion classifies them as having mild, moderate, severe or profound hearing loss. Complete the "Table on Hearing Loss" (DVD > Chapter 2 > Discussion points and exercises > 2.4.2.) with information obtained in page 7 of the Ofcom Study and in the PDF document "Hearing Loss - Decibels and Effect of Spoken Words", also in the same location. Can you fill in a similar table with information of a different country?

According to the information included in page 2 and page 4 of the Ofcom Study, how does the use of subtitles in the UK compare to the use of other access services such as signing and audiodescription?

Has Ofcom published any further studies since "Provision of Access Services" (2006) was released?

2.4.3. Guidelines

In March 2006, Ofcom undertook a review of the Code on Television Access

Services and proposed new Guidelines on access services (subtitling, signing and audio description) for people with hearing and/or visual impairments. You can find these guidelines in DVD > Chapter 2 > Discussion points and exercises > 2.4.3. > Ofcom Guidelines 2006.pdf

SDH is covered in pages 27-29. Although most of the content is focused on pre-recorded subtitling, some parts deal with live subtitling. What do they establish regarding the display mode, delay, speed, accuracy and advanced preparation of live subtitles? Are there any other parts regarding pre-recorded SDH that may also apply to live subtitling? Has Ofcom published any further guidelines since 2006?

Have a look at "NCRA-Realtime Captioning Guidelines" (2008), in the same folder, which set the standard for live subtitling in the US. What are the main differences with the conventions used in Europe?

Can you find any other set of guidelines, in the UK or in any other country, dealing specifically with live subtitling?

2.4.4. Different approaches to live subtitling

Ever since it was formed in London in 1887, the non-profit association Intersteno has provided an international forum for all people who work as professionals or are interested in reporting and text processing. Intersteno is mainly concerned with different approaches to fast writing, be it with stenotype, keyboards, SR technology or any other method. The following video (DVD > Chapter 2 > Discussion points and exercises > 2.4.4. > Live Subtitling Methods 1) was filmed at the 2007 Intersteno Conference in Prague. Although focused on transcription, this video shows many of the approaches to live subtitling included in this chapter. What methods are used in the following excerpts?

- 2:39 to 3:34
- 4:25 to 6:41
- 6:42 to 7:27
- 8:24 to 9:26

The following video (DVD > Chapter 2 > Discussion points and exercises > 2.4.4. > Live Subtitling Methods 2) shows yet another approach to live subtitling used in the Netherlands, but not included in the previous video. Which one is it?

Are some approaches more suited to certain situations or events than others (give examples)? What type of errors can you expect to have with each method? Do you view the different live subtitling methods as alternatives or rather as a progression towards a "perfect" method? Can you envisage a further (and perhaps improved) alternative?

2.4.5. Assessment of live subtitles

Let's have a look at some real examples of live subtitles in the UK: DVD > Chapter 2 > Discussion points and exercises > 2.4.5. > BBC News, Sky News, BBC Weather and Newsnight 1.

Can you describe the subtitles shown in these clips according to the standard definition proposed at the end of section 2.3?: (2) (6) (3) (4) subtitles with (5) correction displayed in (7) mode with (8) for a (1) programme.

Identify for each programme the average delay, speech rate, subtitle rate, accuracy rate and how much has been edited.

<u>Delay</u>: to calculate the average delay between the sound and the subtitles, pick ten different instances randomly. The delay will probably vary throughout the clip, so make sure that half of these instances correspond to the beginning of an utterance and the other half to the last word of an utterance.

<u>Speech rate and subtitle rate</u>: again, you have to do this manually, counting the spoken words to calculate the speech rate and the subtitled words to calculate the subtitle rate. Both rates must be calculated in wpm. In other words, if in the BBC News video the presenter speaks for 22 seconds, this should be counted as 0.37 minutes. During this time, she utters 63 words, so her speech rate is 170 wpm. The same applies to the subtitle rate.

<u>Accuracy</u>: more advanced methods to calculate accuracy rates will be described in Chapter 10. For the time being, all you need to do is to look at the actual errors in the subtitles. You can use the following simple formula:

$$\frac{N(\text{umber of words in the subtitles}) - E(\text{rrors})}{N(\text{umber of words in the subtitles})} \times 100 = \text{accuracy rate}$$

<u>Edition</u>: taking into account the number of spoken words and subtitled words, provide a percentage of how much has been cut in the subtitles.

How do the subtitles of the different videos compare to one another? Which ones do you like better and why? How could they be improved? Can you rate the different videos in terms of the difficulties they pose to the live subtitler? With regard to SDH features, how are speakers identified? Is sound information conveyed in the subtitles? Is there any other type of information that could have been conveyed and has not been included?

In the BBC News video, what is Bruce Hunter's job? Does this problem occur in any of the other videos?

In the BBC Weather video, the live subtitler has had to edit the subtitles heavily in order to cope with the original speech rate. How much information has really been lost (qualitatively)? You can calculate this by identifying units of information throughout the text.

In the Sky News video, what happens in 0:39, where no subtitles are shown for 4 seconds? At least three errors shown in the video were corrected live by the subtitler? Which ones are they and how were they corrected? Do you think these errors needed to be corrected? Are there others you would have corrected instead?

In the Newsnight video, the speakers are identified by means of colours. Are these colours used consistently? Do you think this method works? Look at the use of the dashes in 6:43-6:45 ("- come to that in a second perhaps-"), 6:46 ("already – only defence here") and 6:47 ("-have they got…"). Do all the dashes mean the same? Is this clear when reading the subtitles? Have a look at the digital glitch in 09:54. Where do those subtitles come from?

Finally, watch the videos "Realtime Captions", "Realtime Captions – Teletext" and "Realtime Captions – Spanish" (DVD > Chapter 2 > Discussion points and exercises > 2.4.5), which include examples of how live subtitles are shown in the US. What are the main differences with the live subtitles you have just analyzed?

3. Respeaking as a Professional Practice

3.0. Introduction

Although respeaking is gaining momentum and has consolidated as the preferred method for the production of live subtitles around the world, the respeaking landscape is far from homogeneous. The practice of respeaking, initiated by the BBC (UK) and VRT (Flanders) in 2001, was not immediately followed by academic training or research in this field. As a result, subtitling companies know what they have to do (produce live subtitles) and have the means to do it (respeaking software) but, in the absence of codes of good practice or other conventions, they go about it in many different ways. This chapter includes information about respeaking gathered through questionnaires sent to broadcasters and subtitling companies in the UK, Spain, Flanders, Switzerland, Denmark, France, Italy, Canada and the US between 2009 and 2011. They illustrate many different roads leading to Rome as far as respeaking is concerned.

3.1. Respeaking on TV

3.1.1. Respeaking in the UK

In order to avoid unnecessary repetitions, this section about the UK is taken as an introductory model, with information about companies subtitling by respeaking, the respeakers' working conditions, the procedures of recruitment and training and the respoken subtitles provided. The sections dealing with other countries are briefer and structured by comparison or opposition to the situation in the UK.

3.1.1.1. Companies
Two of the most important subtitling companies providing respoken subtitles in the UK are Independent Media Support (IMS) and Red Bee Media (RBM).
    IMS was founded in 1989 and has offices in London, Newcastle, Cardiff and Stockholm, with 150 full-time staff members plus hundreds of translation freelancers around the world. Its main clients are BSkyB, Channel 5, Disney, Buena Vista and S4C, for which they produce subtitles and subtitling templates for live broadcasts, pre-recorded programmes, commercials, the internet, DVD, video and cinema. Live subtitling operations started in 1999 with dual QWERTY keyboards. Two live subtitlers were on air at all times typing alternate sentences. Although the resulting subtitles were accurate, they were also slow, often falling well behind the action. After some initial testing, respeaking was introduced in 2005. It is currently used for over 200 hours of live subtitles each week. The live subtitling department in Osterley (West London) covers 18 hours per day of Sky News and up to 16 hours per day of Sky Sports News, as well as a wide range of

live sports on Sky Sports 1, 2, 3, and Xtra, including football, rugby, tennis, golf, ice hockey, wrestling, American football, netball and motor sports.

As for RBM, it was formerly part of the BBC Broadcast Limited and became an independent company on 27 October 2005. Its headquarters are in London, but it has offices in Europe, Asia and Australia. As far as accessibility is concerned, RBM provides subtitling, audiodescription, sign language and transcription services to clients such as the BBC, UKTV, Virgin Media Television, ESPN, Community Channel, Setanta Sports News and Channel 4. Live subtitling operations started in 1990 with steno and fast QWERTY keyboards. Respeaking was introduced in 2001 and has quickly become the preferred method, although steno is still used for specific programmes. Overall, RBM produces some 20,000-25,000 hours of live subtitling a year, two thirds of which are produced by respeakers.

3.1.1.2. Working conditions
The number of respeakers has increased (and is still increasing) considerably over the past years. At the time of writing, there are 38 in IMS and over 100 in RBM. Most respeakers work in-house, although RBM also has respeakers working remotely.

Working hours are not very regular and seem more similar to those of an interpreter than a translator/subtitler, especially as they depend on the broadcasting of live programmes. Although a week's work adds up to 8 hours a day, respeakers seldom work from 9 to 5 or in 8-hour shifts, but rather in 10- or 12-hour shifts, with 2-3 days on and 2-3 days off. Usually, respeakers don't spend more than half a day respeaking on air. The other half is devoted to preparation of programmes to be respoken live and to pre-recorded subtitling. The preparation is different in RBM and IMS. RBM respeakers do their own research prior to respeaking a given programme but they also receive wordlists prepared elsewhere. IMS respeakers are encouraged to do their own preparation, the rationale being that this effort results in familiarity with the vocabulary and ultimately better respeaking performance. As for pre-recorded subtitling, respeakers at RBM also use SR, a technique which is known as *scripting*. Firstly, the subtitler respeaks a given programme. Given that this programme is not live but pre-recorded, the subtitler can press play and pause as he or she respeaks. Once the audio has been respoken, a software application synchronizes the respoken script and the audio, which is finally double-checked by a subtitler to ensure that the cueing is correct. When pre-recording subtitling is done in the "traditional" way, with no respeaking involved, the usual ratio of working time versus film duration is 10:1 minutes. When done with respeaking, it goes down to 7:1. Furthermore, it allows subtitling companies to spread their work among different staff members. The idea is to make sure that respeakers don't spend their working day subtitling on air. At IMS, for example, it is believed that high quality live subtitling is difficult to sustain for anything over 20 minutes. In practice, though, respeakers tend to do half hour slots (as this makes it easier to divide programmes fairly) without a serious reduction in quality.

As far as the setting and equipment are concerned, the ideal situation is to have sound-proof booths for respeakers. Another possibility is to have sound-proof rooms where several respeakers can work together, although this may lead to interferences between them. In the UK, respeakers usually have a computer and a TV screen in front of them. They wear headphones to listen to the original programme and they use a USB microphone, with or without a stand. Software-wise, both companies use ENPS, a newsroom application where they can access the scripts that are going to be used in the programmes to be respoken. Although sometimes these scripts are available hours in advance, it isn't uncommon to receive them only minutes before the programme starts. In any case, respeakers in the UK don't usually prepare scripts to launch semi-live subtitles, at least not for the time being, and the norm is to respeak it all live whether or not the script is available beforehand. The SR and subtitling software used by IMS respeakers are ViaVoice and Wincaps, whereas RBM respeakers use ViaVoice and K-Live, developed by the BBC's Research and Development department.[1] K–Live has a small keyboard to change the colour and position of the subtitles, introduce a new line or clear the on-screen text. When on air, respeakers can watch their subtitles either on the computer, as displayed in ViaVoice + Wincaps/K-Live, or on the actual TV screen, as they are being watched by viewers all over the country.

Finally, the respeakers' salary varies across companies. They may start off on roughly £20,000 a year, which can increase to £22-23,000 after a year and £24,000 after two years. Sometimes, allowances of, for instance, £2,000 are given for news respoken at night. More information about the working conditions of respeakers in the UK can be found in "Respeakers' Account – Red Bee" (DVD > Chapter 4 > Discussion points and exercises > Discussion point 4.5.1.).

3.1.1.3. Recruitment and training
Candidates are usually expected to have a degree, preferably in languages, and ideally a postgraduate course on subtitling. Yet, in a company like IMS, the reality is that respeakers' profiles may be as varied as an MPhil in Medieval and Renaissance Literature and a BA in Swahili and African Culture (see "Respeakers' Account – IMS" in DVD > Chapter 4 > Discussion points and exercises > Discussion point 4.5.1.). In this company, the recruitment process starts with a phone interview, followed by a knowledge test on sports and news and another one on spelling. The second stage involves respeaking a 5- to 10-minute piece of news which may be as challenging as to feature overlapping dialogue at some point. Candidates will then be notified whether they have obtained the job.

At RBM, candidates must fill in an application form which includes a brief subtitling exercise. They are asked to watch a TV programme and explain in 300 words how they would go about subtitling it for deaf and hard of hearing viewers. Once they have passed this stage, the recruitment process consists of a series of

---

[1] Plans are afoot to replace ViaVoice with Dragon NaturallySpeaking, which will bring about significant changes both for the respeakers (see Chapter 7) and the viewers (see Chapter 11).

respeaking tests and an interview (Marsh 2006). The tests last between 1 and 3 minutes, with a pause between them, and become progressively longer and more complex, that is, featuring more speakers and faster speech rates. Although neither these respeaking tests nor those carried out by IMS involve the use of SR software (there is no time to train a voice profile for every candidate), it is important to note that candidates are being asked to do something they have probably never done before. As will be explained below, only a few universities have training in respeaking. With this in mind, some instructions are given to provide orientation. Candidates are advised to listen to and repeat the original soundtrack, including punctuation marks. They are reminded that it is important to follow the source text as closely as possible but also that editing may be needed to keep up with the pace of the original soundtrack. In general, the aspects to be monitored are multitasking, language skills, ability to cope with unforeseen challenges and attention to detail.

Once candidates have got the job, training may vary depending on the company and can take anywhere from 3 weeks to 3 months. At RBM, new respeakers start off creating and training their user profile in the SR software. The respeaking practice starts with "easy" genres such as sports (golf, for example), then moves on to news and finally News 24, debates and interviews in programmes such as Newsnight, regarded as the more challenging pieces. This training period can take up to three months. At IMS, newly hired respeakers devote the first week to creating and training their voice profiles as well as to practising respeaking with real-life material. During the second half of the second week they have respeaking tests, often with SkyNews and dictating directly into the speech recognizer without having to change colours for speaker identification. Then they obtain feedback for further training. After this, and depending on each individual case, they may be ready to go on air. Yet, for the first couple of months, a recently trained subtitler's output may be somewhat substandard, as they get used to the demands of the daily routine.

Although more thorough information about respeaking skills will be provided in chapters 4 and 7, some of these companies have a good idea of what must be expected from respeakers, namely a clear, level tone, a consistent rhythm of delivery and the ability to be unflustered by unusual names and to clearly understand the meaning of what they are listening to and saying.

3.1.1.4. Respoken subtitles
Following the classification laid out in Chapter 2, the respoken subtitles provided by IMS and RBM, and thus the subtitles of most live programmes in the UK are live near-verbatim intralingual respoken subtitles with self correction, displayed in scrolling mode[2] with character ID and sound information. A sample of these subtitles is included in the videos "Respeaking at IMS 2" and "Respeaking at the BBC-Red Bee" (DVD > Chapter 3 > Discussion points and exercises > 3.4.1).

---

[2] If the plans to replace ViaVoice with Dragon go ahead, live subtitles may be displayed in blocks instead of word for word (see Chapter 11 for the rationale behind this change).

Even though respeakers at both companies often receive some scripts before the programme is aired, subtitles are not usually cued and launched semi-live, but respoken live. The reason for this, as explained by the staff at IMS, is that even though live scrolling subtitles tend to have more mistakes, prepared cued subtitles cannot take into account last-minute changes in the rundown or breaking news and cannot be corrected as quickly as live scrolling subtitles. A possible alternative would be to combine both, but this has so far been deemed impractical for the subtitler and difficult for the viewer to follow, as it would mean that the same programme would feature subtitles in scrolling and block mode. In this sense, a potential change from ViaVoice to Dragon, which displays subtitles in blocks, would make the combination of live and semi-live subtitles easier.

As far as editing is concerned, respeakers at IMS and RBM are encouraged to follow as close as possible what is being said in the original soundtrack. Yet, given the high speech rates of some programmes, this is hardly ever possible (see Chapter 7), which results in the summary or omission of non-relevant parts of the script.

Although these subtitles have been defined as intralingual, it is important to note that, on some occasions, RBM and IMS also produce interlingual respoken subtitles. This is the case in Wales, where respeakers subtitle live programmes from Welsh into English.

The delay of these respoken subtitles ranges from 3 to 6 seconds and their position varies depending on the type of programme. In weather reports and cricket games, live subtitles are positioned at the very bottom of the screen, so as not to cover the map and the game respectively. This is known as position 20. For news programmes, the position is 16 (or bottom plus 4), which avoids covering the Astons (running labels). Finally, in football matches, which often feature information at the bottom and few close ups, subtitles are normally positioned at the very top.

As for speaker ID, this information is not always provided. For IMS respeakers, for example, Sky Sports News is different to Sky News in that there are almost always two main speakers. Most of the time, it is unnecessary to differentiate between them (i.e. change colour), but it is advisable to do so during asides or brief banter style.

When it is used, character identification may be done by means of colours or tags. As for colours, white is usually allocated to the first speaker, yellow to the second, blue to the third and green to the fourth. When labels are chosen, IMS recommends using capital letters in parenthesis, as in (COMMENTATOR), (STUDIO), (ANNOUNCER).

As well as character identification, another SDH feature included in respoken subtitles is sound information. Whereas RBM opts only for capital letters, IMS recommends capitals and parenthesis, as in the following common labels: (TRANSLATION), (SINGING), (EXPLOSION), (SHOUTING), (CHEERING), (JEERING), (LAUGHTER), (APPLAUSE), (INDISTINCT), (BELL), etc. These labels (and the ones used for character ID) are normally prepared beforehand by the respeakers. The same goes for the music, for which, unlike in pre-recorded SDH, the symbol # is not often used. Instead, labels are prepared in advance to identify the song (MUSIC: "Second Guessing" – Jonny Lang). Nevertheless, respeakers may have to create tags on air, in which case a command like *open bracket all-caps radio all-caps noise close bracket* would yield (RADIO NOISE), whereas *all-caps music colon open quote cap second cap guessing close quote dash Jonny Lang full stop* would yield MUSIC: "Second Guessing" – Jonny Lang.

With a view to saving much-needed dictation time, respeakers are encouraged to create **macros** for recurrent phrases, which in the case of IMS would be "this is Sky News", "these are the top stories", "on our website, www.skynews.com", "thank you for joining us" or "this is Sky News, bringing you all the news and sport in 15 minutes, every 15 minutes".

As far as accuracy is concerned, the target is usually 97% or 97.5%. Anything below that is considered poor and anything above 98% or 98.5% is regarded as very good indeed. When errors do occur, respeakers are expected to correct them themselves, often by using a dash followed by the correct word. Both IMS and RBM conduct regular accuracy checks. In the case of IMS, each subtitler has a random 15-minute section of their output marked a month. Individual logs are taken from a recent section and matched to either a compliance recording or, where available, a tape. After the marking process, subtitlers are emailed with their mark and some feedback. This gives an idea of whether anybody is struggling and may need remedial training. It also gives individual subtitlers a sense of responsibility for their subtitle quality. However, there is not currently an industry-wide standard for assessing accuracy in live subtitling, which means that every company is using their own method and producing results that are not comparable (even though they are often compared). In this sense, more information about this issue and a proposal for a new method to calculate accuracy in live subtitling are included in Chapter 10.

3.1.2. Respeaking in Spain

Although TVE had occasionally provided respoken subtitles for some news programmes before, it was not until RBM acquired the Spanish company Mundovisión in 2008 that a professional respeaking team was put in place in Spain. Although the approach to respeaking is similar to that of RBM UK, there are some important differences too.

As of March 2008, Mundovisión/RBM started providing 10 hours a day of respoken subtitles for news, magazines and entertainment programmes (a figure which is due to increase soon). Although QWERTY and steno have been tested, respeaking (or *rehablado*) is gaining ground as the preferred method. Respeakers at Mundovision/RBM are all in-house professionals and usually deal with both live and pre-recorded SDH. They work 40 hours a week (8 hours a day including weekends) and often form teams of 2 to 4 to respeak a programme, depending on the length. They work in booths, where they have a TV screen, a computer with ViaVoice,[3] Wincaps (Swift, TN, Aptex have also been used) and a desktop microphone with stand.

Candidates applying for a position as respeakers at the company don't need any particular qualification. However, they are expected to have excellent linguistic, communication, editing and team working skills, as well as an interest in TV and issues which affect deaf and hard of hearing people. They are also expected to be highly motivated, resilient and flexible. As in the case of RBM UK, candidates have to do a speech test, grammar and language exams and attend an interview. Once they join the respeaking team, training may take anything between 3 and 6 months, although a subtitler takes up to a year to be considered fully effective.

The respoken subtitles produced by Mundovisión/RBM may be classified as live fairly edited intralingual respoken subtitles with self correction, displayed in blocks with character ID and sound information. It must be said however that, unlike RBM UK, Mundovisión/RBM does resort to semi-live subtitles when scripts are available. Given that the Spanish viewers are not used to scrolling subtitles, a decision has been made to display live respoken subtitles in one- or two-line blocks, which adds delay (ranging from 3 to 10 seconds) but which does not cause any problems when these live subtitles are combined with semi-live ones, as they are both displayed in blocks. Speaker ID is indicated with colours and tags where needed. Sound information has the same format as in pre-recorded subtitles, although it is positioned at the bottom, whereas in off-line subtitling it appears on the top right corner. So far, the respoken subtitles produced by Mundovisión/RBM have been heavily edited, which may be due to the adaptation period rather than a company policy. In any case, accuracy seems to be in the neighbourhood of 97% and is calculated with the same method used by RBM UK.

3.1.3. Respeaking in Flanders

VTM (Vlaamse Televisie Maatschappij) is the main commercial television station in Flanders. It began broadcasting in 1989 and went on to become the Flemish market leader. It can be received on cable or by satellite in Flanders. Live subtitling operations at VTM were initiated by a team of 4 people in 2007. After some tests with velotype, VTM started directly with respeaking, although they use the more general term *live-ondertiteling* (live subtitling), which is more accurate to refer to what they do. For the time being, only the evening news (7pm-7.40pm) are being subtitled live, although plans are afoot to subtitle other news programmes and sports events. Lunchtime news is being used as practice for in-house respeakers and as training for newly hired respeakers, but their subtitles are not aired. This training period usually takes 2 to 3 weeks. After this, trainers know whether a subtitler will be able to work on live subtitling. If that is the case, a further training period of 3 months is usually needed to become a fully trained respeaker.

Currently, VTM has 4 respeakers who normally work in pairs from 12 noon

---

[3] Dragon NaturallySpeaking may be introduced soon.

until 8pm for 4 or 6 days a week. On a normal working day, a pair of respeakers will prepare the lunchtime news from 12 noon to 1pm, carry out a mock respeaking from 1pm to 1.30pm and then check the subtitles. At around 2.30pm, there is a meeting with the journalists in charge of preparing and delivering the evening news (respeakers and journalists are working next door to each other), where respeakers are briefed as to the information that will feature in the news. From 3pm till 5pm, respeakers start preparing the news (reading newspapers, training the software) and, usually after 5pm, they start receiving some of the scripts that will be used by the newsreaders and the correspondents in the newscast. These scripts are to be subtitled in semi-live mode. They are adapted as subtitles by both respeakers (R1 and R2) and then launched live manually by one of them (R1). Meanwhile, the other respeaker (R2) may be preparing new subtitles that have been obtained during the newscast so that R1 can launch them live a few minutes or even seconds later. When no script is obtained, R1 and R2 have to respeak the original soundtrack live. Thus, there are three possibilities, only the third of which involves live respeaking:

- If the video and the text or only the text of a news item is available before the programme, the subtitles are prepared in advance by R1 and R2 (whether manually or by respeaking) so that R1 can launch them live manually;
- If only the video is available, it is first of all respoken, corrected and edited by R2 and then launched live manually by R1;
- If nothing is available, the news item is respoken live by R1. Yet, it is important to note that, in the case of interviews, respeakers often take turns to avoid too much delay in the subtitles. Typically, R1 will do the first question and answer and then R1 and R2 will do a question and an answer each. R1 usually checks and corrects the spoken subtitles before sending them on air. If these subtitles contain a serious error, then R1 will correct the error and R2 will take over.

In sum, unlike what is standard practice in the UK, VTM combines live and semi-live subtitles. Respeaking is thus left for instances when (a) there is no script available and the soundtrack must be subtitled live or (b) the script is available little in advance and subtitles need to be created quickly so that they can be then corrected and launched semi-live. The fact that, as pointed out above, the combination of live (scrolling) and semi-live (block) subtitles may be difficult for viewers to follow is not a problem here, given that VTM uses Dragon NaturallySpeaking, which displays subtitles in blocks. The videos "VTM Video 1", "VTM Video 2", "VTM Video 3" and "VTM Video 4" (DVD > Chapter 3 > Discussion points and exercises > 3.4.2) show different phases of this combination of live and semi-live subtitling.

Another difference between respeakers in VTM and those in RBM and

IMS is that the former use headsets (as opposed to standard microphones) and although they also have a TV screen and a computer in front of them, they use Dragon and Wincaps instead of ViaVoice and Wincaps (IMS)/K-Live (RBM). The reason for this is that ViaVoice is not available in Dutch. VTM live subtitles are thus displayed in blocks, with longer delay (5 to 8 seconds) and often with very few mistakes, which is characteristic of subtitles produced with Dragon. These subtitles are usually shown in one or two lines, although three lines are sometimes used when the newsreader is on screen, given that the visuals are well known by the viewers and do not normally carry essential information. The first words of every respoken subtitle are verbatim, so that hard of hearing viewers can relate the visual words to the sound, but then they are edited significantly. As far as SDH features are concerned, speakers are identified with colours (yellow for the presenter, white for journalists and interviewers, blue for interviewee 1, green for interviewee 2 and blue again for interviewee 3), sound information is displayed in capitals without brackets and music is shown, whenever possible, with a label in capitals, followed by the title of the song in lower case and the lyrics in purple. As for accuracy, it is expected to be somewhere around 95% to 97% and errors are corrected by writing over the misrecognized word, using no dash.

Most live subtitles produced by VTM are intralingual, although a first successful interlingual test was carried out with President Obama's inauguration speech in 2009. This has been followed by other programmes such as *So You Think You Can Dance*, *The X Factor* (English-Dutch) and *Henin* (French-Dutch). Finally, VTM news programmes often feature open subtitles (for example English into Dutch) which are prepared by the journalist responsible for the news item. Respeakers usually prepare back-up subtitles in case there is any problem with these open subtitles.

3.1.4. Respeaking in Switzerland

Since 1984, SWISS TXT has been providing intralingual SDH for SRG SSR, the Swiss public broadcasting corporation, which includes channels in German (SF1, SF2 and SF Info), French (TSR1 and TSR2), Italian (RSI: La 1 and La 2) and Romansh (RTR). The aim is to meet the target set by the Loi fédérale sur la radio et la télévision (LRTV), and more specifically by its ordinance (ORTV), which requires that one third of the programmes broadcast by SRG SSR be subtitled by 2010. At the beginning of 2010, SWISS TXT was providing 1,000 hours of prerecorded subtitles a month, produced by both in-house subtitlers and freelancers. Live subtitling, in this case with keyboards, started in 1984 for the visit of the Pope. Respeaking[4] was introduced in fall 2008 and it has become the preferred method. Currently, SWISS TXT provides 185 hours of live respoken subtitles a month for sports programmes, newscasts, current affairs programmes and any

---

[4] Despite working in German, Italian and French, professionals at SWISS TXT use the English term to refer to respeaking (as well as "to respeak" and "respeaker").

other shows chosen by the office team leader. The goal is to subtitle everything between 7pm and 10pm and all the live events between 12 noon and 12 midnight by the end of 2010.

SWISS TXT works with in-house respeakers. Initially, they were mostly translation graduates with four years training in translation and some training in interpreting. Although they had to learn how to subtitle from scratch, their multitasking skills were particularly valued for the practice of respeaking. Now, subtitlers are also being re-trained to become respeakers. In this case, their main asset is their ability to edit, but overall they seem to need longer training than interpreters. Subtitlers and respeakers at SWISS TXT are asked to provide live, semi-live and pre-recorded subtitles. Live subtitles are intralingual, although respeakers working in German often have to translate the Swiss German spoken on TV to the standard German that must be dictated to the speech recognizer. Semi-live subtitles are used for news programmes whose scripts are available in advance and, finally, tests are underway to see if respeaking can also be used for pre-recorded subtitling, that is, for scripting as is the case in RBM UK.

Respeakers at SWISS TXT work 40 hours a week, including weekends and evenings, and earn about €26 an hour (before income tax and health care). Their shifts vary greatly depending on live emissions but they don't respeak for more than five hours a day. Typically, they work in pairs in a double booth, although they may work in a single booth for semi-live programmes and in a triple booth for particularly tricky programmes. In these booths, they have a TV, a computer and a headset with a microphone. Although at the beginning they used ViaVoice for SR, they quickly changed to Dragon,[5] which they combine with the subtitling software FAB. When they are not respeaking, they either work on pre-recorded subtitling or carry out research for the next programme they have to respeak. The results of this research are then introduced in a database (and in the SR software) so that other respeakers at SWISS TXT can benefit from them too.

As far as recruitment and training are concerned, candidates are expected to write, speak and understand German, French or Italian perfectly, to be able to multitask and to be comfortable in a highly technological environment, finding solutions to the different problems that may arise in a live transmission. So far, the impression at SWISS TXT is that trained interpreters perform particularly well as respeakers, but good results have also been obtained with trained translators and subtitlers. When applying for a position at SWISS TXT, candidates are given a questionnaire on general knowledge and a brief respeaking test of a football programme, including part of the actual game (slow) and an interview (fast and with different speakers). Once they have been selected, newly hired respeakers undergo a training process which can take between one and a half and two months, although it varies greatly depending on the intensity. During the

---

[5] At SWISS TXT, the performance of ViaVoice in French was not considered good enough for on-air subtitle production. The speed of the new Dragon also helped to tilt the balance towards the latter software.

first part of the training, respeakers become familiarized with the SR software: how it works, what tools are available and how these tools can be optimized for respeaking. Indeed, ever since respeaking was chosen as the preferred method for live subtitling, SWISS TXT has placed great emphasis on the importance of using the SR software to its full potential, which may go some way towards explaining the optimum results they have obtained in this field so far. The training for newly hired respeakers, considered as an on-going process, continues with respeaking exercises, firstly using sports programmes and then more challenging genres such as news and chat shows.

As for the respoken subtitles produced by SWISS TXT, they are live near-verbatim intralingual respoken subtitles with self correction, displayed in blocks with character ID and sound information. Similarly to what happens in VTM (Flanders), SWISS TXT combines live subtitling with semi-live subtitling. In the respoken subtitles produced by SWISS TXT in German and Italian, speakers are identified with colours: white for the main speaker or host of a programme and yellow, green and blue for the other speakers. When there are four or more people speaking, respeakers at SWISS TXT use tags, which is the default option applied in the case of their French subtitles. Sounds are displayed with yellow font on blue background. The average accuracy rate of these subtitles is 97.5% to 98% and, when an error occurs, respeakers correct it by introducing a double hyphen followed by the correct word or phrase.

The subtitles produced by SWISS TXT for SF are usually positioned at the top for sports and at the bottom for other live programmes such as news and interviews, and have three lines because German words are usually longer than French or Italian words. For TSR and RSI, the French- and Italian-speaking channels, the subtitles produced by SWISS TXT are shown at the bottom of the screen and on two lines.

SWISS TXT subtitles have an average delay of 3 to 7 seconds, although this depends on the display mode. Up until 2010, most subtitles produced by SWISS TXT were displayed word-for-word. As of this year, two new punctuation-based display modes were introduced: the add-on sentence display mode and the add-on phrase display mode. In the first one, the units uttered by the respeakers are only launched on screen when a full stop is dictated (or when the maximum number of lines defined has been filled). Then, the next utterance (up until the maximum number of lines defined) is added as a new line to the previous one, which remains on screen. For instance, "This is the new display mode used by SWISS TXT. It seems to work." will be shown as follows:

First subtitle:

> This is the new display mode used by SWISS TXT.

Respeaking as a Professional Practice 33

Second subtitle:

> This is the new display mode
> used by SWISS TXT.
> It seems to work.

A sample of this mode can be found in the video "SWISS TXT - Add-on sentence mode" (DVD > Chapter 3 > Discussion points and exercises > 3.4.3).

The main advantage of this mode is that it allows the subtitlers to respeak in units, in this case "This is the new display mode used by SWISS TXT." and "It seems to work". This benefits respeakers (because they can segment the original speech into idea units), the software (which receives these units and performs more accurately because contextual information is given, as explained in Chapter 5) and the viewers (whose comprehension is better with units than single words, as shown in Chapter 11). Besides, it also enables on-air correction, which is a basic requirement for French. Given that most utterances are shown in the software but not launched on screen until respeakers say "full stop", respeakers can read the recognized utterance and correct it in case of errors before saying full stop and launching it live.

In the second display mode, the add-on phrase mode, not only full stops but also commas cause the dictated utterances to be shown on screen and a new line to be introduced. So "As you can see, this is a new display mode. It seems to work." will be shown as follows:

First subtitle:

> As you can see,

Second subtitle:

> As you can see,
> this is a new display mode.

Third subtitle:

> As you can see,
> this is a new display mode.
> It seems to work.

A sample of this mode can be found in the video "SWISS TXT - Add-on phrase mode" (DVD > Chapter 3 > Discussion points and exercises > 3.4.3).

The advantage of the add-on phrase mode over the add-on sentence mode is that delay is reduced, as the software doesn't have to wait for a full stop to show the subtitle. The main disadvantage is that it doesn't lend itself easily to on-air corrections. At SWISS TXT, the idea is to use both display modes depending on the particular features of each programme.

3.1.5. Respeaking in Denmark

TV2 is a publicly owned Danish television station based in Odense. The station began broadcasting on 1 October 1988. Foreign programmes and pre-recorded Danish programmes are subtitled by in-house subtitlers, whereas live subtitling is carried out by freelancers or part-time professionals. Live subtitling at TV2 started in 2004 using a dual keyboard system (Wincaps). In the summer of 2006, this was replaced by respeaking (which, incidentally, is the term used in the company even when speaking in Danish), which was first used to subtitle a news programme. According to the current national legislation, TV2 must subtitle one daily newscast from Monday to Friday plus national events like elections and royal weddings. The daily newscast is the 7pm news and the subtitling of national events is discussed on each occasion. Yet, by 2012 the Danish government expects TV2 to subtitle all its live programmes. Currently, TV2 has 9 freelance respeakers who work from 6pm to 8pm from Monday to Friday, except for some national events which take place at the weekend. Overall, each respeaker works an average of 10 hours a month and is paid DKK 240 (€32) an hour. From 6pm to 7pm, respeakers prepare the programme and obtain the research facilitated by the broadcaster. From 7pm to 8pm they respeak the news, which last 27 minutes and are subtitled by two respeakers. The respeakers decide how long the shifts are, often depending on the length of each news item. Typically, turns last for 5 to 8 minutes. As far as setting, hardware and software are concerned, respeakers at TV2 do not have booths and, unlike in the UK, they use headsets. They have a TV screen in front of them as well as a computer with Inews, the SR software Speech Magic, by Philips, and Wincaps as a subtitling application. The choice of Speech Magic as SR software, unique in the respeaking landscape, is due to the fact that neither ViaVoice nor Dragon is available in Danish.

As for recruitment and training, no special qualification is required for candidates who apply to work as respeakers, although special emphasis is placed on good spelling, accuracy, general (and up-to-date) world knowledge and technology skills. Training at TV2 is expensive and intensive and so candidates are expected to stay for more than a year. Currently, the respeaking staff is made up of trained secretaries and linguists. During the application process, candidates are asked to complete a split attention test and another one to measure natural ability to understand, edit and paraphrase. Once they have been selected for the job, respeakers undergo a training period of an average of 75 hours, mostly devoted to creating and developing their voice profile in Speech Magic by reading relevant texts into it, finding their way around the system and doing editing exercises and preparation for the 7pm newscast. Respeaking exercises are done first of all with political speeches, for which Speech Magic has been particularly tuned, and then with more challenging genres.

As for the respoken subtitles produced by TV2, they may be classified as live near-verbatim intralingual respoken subtitles with self correction, displayed in scrolling mode with character ID. Indeed, TV2 respoken subtitles are always launched live, they are verbatim insofar as it is possible for respeakers to keep up with the original soundtrack and are usually intralingual. Yet, for important international events such as President Obama's inauguration speech, interlingual subtitles are produced, respeakers subtitling live from English into Danish. As for their delay, these subtitles have an average delay of 4 to 9 seconds, slightly higher than in the UK. They are positioned at the bottom and raised (via the keyboard) whenever a label appears on the screen. Speakers in the news programme are identified with colours (white for the host, yellow for reporters and blue and green for other people and interviewees) and no information is provided for sound or music. As for accuracy, it is usually 97% but some of the best respeakers achieve up to 98.5%. Unlike in the UK, accuracy is measured by character and not by word. Records are kept of every programme respoken but calculations are only conducted on selected weeks. Recent results show that two thirds of the errors are normally due to missing words or syllables and the rest to unclear or wrong pronunciation. When an error occurs, TV2 respeakers use a feature called "slet-word" (erase word), which causes the misrecognized word to disappear so that the right word can be respoken instead.

3.1.6. Respeaking in France

Facing a similar situation to other countries regarding the need to provide subtitles for live programmes (see Chapter 2), some French channels have opted for a slightly different approach, albeit also based on respeaking. Since early 2007, TF1, France 2 and France 3 are subtitling news, current affairs programmes and weather reports with a three-people team. A respeaker (*perroquet*) listens to the original soundtrack of a programme and respeaks it in the "traditional" sense, verbatim in so far as possible and allocating colours: white for on-screen speakers and yellow for off-screen speakers as per SDH conventions in France. Although the script is sometimes available, subtitles are not prepared beforehand and sent semi-live, but rather produced live. Sitting next to the respeaker, a prompter/whisperer (*souffleur*) checks what is being said by the respeaker against what is being displayed on the screen and, should a sentence need to be modified, warns the corrector about it. Finally, the corrector (*correcteur*), sitting beside the prompter, is mainly in charge of correcting misrecognitions or those problems found by the whisperer and validating the subtitles so that they can go on air. Although the whisperer is sometimes removed from the equation, this type of respeaking clearly tilts the balance towards 100% correction to the detriment of cost and delay, which are higher than in more standard approaches. In some programmes, such as interviews in France 3, live subtitles are displayed with virtually no errors but with a delay of up to 16 seconds, as can be seen in the video "FR3 - Respoken subtitles" (DVD > Chapter 3 > Discussion points and exercises > 3.4.4). Yet, according to TF1, this is not always the case, as this two or three-people approach to respeaking can also be done with much less delay.

Be that as it may, other broadcasters in France have opted for a more standard respeaking method. In 2007, M6 signed a contract with RBM France for the provision of live subtitles, in this case using a similar method to the one applied in RBM UK. Judging by a random sample analyzed in May and June 2009, M6 subtitles do not seem to have more than 4 to 5 seconds delay although, it must be said, they feature more errors and grammar mistakes than those provided by TF1, France 2 and France 3. A choice is thus being made between error-free respoken subtitles with high delay and not-so-error-free (97% accurate) respoken subtitles with less delay.

3.1.7. Respeaking in Italy

Another peculiar approach to respeaking is that of Colby, which has been working in the broadcasting field in Italy since 1988 and has introduced the touch screen for the production of live subtitles. Respeakers, who wear headsets and use Dragon to respeak, have in front of them a touch screen which they use to introduce punctuation marks as well as keywords that may crop up in the programme they are subtitling. This method is similar to the joystick used in Canada by TVA (see section 3.1.8 below) but in this case the touch screen allows for the inclusion of many more words and punctuation marks and, most importantly, it can be customized for every programme. This is shown in the video "Respeaking at Colby", in DVD > Chapter 3 > Discussion points and exercises > 3.4.3. At Colby, a programme of 30 to 90 minutes is usually respoken by two respeakers (one at a time). A coordinator, sitting alongside them, decides on the alternation of the two respeakers based on the complexity and the flow of the subtitles. The coordinator is also in charge of launching semi-live subtitles if the script of a programme is available beforehand as well as deciding which icons, symbols and names must be included in the touch screen. As for recruitment, candidates are expected to have an extremely high level of concentration, excellent diction and outstanding listening skills, and are trained by narration coaches and teachers of simultaneous interpreting.

The introduction of the touch screen by Colby is similar to the three-people team used by TF1, France 2 and France 3 in France in that it favours accuracy to the detriment of delay. Thus, in the same way that the latter approach guarantees error-free subtitles, the use of the touch screen means that virtually no errors will be made with specific or out-of-vocabulary words, always problematic in SR. Yet, something has to give, and when Colby respeakers touch the screen to insert punctuation marks or key terms, they have to pause and interrupt their flow, which necessarily adds delay to the subtitle. In any case, they manage to produce, as in the case of the French broadcasters, accurate live subtitles. The only difference is that in France the extra strain takes place after the respeaking process (with corrections by the whisperer and the corrector) whereas here it takes place during the process (pausing to touch the screen).

3.1.8. Respeaking in Canada

Short for *Téléviseurs associés* (associated telecasters), TVA is a Canadian French language privately owned television network based in Quebec. It is owned by Groupe TVA Inc., which also operates a series of cable specialty channels, including ARGENT, Les idées de ma maison, Mystère, LCN, Prise 2, Canal Indigo and Shopping TVA. Pre-recorded subtitling at TVA Network is carried out by a team of 35 subtitlers (or captionists), one supervisor and one closed captioning director. Each of the TV licences included in the network has a different subtitling target: 90% (live and pre-recorded) for TVA, 100% (pre-recorded) by 2012 for Prise 2, 90% (pre-recorded) for Mystère, 50% (pre-recorded using respeaking) for Idées de ma maison and 50% (pre-recorded and live) for ARGENT. The first developments regarding live subtitling at TVA Network started in 2002 and two years later, in 2004, the first newscast was subtitled live by respeaking (which they refer to simply as *reconnaissance vocale*, respeakers being *locuteurs* or *sous-titreurs vocaux*). Currently, the programmes broadcast with live subtitles are morning shows, newscasts and public affairs programmes, all of them chosen by the team supervisor.

Respeakers at TVA Network work 5 days a week, including weekends, for an average of 8 hours a day. Five of these hours are devoted to live respeaking and the rest is used for research, normally up to an hour for every programme. The starting salary is CAN$21 per hour and given that the company is unionized, respeakers are paid 1.5 times their salary on holidays. With the exception of breaking news, respeakers work on their own in the three booths (2 single, one double) available at the network. Their working station consists of a computer, a headset with microphone, a joystick (which they use to include punctuation and sound information) and an audio box. Software-wise, TVA use the SR engine STDirect, developed by CRIM (Centre de recherche informatique de Montréal) in 2002. The main advantage of this software is that it has no limit on the number of respeakers who can use it or on the number of words in the dictionary and especially that it updates itself by automatically checking relevant websites in order to add new words and rule out others on the basis of (re-)occurrence. The subtitling application used by TVA since 2001 is called ProCAP and allows subtitlers who are respeaking off-line to simultaneously do the transcript and edit the timecodes.

TVA expects its respeakers to write and speak French perfectly, to be comfortable in a highly technical environment and to be capable of managing their stress while multitasking (listening, respeaking, using the joystick), finding solutions to technical problems and bringing new ideas to the team. Many of the current respeakers are in-house off-line subtitlers who have been trained in respeaking. In general, training is conducted by one of the experienced live subtitlers in the network, who starts off with general training on SDH and then moves on to the use of the SR software for subtitling.

The respoken subtitles produced by TVA may be defined as live or off-line near-verbatim intralingual respoken subtitles without corrections, displayed in scrolling mode with character ID and a limited use of sound information. Respeaking is used at TVA for all live subtitles (semi-live subtitling, as done at VTM in Flanders is not considered) and, since 2008, also for **offline subtitling** in order to increase productivity.

The scrolling words, displayed with an average delay of 3 to 5 seconds, form up to three lines that roll up one by one. Particularly worth noting here is that TVA has managed to delay the video signal so that respeakers can listen to the audio of a programme before the viewers, which reduces the overall delay. Unlike in the other countries surveyed in this chapter, speaker identification is done with dashes and the few labels used for sound information are introduced with a joystick, which displays them in brackets and lower case, i.e. (music) and (foreign language). Finally, no corrections are introduced on air, although the sign (…) is used when an incomplete subtitle is displayed on the screen. Corrections may however be implemented for reruns of the programmes. As for error rates, TVA does not run tests to find these out, at least not unless asked by CRIM.

A video of how respeaking is done at VTA can be found in DVD > Chapter 3 > Discussion points and exercises > 3.4.4.

3.1.9. Voice Writing in the US

In the US, stenotyping has always been the preferred method to provide real-time transcription, initially in courts and then on TV as well as for **CART** (Communication Access Realtime Translation) services such as counselling sessions, meetings, teleconferences, seminars, classrooms and conventions. The American audience is thus used to reading verbatim or near-verbatim transcriptions and subtitles with an average accuracy of 98.5%. As has been explained, respeaking (or [realtime] voice writing, as it is known in the US) can only sometimes achieve this accuracy and is not as fast as steno. This goes some way towards explaining why, unlike in Europe, it is still the second choice in the US.

Yet, over the past years voice writing has gained considerable ground and is increasingly being used in courts, for CART services and to a lesser degree on TV. The reasons are summed up in Table 3.1, published by the National Verbatim Reporters Association:

Fact Sheet		
	Automated Speech Recognition (ASR)	**Stenography**
Cost of Equipment	$3,000 – 4,000	$10,000 – 12,000
Duration of Training	9 months	33 months
Dropout Rate	10% or less	90% or more
Training Programs	Few, but Growing	134 and Declining
Accrediting Organization	National Verbatim Reporters Association	National Court Reporters Association
Accuracy Rate	90-99%	90-99%
Speed	200-260 WPM Depending on CPU Speed	180-260 WPM Depending on Manual Speed

Table 3.1: Voice writing vs. stenography

One of the companies using voice writing to provide **realtime captions** (the term used for live subtitles in the US) is Mark Hall Associates (MHA). Since it was founded in 2002, MHA has sold its software Caption Mic to, and provided training on voice writing for, over 70 broadcasters, colleges, religious institutions, theatres and companies offering conference and webcast captioning across the whole country. The professionals are known as "voice captioners", who "echo", "shadow" or "respeak" the original speech. Most of the terminology used in-house has been borrowed from the court reporter or CART fields.

Voice writers using Caption Mic for live captioning work between 25 and 40 hours a week, including weekends when required, and earn $12 to $15 per hour. Their working station consists of a monitor, a headset (usually a Sennheiser PC-166) and a computer with Caption Mic, which is an integrated captioning software that uses ViaVoice as the underlying SR engine. Voice writers usually devote up to 30 minutes to research prior to a programme and they share this research with the rest of the captioners. Whenever possible, they are also provided with a script or at least an outline of the upcoming programme. If a full script is available, semi-live captioning is combined with live captioning.

Candidates wanting to use Caption Mic for live captioning are expected to have basic computer knowledge, a clear speaking voice, willingness to learn, extensive vocabulary and the ability to overcome the frustration caused by the occurrence of errors. Memory skills are also highly valued, which is why candidates with backgrounds on music, theatre, shorthand, steno, language and sign language interpreting have proved particularly successful. Initially, candidates are given a 10-minute respeaking test to see whether they can enunciate clearly while keeping up with the original soundtrack and recovering from occasional slip ups. Typically, out of a random group of 10 candidates, 6 do quite well, 2 are borderline and 2 are unable to do it, which has led the professionals and trainers working for MHS to believe that 60% to 70% of the general population have the ability to respeak. Once the candidates have obtained the job, they undergo 3 to 6 weeks of training, consisting of an in depth walkthrough of the software and the main concepts of voice writing, applying, whenever possible, the NCRA guidelines for Realtime Broadcast Captioning (2008).

The subtitles provided with Caption Mic are real-time or semi-live near-verbatim intralingual respoken subtitles with self-correction, displayed in scrolling mode with character ID and a limited use of sound information. The scrolling words are displayed in capitals, following the conventions of live captioning in the US, and in 2, 3 or 4 lines. The average delay is 3 to 5 seconds, and is mostly down to the time it takes the voice captioner to hear and respeak the utterances. After that, the display occurs within 1 to 2.5 seconds. As for character ID, known speakers are identified with name tags in capitals followed by chevrons (PRESIDENT OBAMA >>), whereas unknown speakers only take chevrons (>>). Finally, as far accuracy is concerned, it is difficult to meet the standards set by the above-mentioned NCRA guidelines, which state that realtime captioning must achieve an accuracy rate of "over 98% and may be performed at speeds up to and possibly exceeding 300 wpm" (2008:7). The average accuracy of live captions with Caption Mic is 95% to 98%, most errors consisting of single syllable words and homonyms. Corrections are only made (by introducing a dash) when the meaning of a whole sentence is changed.

Finally, although voice writers at MHA only use Caption Mic (that is, ViaVoice), it is worth noting that most voice writers in the US are now using Dragon NaturallySpeaking. Unlike in other countries, several attempts have been made in the US to solve the issue of the delay caused by Dragon. A case in point is the combination of Dragon with specialized software such as EclipseVox that speeds up the delivery while maintaining and even increasing the accuracy. As can be seen in the video "EclipseVox with Dragon" (DVD > Chapter 3 > Discussion points and exercises > Discussion point 3.4.4), the increase in speed is noticeable but the inconsistent display mode of the subtitles raises serious issues regarding legibility from the viewers' point of view (see Chapter 11).

3.2. Respeaking training at University

3.2.1. Universitat Autònoma de Barcelona (Spain)

The Universitat Autònoma de Barcelona (UAB) was the first university to offer respeaking training in Spain and the first one to offer online respeaking training in the world (excluding the voice writing courses in the US described below).

In the on-campus MA on Audiovisual Translation (MTAV, http://www.fti.uab.es/pg.audiovisual), respeaking is part of the 4-credit module "Subtitulació per a sords" (Subtitling for the Deaf and Hard of Hearing), which comprises SDH theory, pre-recorded SDH and respeaking, for which the SR software Dragon and the subtitling software Isis (developed by Starfish) are used. As far as respeaking is concerned, students have first of all an introductory session where they are taught how to create a user profile in Dragon and how to train it. Several months later, once the profiles are properly trained and students are familiarized with Dragon, they have an intensive hands-on 6-hour course where they learn the practical skills of respeaking. The assessment consists of three clips of different complexity (a narration, a sports commentary and a news item) to be done under time constraints.

In the online European MA on Audiovisual Translation (METAV, http://mem.uab.es/metav), respeaking is a 10-credit module lasting for three months and divided into 10 units. Each week, students read a unit on the online platform and perform the relevant task, for which they obtain feedback. Among many other applications, the platform has a forum where different respeaking-related aspects are discussed. This platform also allows for synchronous communication between lecturer and students, which in this case is done via shared-desktop applications such as GotoMeeting or Dimdim. In this way, students can not only chat with their lecturer (and among themselves) but also see the teacher's computer screen, which is particularly helpful for solving software-related issues. So far, both ViaVoice and Dragon have been used in this module.

3.2.2. Roehampton University (London, UK)

Roehampton University is the only university so far to offer respeaking training in different languages (English, Spanish, French, Italian and German) as part of the module "Subtitling for Accessibility: SDH and Respeaking" included in its multilingual MA on Audiovisual Translation (http://www.roehampton.ac.uk/postgraduate-courses/audiovisual-translation). The programmes used are the multilingual versions of ViaVoice and Dragon, which allows students to become familiarized with different approaches to respeaking. During the module, students acquire first of all awareness of the different methods currently used to produce live subtitles and are then provided with the necessary theoretical and practical skills to begin work as respeakers in a professional context. This comprises the creation and development of a user profile and practical exercises to respeak different audiovisual genres, public events as well as some training on interlingual respeaking.

3.2.3. Higher Institute for Translation and Interpreting of Artesis University College (Antwerp, Belgium)

A pioneer in the training of respeaking at university level, the Higher Institute for Translation and Interpretation at Artesis University College includes respeaking in Dutch as an option within its Master in Interpreting. This respeaking module bears 3 ECTS credits and is taught for 2 hours a week over a year. The programmes used in the course are Dragon and Swift. Most students who take the course already have an MA in translation, specializing in Audiovisual Translation, which means that they have already been trained in subtitling. If not, they take a practical subtitling course in the first semester within the MA in Translation. The inclusion of respeaking in the MA on Interpreting is based on the belief that the two disciplines have much in common and that students with interpreting skills often perform very well as respeakers.

3.3. Respeaking training In the US

In the US, the NVRA offers a certification programme to its members in various locations around the country. The NVRA provides three national certifications: Certified Verbatim Reporter, Certificate of Merit and Real-time Verbatim Reporter. They are all clearly focused on the use of voice writing in court, but the skills acquired are very relevant to live captioning.

In any case, most of the training on voice writing provided in the US is online. Some examples are Learn2Voice, developed by the voice writer Chris Ales, and the courses on real-time voice writing offered by the Verbatim Careers Institute and the Real-Time University.

Learn2Voice is taught in a Moodle-based online learning environment and is divided into three modules, each of which requires 24 to 26 weeks to complete (based on a student schedule of 5 days per week, 4 hours per day). After an initial introduction, students receive in-depth training on voice theory, which is followed by dictation practice. As this practice becomes harder, students are provided with speed-building techniques using different software applications. By the end of the course, they should be equipped with a comprehensive skill set to perform effectively in captioning, court and CART settings.

The voice writing course developed by Ardith Spies, the director of Verbatim Careers Institute, is a 10- to 12-month distance learning programme offering students specialized training for captioning, webcasting, off-line captioning, CART services and/or court reporting. Students are first of all asked to train their software and then they receive a CD with training materials in both text and audio format. A study guide shows students how to work with the material, which becomes increasingly difficult and faster (from 140 wpm to 180 wpm). Once the exercises are completed, they must be sent to the instructor for evaluation. In all cases 95% accuracy is required. When the final speed level has been reached, unfamiliar testing material is emailed to the student in mp3 format and the student is expected to voice write the material and immediately email the unedited, uncorrected test to the instructor for grading.

Finally, another institution providing online training on voice writing is the RealTime University. Its course has been developed by Bettye Keyes, author of the key book in this field: *Voice Writing Method* (2005). The course is divided in a series of modules: SR basics, voice writing theory, captioning, court reporting and CART. The module on SR basics aims to provide students with the necessary skills to use Dragon with 95% accuracy at a speed of up to 150 wpm within two weeks. The module on voice-writing theory covers the content of the above-mentioned book by Bettye Keyes. Once these two modules have been completed, students can choose to take any or all of the other three modules. The one on captioning provides students with skills to subtitle a wide range of programmes, prepare specialized dictionaries and stream realtime text.

3.4. Discussion points and exercises

3.4.1. Respeaking in the UK

You can find the videos and pictures that you need for this section in DVD > Chapter 3 > Discussion points and exercises > 3.4.1.

Have a look at the pictures "Red Bee Pic 1", "IMS Pic 1" and "IMS Pic 2". What are the main differences between the workstations of respeakers at RBM and IMS?

Watch the video "Respeaking at the BBC-Red Bee", made by the BBC Research and Development department. Try to focus on those instances where you can see the subtitles appearing on the screen as you can hear the respeaker's and/or the speaker's voice: 0:27-0:34, 0:44-0:51, 1:34-1:41 and 1:46-1:58. What is the average delay between the speaker and the subtitles? And between the respeaker and the subtitles? With regard to SDH features, what method is used to identify speakers? Are sound effects subtitled? If so, how are they displayed? With the help of the picture "Red Bee Pic 2", can you tell what key the respeaker presses in 1:34 and for what purpose? How does the respeaker create the tag displayed on the screen in 1:38?

Watch the video "Respeaking at IMS 2". What are the main differences and similarities with the previous video in terms of the job done by the respeaker? What is the average delay of the subtitles? Are there any recognition errors? What SDH features are used and how? How does the respeaker manage to get "Manchester United" displayed on the screen?

3.4.2. Respeaking in Flanders

You can find the videos and pictures that you need for this section in DVD > Chapter 3 > Discussion points and exercises > 3.4.2.

Have a look at pictures "VTM Pic 1", "VTM Pic 2" and "VTM Pic 3" to see how the respeaking working station at VTM in Flanders compares to the previous ones in the UK.

Watch the videos "VTM Video 1", "VTM Video 2", "VTM Video 3" and "VTM Video 4". They capture in chronological order the different stages of the production of live subtitles for a news programme broadcast by VTM. Taking into account the description provided in section 3.1.3, what are the respeakers doing in each of the videos? Bear in mind that only the respeaker on the right-hand side is actually producing live subtitles.

3.4.3. Respeaking in Switzerland and Italy

You can find the videos that you need for this section in DVD > Chapter 3 > Discussion points and exercises > 3.4.3.

Watch the videos "Respeaking at SWISS TXT", "Respeaking at SWISS TXT -SF", "Respeaking at SWISS TXT –SF Sports" and "Respeaking at SWISS TXT-RS1 La 1" to see how respeaking is done at SWISS TXT both in German and Italian and how it compares to respeaking in the UK and Flanders.

The videos "SWISS TXT - Add-on Sentence Mode" and "SWISS TXT - Add-on Phrase Mode" show two new display modes introduced by SWISS TXT. What are their main advantages and disadvantages with regard to the more traditional scrolling and block modes?

Watch the video "Respeaking at Colby". What is the average delay of the subtitles produced by Colby's respeakers in the video? In those instances in which the respeakers use the touch screen to introduce punctuation marks or key words (for example Miss Italia, Barrichello, "La vitta in diretta", Clooney), does the delay vary?

3.4.4. Respeaking in Canada, France and the US

You can find the videos that you need for this section in DVD > Chapter 3 > Discussion points and exercises > 3.4.4.

In "Respeaking at VTA", you can see a different approach to respeaking, using a Nintendo 64 joystick to introduce punctuation marks.

Let's have a look now at another method used by TF1, France 2 and France 3. The videos "TF1 – Live Subtitling Commercial" and "FR3 – Respoken Subtitles" show an advertisement of these subtitles and their final appearance on screen respectively. What is the main difference between the subtitles shown in both videos? How have the subtitles on the commercial been made? What is the average delay of the subtitles shown in the FR3 video?

Watch the video "EclipseVox with Dragon". What is the average delay of these subtitles as opposed to other respoken subtitles produced with Dragon? What do you think about the display mode of the subtitles?

3.4.5. Respeaking at University

Finally, the video "Respeaking in Class – UAB" (DVD > Chapter 3 > Discussion points and exercises > 3.4.5) shows a respeaking class in the on-campus MA on Audiovisual Translation at the Universitat Autònoma de Barcelona (UAB). The fact that there were 15 students respeaking simultaneously in the same classroom did not seem to affect recognition. What do you think are the challenges of teaching respeaking in a classroom as opposed to a professional environment?

4. Respeaking Skills[1]

4.0. Introduction

In Chapter 1, a series of questions were left unanswered as to the extent to which respeaking equals repetition of the source text and whether respeaking is closer to subtitling or interpreting. Having covered the terminology (Chapter 1), the origin of respeaking as a live subtitling method (Chapter 2) and especially the different respeaking practices around the world (Chapter 3), it now seems clear that respeaking is no mere repetition of the source text. Likewise, although the end product of respeaking are subtitles, the process is closer to interpreting, in this case simultaneous intralingual (and sometimes interlingual) interpreting with punctuation marks and some SDH features. In many ways respeaking is to subtitling what interpreting is to translation, namely a leap from the written to the oral without the safety net of time.

The problem here is that whereas respeakers are regularly carrying out the process of respeaking (listening to the source text and transcribing/reformulating it as they dictate punctuation and introduce SDH features), they only seem to achieve recognition for what they produce (subtitles displayed on the screen):

> Respeaking is not yet recognised as a job in its own right, but merely as a branch of subtitling. Respeakers and subtitlers are in the same salary bracket, even though their jobs entail very different things; remuneration for respeaking, however, is significantly lower than for stenography, even though the two jobs are very similar. (Marsh 2004:26)

More attention needs to be paid to what is really involved in respeaking so that respeakers can obtain the credit they deserve for their work. With this purpose in mind, this chapter is devoted to positioning respeaking in relation to simultaneous interpreting and subtitling. The aim is to outline the skills that are required to carry out this job and then, in subsequent chapters, to explain how these skills can be provided.

4.1. Respeaking and interpreting

The comparison between respeaking and interpreting is a common discussion in respeaking classes: which one is more difficult? Although the question is probably too reductionist to be dealt with in depth, attempting to answer it helps to outline some of the complexities involved in interpreting and, more importantly, in respeaking. Those who choose interpreting as an answer often argue that, while both disciplines feature split attention and multitasking, only interpreting

---

[1] This chapter draws heavily on Arumí Ribas and Romero-Fresco (2008).

requires necessarily a change of language. Yet, what is overlooked here is that respeaking may entail interlingual translation and that the multitasking involved in respeaking is more complex than that required in interpreting. Interpreters, activating immediate verbal agility and speed upon receiving the message, must listen to the source text and speak the target text at the same time while they also listen to their own voice (the target text again) to monitor what they are saying. Respeakers must also listen (to the source text), speak (the target text) and listen (to the target text), but their job is not finished there. Rather, it is passed on to the software, which means that respeakers also have to read (what is being displayed on the screen in case there are errors) and sometimes write or rather type (correcting the errors, changing the position of some subtitles, etc.). As will be explained in Chapter 7, the complexity here does not only lie in the multiplicity of tasks, but in the fact that, although happening at the same time, these tasks do not overlap fully.

In any case, leaving aside the which-one-is-more-difficult discussion for a more traditional comparative approach,[2] it seems that the two activities share clear time constraints, namely real-time production, little or no margin for correction or improvement and the need for the practitioners to control their voice while listening. Another common feature is the thematic and lexical preparation, achieved in both disciplines through extensive glossaries, databases and terminology searches. Finally, yet another similarity lies in the working set-up. Simultaneous interpreters and respeakers alike often work unpredictable hours, including weekends. They work in booths with a microphone and a headset and often with another colleague, both team members working for no longer than 30 minutes so as to achieve a good performance.

As for the differences, an important one is that whereas interpreters must have good diction, timbre and articulation so that listening is pleasant and comfortable for the audience, respeakers' voices are usually flat and monotonous, as they are not addressing a human audience but a computer programme that must recognize their message. This aspect will be dealt more in detail in Chapter 6. Suffice it to say here that although interpreting students tend to perform well as respeakers, they sometimes struggle to eliminate the pleasant tone they have been trained to use. Another difference lies in the type of work covered by a simultaneous interpreter and a respeaker (Marsh 2004). Meetings, conferences, summits and court cases form the staple diet of simultaneous interpreters, whereas respeakers work mainly on live television broadcasts such as news, parliamentary sessions, sport events and magazines. The use of respeaking in public events may change this trend (see Chapter 9). Finally, as anticipated above, the main difference between interpreting and respeaking is a linguistic one. Interpreting is always interlingual and requires decoding in the source language and simultaneous recoding in the target language, whereas respeaking is usually an intralingual activity. This does not make respeaking a repetition of the source text, as it requires the introduction

---

[2] See also Marsh (2004) and Remael and van der Veer (2006).

of pauses and punctuation in speech, editing and a careful selection of the terminology that the SR software can best process. Additionally, extra-linguistic aspects have to be dealt with, for example, by selecting different colours or making use of labels indicating a change of speaker. All of this means that the respeaker, far from being a mere parrot, has to perform a process of message comprehension and reformulation that often requires a certain distancing from word-for-word formulation.

It is this aspect that separates respeaking from shadowing, a technique that has long been used in the initial phases of simultaneous interpreting training and that consists in simultaneously repeating a speech in the same language, using the same words. Authors such as Schweda Nicholson (1990) and Lambert (1992) argue that shadowing helps students in their initial phases to master the technique of listening and speaking at the same time, in addition to following a pace set by an external source. Yet, notwithstanding this tradition, the usefulness of shadowing has often been questioned (Kurz 1992) or rejected outright (Seleskovitch and Lederer 1989). The rationale here is that simultaneous interpreting consists of deverbalizing the original and that this exercise leads students to focus too much on the words and not on the idea being conveyed. In his studies on the levels of information processing, Lambert (1993) showed that comprehension and recall are significantly higher in interpreting than they are in shadowing, which is merely a literal repetition of the source message.

As far as respeaking is concerned, the interest of this discussion lies in whether shadowing may be useful for training purposes. In this sense, although it should not be considered as the purpose and product of respeaking, it may be useful as an exercise to help future respeakers grapple with the difficult task of listening and speaking at the same time. As in simultaneous interpreting training, it would be recommendable to set, as early as possible in respeaking training, exercises that help the student to avoid following the speaker blindly, such as the introduction of punctuation marks or editing and reformulation techniques that force students to keep enough distance to understand the meaning of the unit to be respoken.

4.2. Respeaking and subtitling

Of all the different types of subtitling available (interlingual subtitling for hearing viewers, SDH, karaoke subtitling or even subtitling for therapeutic purposes (Porteiro-Fresco 2009), ordinary pre-recorded SDH is the one that bears more similarities with respeaking. Indeed, they both aim at creating the same product (comprehensible written subtitles, usually in the source text language) for the same audience (mainly deaf and hard of hearing viewers, but also hearing viewers who may use subtitles for language-learning purposes or in situations where no sound is heard on screen, such as a waiting room or a pub). For this purpose, respeakers and subtitlers usually have to reformulate or edit in their own language, often applying text reduction strategies. Good grammar and spelling skills are needed for both disciplines, with particular focus on punctuation, which will have to be delivered orally in the case of respeakers. Besides, the source text often poses the same type of difficulties for respeakers and subtitlers, namely multiple turn-taking, overlapping dialogue, use of realia (famous names, geographical references, names and institutions), etc. Regarding the audience, both respeakers and subtitlers need to be aware of their viewers' needs and requirements so as to, for instance, produce appropriate extralinguistic information.

As far as the differences are concerned, the most important are two: the translation situation (offline/live) and the translation mode (written/oral). As regards the former, whereas subtitlers may have more or less time to produce their work, respeakers have to deal with the pressure inherent in a live situation. Thus, all the difficulties involved in the subtitling process that may be shared by subtitling and respeaking, such as the need to deal with technological vagaries, become increasingly demanding in respeaking, where pause, re-thinking and correction are usually not an option. As for the translation mode, it is often very different: whereas subtitlers (when they have access to the written script of the source text) provide a written-to-written translation, respeakers (considering respeaking as a process) provide an oral-to-oral translation. This is the reason why, as mentioned in the introduction, it may be argued that respeaking is to subtitling what interpreting is to translation, i.e. a leap from the written to the oral without the safety net provided by time.

4.3. The specificity of respeaking

As well as subtitling and interpreting skills, respeaking also calls for other abilities that may be regarded as specific to respeaking (Remael and van der Veer 2006). First of all, respeakers must be fully familiarized with the SR software they are going to use, which becomes an indispensable co-worker for them. Not only is it a tool, but a partner which, if no corrections are made, is going to have the final say about the subtitle that will be displayed on the screen. Thus, in the same way that SR software is often described as speaker-dependent (a respeaker is needed as an intermediate step between the source text speaker and the software), the respeaker can be said to be software-dependent.

First of all, respeakers are expected to know how SR technology fits in the bigger respeaking picture, that is, how much of the end-result hinges upon the performance of the software. This is very important, as the amount of work carried out by this software in the respeaking process is directly proportional to the amount of work that must be carried out by the respeaker to constantly train it and improve it. Likewise, respeakers are expected to have a basic understanding of how SR technology processes acoustic data, which is very different to the way humans do. As Keyes (2007) points out, we adopt a top-down approach to recognizing speech, thus resorting to concepts and circumstantial knowledge to distinguish words. Computers adopt a bottom-up approach, analyzing sound structures, the most basic of which is the phoneme, to be able to recognize speech. This, which will be explained in detail in Chapter 5, is of paramount importance for the delivery of the target text, as respeakers are expected to pronounce words carefully, setting clear boundaries between them to minimize misrecognitions. Overall, respeakers must feel at ease when dictating to the SR software, which requires familiarization with the software demands and limitations.

Once these limitations are identified, respeakers must try either to overcome them or at least to minimize them through training, which is possibly the most important part of the preparation stage in respeaking. In general, the main aim of this training stage is to obtain a conflict-free outcome (Keyes 2007), that is, to make sure that the SR software departs as little as possible from what the respeaker has dictated. At least three tools are available for this purpose: individual voice models, vocabularies and macros. First of all, respeakers have their own voice models or user profiles, which they create and enhance through continuous dictation, thus helping the software to get used to their speech patterns. Although current SR software such as the English version of Dragon NaturallySpeaking has a sizeable corpus of some 150,000 words, many specialized terms or proper nouns needed to respeak a specific (audiovisual) programme are likely to be missing (the so-called out-of-vocabulary words). Respeakers must introduce them manually or through dictation, thus fine-tuning their voice models and minimizing the error rate. Yet, as pointed out by Marsh (2004), the software is bound to have problems when deciding between homophones or near-homophones such as *bunker* or *banker*. In this case, respeakers can make use of a second tool – the creation of specific vocabularies for specific topics. Thus, for the golf vocabulary they will introduce most of the specific terms used in this sport and, once it is activated, the SR software will choose *bunker* instead of *banker*, in the same way that it would opt for the latter should the financial vocabulary be selected.

Also very useful are the so-called macros. In this case, respeakers can set the software to display a word or group of words every time they utter a given command, which they prepare in advance. This can be helpful to save much-needed time when respeaking (for instance, the command *Queen macro* could trigger 'Her Majesty the Queen Elizabeth II'), but also to avoid potential misrecognitions (*Bor-macro* to trigger the surname Borowski as opposed to, say, 'brought ski'), to improve punctuation (*mac-ex* for exclamation mark) and to change the subtitle colour orally (*macroyellow*). It thus follows that a great deal of the preparation work to be carried out by respeakers beforehand lies in being able to anticipate the potential problems that may be faced by the software and in using the available tools as effectively as possible to solve them. As for the respeaking skills included within the "crossover" category, one that is worth noting is mental pre-editing (Remael and van der Veer 2007). Indeed, apart from the multitasking process involved in listening (source text) while speaking (target text), reading (the subtitles, trying to pay attention to the potential errors) and typing (corrections, subtitle position and colour), respeakers are also expected to anticipate what will or will not be recognized by the software. Many terms may come up that have not been prepared beforehand, and so respeakers will have to find a way round them to avoid potential misrecognitions.

Finally, although the delivery skills needed for respeaking are fairly self-explanatory (see table 4.1 below), it should be pointed out that they may also depend on the SR software used and even on the way it displays the subtitles on the screen. ViaVoice, for example, has a word-for-word display mode, whereas Dragon or Vista display subtitles in chunks which usually correspond to full sentences or phrases. There may be in this case a bigger delay, as the software waits for the respeaker to pause after dictating the last word of a chunk/sentence to show the whole utterance on the screen. Thus, when respeaking with ViaVoice, respeakers are basically concerned with being able to split their attention to listen as they speak, type, and read. With Dragon or Vista, respeakers may be expected to minimize the inevitable delay by producing short phrases or sentences that will be shown as subtitles. They then need to bear in mind the appropriate length of these units and other relevant features, which means that they need "insight into subtitling concepts such as reading speed and spotting" (Remael and van deer Veer 2006). Therefore, although all the skills included in the table below are necessary, respeaking with ViaVoice requires mainly those that are common to interpreting, whereas respeaking with Dragon or Vista also draws heavily on subtitling skills.

4.4. Respeaking skills summarized

After comparing and contrasting respeaking, simultaneous interpreting and subtitling, the next step is to identify the competencies inherent in each of the practices in question that respeakers must master to do their job. Needless to say, the identification of these skills is a fundamental step for the design of any respeaking course. Table 4.1 outlines the most relevant skills required for a professional respeaker and arranges them in a double-entry matrix. The vertical columns delimit the fields from which the competences are obtained, be it subtitling, simultaneous interpreting or respeaking, in the case of those that are inherent to this discipline. The horizontal rows feature other elements of classification. The first of them is temporal, and is related to the process carried out by the respeaker. A distinction is made here between the skills required before the process, those to be applied after the process and those to be activated as the process is taking place. In turn, the latter are further divided into those skills that are related to the source text, the target text or the transition between the two, which is referred to as crossover.

RESPEAKING SKILLS				
		FROM SDH	FROM SIMULTANEOUS INTERPRETING	SPECIFIC TO RESPEAKING
PRIOR TO THE PROCESS		Software-related skills -Ability to use industry-standard subtitling software.	Preparation skills - Fostering of research capacity; - Ability to develop subject matter glossaries and databases; - Familiarity with terminology in specialized fields; - Compliance with the Code of Ethics. Strategic skills -Ability to work as part of a team.	Software-related skills * General knowledge - Understanding of how it fits in the bigger picture; - Understanding of how speech recognition technology works (bottom-up as opposed to top-down); - Comfort dictating to speech recognition software; - Awareness of software demands and limitations; - Confidence in new technology (working with it, not against it). * Preparation of the software - Ability to search for a controlled outcome, anticipating possible errors; - Ability to constantly improve both voice model and vocabulary; - Mastery of the skills required to develop macros; - Readiness to test and report benefits and drawbacks.

Table 4.1: Taxonomy of respeaking skills (continued)

RESPEAKING SKILLS				
		FROM SDH	FROM SIMULTANEOUS INTERPRETING	SPECIFIC TO RESPEAKING
DURING THE PROCESS	ST	General source text-related skills - Ability to reformulate/edit; - Ability to apply text reduction strategies; - Spotting skills. Specific source text -related skills - Ability to cope with multiple turn-taking or overlapping dialogue; - Attention to realia; - Ability to adapt to different programme genres.	Listening comprehension skills - Attention to concentrated listening; - Familiarity with accent recognition: geographic and social variants; - Familiarity with the cultural context; - Ability to develop short term memory; - Ability to develop emergency strategies when source text is not understood. Analysis, synthesis and reformulation skills - Ability to understand the communicative intention of the source message; - Ability to understand the red thread of the discourse; - Capacity to select and focalize the relevant information; - Ability to divide between main and secondary ideas; - Capacity to identify the discourse connectors; - Capacity to deduce meaning through context and extralinguistic elements; - Ability to condense information; - Ability to segment information in sense units.	

Table 4.1: Taxonomy of respeaking skills (continued)

RESPEAKING SKILLS				
		FROM SDH	FROM SIMULTANEOUS INTERPRETING	SPECIFIC TO RESPEAKING
	CROSS-OVER	Synchronization skills - Ability to synchronize oral dialogue and subtitles.	Multitasking skills - Ability to speak while listening; - Capacity to receive analytically the incoming message; - Capacity to monitor the outgoing message; - Ability to keep up with rapid dialogue; - Confidence in maintaining décalage. Live skills - Ability to show calmness and accuracy under pressure; - Capacity to manage stress: no second chances; - Ability to correct one's own mistakes; - Attentiveness to keep target text audience in mind.	Multitasking skills - Ability to cope with up to four types of simultaneous intersemiotic tasks: Listening while speaking, writing and reading. Live skills - Ability and speed to change the subtitle colour/label; - Ability and speed to change the subtitle position; - Mental-pre-editing skills; - Ability to cope with visual feedback from screen; - Comfort in dealing with no feedback from the audience; - Confidence in dealing with technological vagaries.
	TT	Production skills -Accurate grammar; - Accurate spelling (including punctuation); - Ability to produce comprehensible subtitles.	Delivery skills - Ability to express thoughts clearly and concisely; - Extensive vocabulary; - Ability to control one's own voice; - Ability to communicate fluently; - Ability to communicate with accuracy; - Capacity to reproduce the same tone and register as in the source text; - Capacity to transmit conviction and self confidence; - Ability to communicate with good voice projection without hesitations, unnecessary repetitions and corrections; - Ability to communicate with good diction.	Delivery skills - Ability to produce a consistent delivery, enunciating every word clearly; - Attentiveness to avoid pauses between each word; - Ability to set word boundaries clearly; - Attentiveness to enunciate sounds within small words; - Ability to speak in short stretches of text (respeaking units) that can lend themselves to accurate recognition by the software (phrases as opposed to single words) and to comfortable reading for the viewers; - Ability to dictate at higher than average speed; - Accurate oral punctuation.

Table 4.1: *Taxonomy of respeaking skills (continued)*

		RESPEAKING SKILLS		
		FROM SDH	FROM SIMULTANEOUS INTERPRETING	SPECIFIC TO RESPEAKING
		Awareness of target audience -Understanding of Deaf people's difficulties when watching TV; -Knowledge about the required reading speed (intuitive sense of reading speed for segmentation); - Ability to convey extra-linguistic information; - Awareness of style sheets and norms.		
AFTER THE PROCESS		Assessment skills - Ability to analyse one's own (or somebody else's) subtitles, provide feedback and draw conclusions to improve future practice.	Assessment skills - Capacity to cope with frustration caused by the inevitability of mistakes; - Ability to reflect on the live performance and think of ways to improve it for next time.	Assessment skills - Knowledge of different methods to calculate accuracy rate as well as the situations for which they are better suited; - Ability to assess the accuracy of respoken subtitles providing not only a percentage of errors but also feedback on what aspects were (un)successful and how they can be tackled in the future.

Table 4.1: Taxonomy of respeaking skills

4.5. Discussion points and exercises

4.5.1. Respeaking skills as viewed by respeakers and employers

You can find the documents that you need for this section in DVD > Chapter 4 > Discussion points and exercises > 4.5.1.

Read the accounts given by respeakers at IMS and RBM. What are the main differences between them? How do these respeakers view their job? Do they mention any skill required for the job that has not been included in the table presented in this chapter?

In the same folder, there are two more descriptions of what respeaking involves ("Respeaking Job at Red Bee 1" and "Respeaking Job at Red Bee 2"). How do these descriptions, especially the second one, compare to the above accounts given by the respeakers? Do they mention any further skills?

For similar information about respeaking in France, you can read "Journée Type" and "Descriptif du Poste Paris".

Finally, "Colby-Live Subtitling" also covers some of the skills called for in respeaking. Yet, when it deals with the training of respeakers, it mentions a professional figure that has so far been overlooked. What figure is it? To what extent do you think this is important in respeaking?

4.5.2. Research

Look for other websites (of subtitling companies, universities, deaf associations) outlining the skills needed to become a respeaker. Do they mention any new skills that can be added to the table?

Look up on the Internet universities and schools offering training in respeaking. What skills do they identify as being the most relevant? Is respeaking included as part of subtitling courses, interpreting courses or as a separate component?

5. Respeaking Skills Applied before the Process
General Knowledge of SR

5.0. Introduction

Put simply, SR is just another input method, like using a mouse or a keyboard, albeit in this case the input is provided by means of speech, as opposed to clicks or strokes. For some years now, SR has been regarded in the field of technology as the next big thing that, alas, doesn't work. In its wide and perhaps somewhat hasty release in the early 90s, SR software failed to live up to its promise, causing first disappointment and then scepticism among the many professionals from different walks of life who tested the technology. The accuracy offered by these applications ranged between 90% and 95%, which sounded high on paper but proved too low to be used on a daily basis. As far as respeaking is concerned, this must be added to the average results usually obtained in respeaking workshops at Audiovisual Translation conferences, which is inevitable, given that there is no time to train the software. This has often resulted in reservations as to the reliability of respeaking and in the consideration of this technique as "a glimpse of the future".

Yet, the current professional practice of respeaking in many TV channels as well as the results obtained by the most modern SR applications shows that this is very much a present reality. The new generation of SR software has benefited from more powerful computers with massive technological improvements, which have increased recognition up to 98% and 99%. Users seem to have regained confidence in SR and so have leading companies such as Google, whose Vice-president, Vint Cerf, has pointed to SR as one of the main future pillars for the Web, given its potential for solving health and disability issues.

This chapter includes a description of how SR works (components and process) and how it can be applied to respeaking, as well as an overview of the past, present and future of this technology. However, before moving into this, three important aspects must be clarified:

SR recognizes what we say, not what we mean
Contrary to Star Trek-based misconceptions, there is no artificial intelligence involved in SR technology (yet). When we speak, the software recognizes our utterance and reacts as programmed but does not enable us to hold a conversation with our computers.

SR is different from voice recognition
Although they are often used interchangeably, there is a clear distinction between these two types of technology. SR recognizes *what we say* and displays it on the screen (or executes a certain command if what we dictate is a command). **Voice recognition** recognizes *who says what*. It is a form of biometrics mainly

used for security purposes to identify a specific individual on the basis of the unique characteristics of his/her voice.

SR can be speaker-dependent or speaker-independent
Speaker-dependent SR requires users to train the software so that it learns about their pronunciation, speech patterns etc. This technology allows for the use of very large vocabularies with high recognition (98% to 99%) and is the one chosen for respeaking so far. **Speaker-independent SR** can recognize different speakers without any training. In order to achieve optimum accuracy, it is often used with small vocabularies, such as telephone menus. Speaker-independent SR is also being tested with large vocabularies (see section 5.4.5) but the results are so far worse than those of speaker-dependent SR and not deemed good enough for live subtitling.

5.1. How it works: main components and process

5.1.1. Main components

All SR applications employ 3 basic speech models:
- Acoustic model
- Grammar / vocabulary / lexicon / dictionary
- Language model(s)

Acoustic model
This is a collection of speech data located in the speech engine and comprising (a) a large amount of audio material, (b) its exact proofed and corrected transcription and (c) the digital representation of that audio material in the way of waveforms of individual sounds; in other words, what this audio material looks like mathematically. In the case of Dragon, the speech data collected as far back as 1999 (Dragon Systems) from the US Defense Advanced Research Projects Agency (DARPA) and all the speech data collected by L&H and Nuance consists of over 15,000 speakers and includes 10 million words. The speakers from whom this data was compiled are a combination of male and female end-users, newscasters and professional speakers of all ages.

Grammar / vocabulary / lexicon / dictionary
This is the list of words among which the speech engine can choose so as to recognize the speaker's utterance. This list of words is specified in advance by the software developers. If the speaker's utterance is not on the list, it will not be recognized or rather it will be misrecognized.

Although grammar, vocabulary, lexicon and dictionary are sometimes used interchangeably to refer to this component, they are not exactly the same. For example, it is possible to load different grammars for different purposes, such as a grammar for sports and a grammar for news, with different words. The vocabulary is the sum of all of the loaded grammars and so 5 grammars with 50 words each will yield a total vocabulary of 250 words. Finally, other experts refer to the vocabulary as dictionary and others prefer the word lexicon as, they note, the only difference between a dictionary and a lexicon is the fact that a lexicon contains no definitions, which applies to this particular case.

Language model
A language model is a probabilistic mechanism for generating text that calculates the likelihood of occurrence of a word string. In other words, it analyzes the word recognized by the acoustic model and calculates how likely it is to have occurred after the previous words and before the next words in the speaker's utterance. The next section includes an explanation of how this model works.

5.1.2. Process

(a) From analogue sound to phonemes:
Let's see how a phrase such as "New York City" is handled by a speech recognizer. First of all, the microphone transforms our utterance into an analogue signal and feeds it to the PC's sound card. An analogue-to-digital converter takes the signal and converts it to a stream of digital data (ones and zeros), i.e. the type of language a computer can understand. Here is when the SR software comes in. The acoustic model analyzes the sounds of our voice and coverts them to phonemes, the smallest units of sound (the English language contains approximately 45 phonemes). This process happens as follows: first, the acoustic model removes noise and unneeded information such as changes in volume. Then, using mathematical calculations, it reduces the data to a spectrum of frequencies (the pitches of the sounds), analyzes the data, and converts the words into digital representations of phonemes.

(b) From phonemes to words
The phonemes obtained in the acoustic model are checked against the words available in the dictionary to see which word the phoneme(s) correspond to. It is important to note that the SR software is usually not sure about what the speaker has said. This uncertainty is handled by using a method based on probabilities. The Speech Engine returns a *confidence score* for any audio it attempts to recognize. This score represents how likely it is that the engine's recognition result matches what the speaker said. In this case, the first choice by the acoustic model in the confidence score will be "New York City" but it is possible that the acoustic model is also considering another option such as "New York Sid", depending on how we have pronounced this phrase. Before the acoustic model makes its choice, the language model often steps in to refine the recognition.

(c) From words to phrases
The language model calculates the probability of a dictated word, for example "City" or "Sid", occurring after "New" and "York". For example, if the large

corpora included in the language model yield 553 occurrences of "New York City" and only 1 of "New York Sid", this will modify the confidence score yielded by the acoustic model. Now, the speech recognizer is almost sure that the speaker has said "New York City" and will offer that as a result. Therefore, although the acoustic model may have chosen "New York Sid" as number one option, the speech recognizer has displayed "New York City" on the screen.

In order to reach this conclusion, the language model applies the so-called **n-gram models** or HMM (Hidden Markov Models) to improve recognition on the basis of contextual information. There are different types of n-gram models. Bigram models analyze 2 words before and after the dictated word; trigram models analyze 3 words before and after the dictated word and finally quadgram models, used by modern speech recognizers such as Dragon (but not ViaVoice), span 4 words before and after the dictated word. The context analysis is conducted word by word through an entire utterance. Each word is selected as a target word and the analysis spans the previous and following two, three and four words. It is for this reason that SR users are expected to dictate in long utterances, so that not only bigram models but also trigram and even the quadgram models can be applied.

Using this method, the language model manages to reduce the error rate by a factor of four, taking accuracy from 80% to 95%. This accuracy may improve if the topics covered by the corpora of texts included in the language model are similar to those being dealt with by the speaker. In other words, a SR system will cope with news programmes more efficiently if it has been trained on such texts. Likewise, if we want the recognizer to cover many areas, it will require a wider range of training texts and it will be less accurate, as the range of likely word sequences increases.

Figure 5.1 shows how an utterance such as "I speak to my" is recognized. Once the analogue signal is digitized, the acoustic model turns it into phonemes. Then, checking it against the lexicon, the acoustic model yields different words in its confidence score (eye, I, eyes, ice / speak, peaked, pig, pick / tomb, to, too, two / my, mike). Finally, the language model calculates, on the basis of statistics, the most likely phrase. In this case, the application of a brigram (I + speak to) and even a trigram model (I + speak to my) yields "I speak to my" as the most likely result:

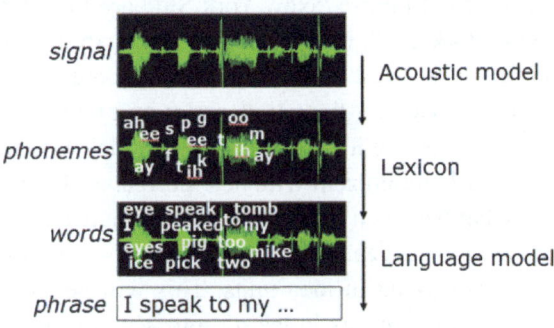

Figure 5.1: The process of SR

5.2. How it works for respeakers

A brief note is in order regarding the use of SR software for the production of live subtitles. It is important to highlight that this type of software is originally intended for dictation, not for respeaking. The focus in this type of technology has so far been placed on increasing accuracy and not necessarily on reducing **latency**. Users who want to type documents with their voice are not bothered by having to wait a couple of seconds until the words are displayed on the screen as long as those words are correct. Respeakers, however, need subtitles to be displayed quickly on the screen. If there is too much delay, viewers will not be able to keep track of what is going on in a given programme. This discrepancy between the traditional goals of SR software and those of respeakers tends to cause problems for subtitling companies, which often have a hard time trying to liaise with SR developers to make their software faster and, in general, more respeaking-friendly. In any case, there are ways in which respeakers can improve the performance of any SR software. This could be done by fine-tuning the acoustic and language models.

The acoustic model is first of all fine-tuned by performing the initial training, in which the model gathers data about the specific speech patterns of the user. Respeakers must make sure that they train the software in as similar a manner as possible to the way they intend to respeak. Training the software at a very low speed to make sure everything is understood does not help if respeakers are later on going to speak at a much faster speed. After the initial training, the acoustic model may be further optimized by training specific words or phrases. Whether these terms are new (out-of-vocabulary words) or they are included in the vocabulary but tend to be misrecognized, respeakers can train them again and thus improve the performance of the acoustic model.

As for the language model, it can be optimized in different ways. Firstly, respeakers can introduce in the software texts that are relevant to the type of programme they usually subtitle. The language model will then include in its statistical calculations those texts when trying to produce an accurate result for what has been dictated. Thus, taking up the example mentioned above, if texts with a high occurrence of the phrase "New York Sid" are introduced, once the software "hears" "New York Sid", it will be more likely to display this phrase as opposed to correcting it to "New York City". In the same way, if respeakers manage to get hold of, for instance, the whole script of a news item before it is broadcast, they can also introduce it in the language model. When they respeak it live, the SR software will recognize it with near perfect accuracy, as in case of doubt it will resort to what has been introduced in the language model.

Another way in which respeakers can optimize the performance of the language model is by respeaking in idea units. This will be further explained in Chapter 7, but it basically consists in taking into account how the language model works and making the most of its potential by dictating, when possible, in phrases. For example, say that the original speaker utters the phrase "meet, as Peter mentioned, the requirements…". If the respeaker utters this verbatim, the software will analyze the word "meet" individually. Only the acoustic model will come into play and it will probably doubt between different similar-sounding words such as "meat", "mead" and even "mid". The language model will not help, as the software will not be able to recognize that this utterance contains the phrase "meet the requirements". If, however, the respeaker decides to utter this as "meet the requirements, as Peter mentioned", the situation will be different. The acoustic model may have doubts as to how to recognize "meet" but the language model will quickly identify the phrase using a bigram model that will point out that "meet + the requirements" is much more likely to occur than "meat + the requirements", "mead + the requirements" or "mid + the requirements". It is for this reason that respeakers must try to speak in idea units, which will improve the performance of the software. As often pointed out by experts,[1] around 70% of SR performance depends on the users, i.e. on their dictation (enunciation, style, length of the utterances, etc.); between 20 and 25% is based on the hardware, that is, the computer (which may or not meet the required specifications) and the microphone (which may or not have been designed for SR); finally, the remaining 5 to 10% depends on the actual software used: Dragon, Viavoice, etc.

5.3. The origins of SR[2]

The first efforts in the field of SR may be recorded as far back as the late 19th century, when Alexander Melville Bell created a phonetic system to teach the deaf to speak called *visible speech*. His son, Alexander Graham Bell, used this system in 1871 to teach instructors of the deaf in Boston and built the so-called phonoautograph to communicate with his deaf wife. Although this system didn't work, it turned out to be an initial stage to one of the major breakthroughs in the history of mankind – the invention of the telephone.

In general, however, although speech technology dates back to 1936, when AT&T's Bell Laboratories produced a device that could emit speech using a keyboard and foot pedals, SR technology did not start until 1952. In this year, Davis, Biddulph and Balashek, also at Bell Labs, devised a system that could recognize isolated digits for a single speaker. In 1956, Olson and Belar (RCA Labs) came up with a system to recognise 10 syllabes of a single speaker. Three years later, in 1959, two other important developments followed: Forgie and Forgie (MIT Lincoln Lab) built a speaker-independent 10-vowel recognizer and Fry and Denes (University College in England) produced a phoneme recognizer to identify 4 vowels and 9 consonants, incorporating for the first time *statistical syntax* in automatic SR.

---

[1] http://www.knowbrainer.com/pubforum/index.cfm?page=viewForumTopic&topicId=10413
[2] This section draws on Kurzweil (1996), Juang and Rabiner (2005), Grabianowski (2010) and IBM (2010).

Recognition at vowel and phoneme level was pursued further in the 1960s by Suzuki and Nakata (Radio Research Lab in Tokyo) and most notably by Sakai and Doshita (Kyoto University), whose work is generally considered a precursor to *continuous SR* software, which doesn't require users to pause after every word. In 1964, IBM, which had started research on SR in the late 1950's, demonstrated recognition of spoken digits at the World's Fair with a product called "shoe box recognizer".

In the 1970s, Tom Martin, a former researcher in RCA Labs, founded the first SR commercial company, Threshold Technology, which developed the first real SR product called the VIP-100 System. Used for TV quality control and by the logistics services company FedEx, the main contribution by VIP-100 is to have influenced the DARPA to fund the Speech Understanding Research (SUR) programme during the early 1970s. Several systems were developed under DARPA'S SUR programme. Harpy, created at Carnegie Mellon University, achieved good accuracy recognizing speech with a vocabulary of 1,011 words, whereas other systems called Hearsay-II and HWIM (Hear What I Mean) failed to meet the goals set.

Also in the 1970s and in parallel to the work carried out by DARPA, IBM and AT&T Bell Laboratories initiated two different schools of thought regarding the commercial application of SR systems. Developed by Fred Jelinek, IBM's recognition system Tangora was designed as a "voice-activated typewriter" which required training by every user. In other words, it was a speaker-dependent application that placed its focus on the size of the vocabulary and the use of n-gram language models to ascertain the probability of occurrence of spoken words. In contrast, the work carried out by AT&T Bell Labs was focused on providing automated telecommunication services for millions of speakers without the need for individual training, that is, speaker-independent SR.

The 1980s brought about the introduction of the Hidden Markov Model (HMM), a probabilistic mechanism used to calculate the likelihood of occurrence of speech. Although the idea of the HMM was first developed in the late 1960s at the Institute for Defence Analyses (IDA) in Princeton, it was not completed and published widely until 1983. Thirty years later, it remains as the preferred method for SR. The 1980s also brought about the foundation of two leading SR providers, Dragon Systems (1982), speaker-dependent system for commercial use, and SpeechWorks (1984), main provider of over-the-telephone automated SR solutions. IBM also pursued its research in the field, releasing in 1984 the world's first 5000-word vocabulary SR system, which could handle discrete dictation (one word at a time) from a trained speaker with up to 95% accuracy.

Following the successful application of the HMM to SR, DARPA re-doubled its efforts on speaker-independent SR in the late 1980s and early 1990s with several projects, notably the Sphinx system from Carnegie Mellon University, the BYBLOS system from BBN Technologies and the DECIPHER system from SRI. Intensive evaluations of the performance of SR technology were carried out during this period with vocabularies of over 20,000 words. Three main problems were identified: the natural and not grammatical speech patterns of most users, the existence of ambient noise and interfering speech in recordings and the need to enable dialogue between the user and the machine to reach some desired state of understanding. Different applications launched in the early 1990s, such as Pegasus and Jupiter (MIT), and in the late 1990s, such as United Airlines' automatic flight information system and AT&T's "How May I Help You? (HMIHY)" call routing system, attempted to solve these problems.

As far as speaker-dependent SR is concerned, the 1990s were also very prolific. In 1990, Dragon introduced DragonDictate 30K, the first large-vocabulary, speech-to-text system for general-purpose dictation, which also allowed control of a PC with voice commands. Although popular among disabled users, it failed to attract a wider audience, possibly because it required the speaker to pause between words. It was thus clear for Jim and Janet Baker, founders of DragonSystems, that continuous SR was needed. Two years later, in 1993, they received a federal Technology Reinvestment Project award to develop this technology. As a result of this research, in July 1997 Dragon presented the award-winning Dragon NaturallySpeaking, a continuous SR programme for general-purpose use with a vocabulary of 23,000 words. One month later, in August 1997, IBM followed up the creation of its discrete dictation system VoiceType 3.0 (1996) with the release of the continuous SR application ViaVoice, which would go on to become Dragon's main competitor in the speaker-dependent SR market.

5.4. The present: state of the art and software available

Although there is an increasing number of free SR programmes available (CVoice Control, PerlBox, Sphinx, Open Mind Speech), often for Linux and thus open source, their performance is still not reliable enough to be used for respeaking. For this purpose, commercialized SR applications are still the most viable option.

5.4.1. Viascribe

Viascribe is the software used by the Liberated Learning Consortium (LLC). Initiated in 1998 at Saint Mary's University (Halifax, Canada) and composed of more than 21 universities and research centres from all over the world, the LLC sets out to create and foster barrier-free learning environments where all students have equal access to information. The particularity of the LLC is that it doesn't envisage the use of a respeaker to make classes accessible. Rather, lecturers speak directly to a microphone connected to a computer with Viascribe, which transcribes what the lecturer has said on a screen for all students to read. From the beginning, this approach posed two main difficulties: the need to convince lecturers to train the software in advance and the dictation of punctuation marks. To solve this, researchers at IBM T.J. Watson Center (also a partner of the LLC) adapted the ViaVoice technology to create Viascribe, which is available in UK and US English, Japanese, Chinese (Mandarin), French, Italian, Spanish and German. Unlike ViaVoice, Viascribe can be trained by feeding recordings of the user's voice, in this case university lectures. In this way, lecturers don't have to spend time training the software. Besides, Viascribe has an in-built application which introduces new lines and paragraph breaks when speakers make a pause in their speech, which means that there is no need to dictate punctuation marks. Furthermore, Viascribe saves the SR-generated transcript and creates media files that are accessible to hearing, hearing impaired and even blind students, as the audio of the transcripts is also saved. However, all these features that enable the use of Viascribe in class hinder its use for respeaking. A key factor in this sense is that its current average accuracy (between 75% and 85%) may be acceptable for a class, but is far from the 97% currently required for live subtitling. Two videos describing how Viascribe works are included in DVD > Chapter 5 > Discussion points and exercises > 5.6.1.

5.4.2. Windows Speech Recognition

Microsoft researchers have been working on speech technologies since 1993, when they hired three of the four experts from Carnegie Mellon University responsible for the successful Sphinx-II SR system in 1992. Research at Microsoft led initially to the development of the Speech API (SAPI), designed so that software developers could write an application to perform SR. Although SR technology had been used previously by Microsoft in some of its products, the first mainstream version of Microsoft Windows to offer fully-integrated support for SR, known as Windows Speech Recognition (WSR), was Windows Vista, released in 2006. Windows 7, released in 2009, also has WSR.

As is the case with ViaVoice and Dragon, WSR allows users to control their computers with voice commands and to dictate into different applications. The languages currently supported are English (U.S. and British), Spanish, German, French, Japanese and Chinese (traditional and simplified). Although WSR is often said to achieve high accuracy, it has so far not been used for respeaking. This may be due to the fact that, by the time it was released, broadcasters who were resorting to respeaking were already using ViaVoice or Dragon. Besides, its combination with a subtitling application may not be entirely straightforward.

In any case, it is worth noting that, like Dragon (and unlike ViaVoice), WSR requires the user to pause his/her dictation so that the utterance is shown on the screen. The display mode is in blocks, as opposed to the word-for-word mode of ViaVoice. From the point of view of respeaking, the main disadvantage of WSR is its latency, i.e. the time it takes for the software to display on the screen what the user has said. This latency, longer in Dragon than in ViaVoice, is even longer in the case of WSR. Taking into account that ViaVoice-based subtitles have an average delay of 3 to 6 seconds and those produced with Dragon somewhere around 4 to 7 seconds, the use of WSR for respeaking could result in a 7- to 10-second delay. In any case, and given that it is bundled for free with Vista and Windows 7, further tests are needed to see whether WSR may be used for respeaking, if only for training purposes. Videos showing how WSR works can be found in DVD > Chapter 5 > Discussion points and exercises > 5.6.2.

5.4.3. ViaVoice

In 2003, IBM gave ScanSoft (owner of Dragon) exclusive global distribution rights to ViaVoice for Windows and MAC. In 2005, Nuance merged with Scansoft and now ViaVoice is a Nuance product. Yet, unlike Dragon, ViaVoice has been discontinued. The latest version, ViaVoice 10, can still be acquired in UK and US English, German, Italian, Japanese and Spanish, but the software is no longer being developed. As described in Chapter 3, some companies still use it for respeaking, but many others are changing or have already changed to Dragon.

Produced before the release of Windows Vista, ViaVoice was designed to run on Microsoft® Windows 98SE, 2000 Professional (Service Pack 2) and XP Home & Professional Editions with the following system requirements:

- Intel® Pentium® 300 MHz processor and 256K L2 cache or equivalent (including AMD-K6® with 256K (L2 cache);
- 64 MB RAM for Windows 98 Second Edition and Windows Me;
- 96 MB RAM for Windows 2000;
- 192 MB RAM for Win XP Home and Professional;
- USB port for USB microphone input;
- 510 MB of available hard drive space;
- Quad-speed CD-ROM drive or faster.

In order to run it in Windows Vista, it is necessary to turn off Windows Firewall and install ViaVoice using the compatibility mode.[3]

ViaVoice 10 has the following editions: Pro USB Edition, Advanced Edition, Standard Edition, Personal Edition, ViaVoice for Mac OS X Edition and Simply Dictation for Mac. Of all these, the most suitable for respeaking is ProUSB Edition (currently around £115 or €140), as it is compatible with different Windows systems and it allows the use of macros and specialized vocabulary topics.

As far as respeaking is concerned, ViaVoice has so far yielded very good results, as attested by the subtitles produced by RBM and IMS. Following a brief enrolment to create the voice profile (a short paragraph) and a longer training process (four short stories, an hour long overall), users may expect to achieve 95% accuracy in their dictation. Further training may allow users to achieve 98% to 99% in dictation, which usually drops to 97% to 98% in respeaking. The main advantage of ViaVoice for respeaking is its speed and short latency. As shown in

---

[3] Screenshots and a description of this process can be found in "ViaVoice–Vista–Install" (DVD > Chapter 5 > Discussion points and exercises > 5.6.2).

the videos "ViaVoice 1" and "ViaVoice 2" (DVD > Chapter 5 > Discussion points and exercises > 5.6.2), it takes very little time for the words to be displayed on screen. The words appear on scrolling mode but not regularly: sometimes one word at a time and other times in bursts of two or three words. ViaVoice-based subtitles have a short delay of 3 to 6 seconds, which includes the transmission from the SR engine to the subtitling application as well as from the latter to the TV screen. Another key advantage is that, unlike with Dragon, no pause is required for the utterance to be displayed on the screen. Respeakers can thus concentrate solely on listening and speaking at the same time, without having to think of when they must pause.

However, the fact that ViaVoice has been discontinued and has not been developed for eight years (a long time in SR terms) poses several problems regarding its use for respeaking. First of all, ViaVoice's language model is less powerful than the one included in Dragon, which may explain why Dragon's accuracy is generally considered to be higher. Furthermore, ViaVoice requires a more robotic delivery than Dragon, is more sensible to noise and microphone issues and allows fewer options in terms of specialized vocabularies and macros, which are essential for respeaking.

All in all, although ViaVoice has contributed to the successful past and even present of respoken subtitles, its future contribution looks more uncertain.

5.4.4. Dragon NaturallySpeaking

5.4.4.1. Dragon 10
Many of the exercises included in this book and some of its contents, especially Chapter 6, are based on Dragon NaturallySpeaking 10, released in 2008 and available in US English, UK English, Australian English, Southern Asian English, Indian English, Teen English, Spanish, French, German, Italian and Dutch. Dragon 10 is compatible with any Windows version and its update, Dragon 10.1, is also compatible with Vista 64-bit operating systems.

The recommended specifications for Dragon 10 are:

- CPU: Intel® Pentium4® / 2.4 GHz (1.6 GHz dual core) or equivalent AMD processor. (SSE2 instruction set required).
- Memory: 1 GB RAM
- L2 Cache: 1 MB

As was the case with previous editions, Dragon 10 has four different versions: Standard, Preferred, Professional and MacSpeech Dictate, for Macintosh.

Standard is the most affordable option (currently £80 or €100) and can be used for respeaking, but has some important limitations. First of all, it does not feature playback dictation, that is, it cannot play back what the user has dictated, which is sometimes useful to find out what respeakers have said and where they have gone wrong. Most importantly, though, with this version it is not possible to import or export voice profiles, which means that users can only use Dragon in one computer. In contrast, Dragon Preferred (£150, €199) does have the playback dictation function and allows to import and export files. In this way, respeakers can, for example, train their profiles at home in their PC or laptops and then import them into their office computers to respeak a given programme. Besides, Dragon Preferred is usually bilingual, including the language of the country where it has been bought and English by default. This is also the case with Dragon Professional (£630, €800), which offers on top of this the possibility of creating custom voice commands, importing and exporting commands and vocabularies as well as purchasing specialized vocabularies developed by Nuance.

Although subtitling companies may want to choose Dragon Professional, for more modest budgets (whether for personal use or for teaching purposes) it makes sense to opt for Dragon Preferred as opposed to the Standard version, given the importance of being able to import/export files from and to different computers.

According to Nuance, Dragon 10 is 20% more accurate than previous editions, regularly achieving 99% in dictation, and more than 50% faster displaying the dictated words on the screen. It has new acoustic models to cover non-native and regional accents and new formatting features, which may come in really handy for respeakers. One of the main advantages of Dragon is its remarkable out-of-the-box accuracy, which means that it requires very little training. The fact that it is constantly being developed on the basis of identified problems also helps considerably. The latest edition, for example, includes the "nothing-but-speech feature", which increases accuracy by disregarding the user's hesitations (uh, um, er) as opposed to trying to transcribe them as other words on the screen (a, am, err, etc.). An example of how Dragon 10 works is included in the video "Dragon 1" (DVD > Chapter 5 > Discussion points and exercises > 5.6.2).

As far as respeaking is concerned, subtitling companies have traditionally chosen ViaVoice over Dragon, even acknowledging that the latter is more accurate than ViaVoice. This is based on the belief that Dragon is much slower to show the text on the screen and that it displays the subtitles in blocks, whereas viewers are said to prefer a word-for-word mode. Yet, as explained in Chapter 11, this preference is being reconsidered in the light of recent studies. Furthermore, Dragon 10 is considerably faster than previous editions, particularly if it is adjusted with the right settings. Also, it can be used with subtitling applications such as FAB that allow its display in scrolling mode, as done by Colby in Italy. The above-mentioned increase in accuracy is due among other reasons to the development of the language models in Dragon, which use not only bigram and trigram models, as ViaVoice, but also quadgram models. They thus analyze up to four words before and after the dictated word, which increases the likelihood of accurate recognition.

Having said this, Dragon also presents difficulties for respeaking. The most noticeable one is the fact that, like WSR, it requires the users to pause their dictation so that the utterance is shown on the screen. Unlike what happens with ViaVoice, if respeakers speak for ten seconds without making any pause, nothing will be displayed on the screen. Once they stop, a block of say thirty words will suddenly appear, filling in the subtitle lines and passing on to the next lines so quickly that viewers will not be able to read them. Respeakers using Dragon must thus bear in mind this issue and find a balance between speech and pause in order to produce readable subtitles. For this reason, whereas respeaking with ViaVoice mainly depends on multitasking, respeakers using Dragon also need to perform oral segmentation of their subtitles. As will be explained in Chapter 7, the notion of *respeaking units* may well be a solution for this problem which benefits the respeaker, the viewers and even the performance of the software.

5.4.4.2. Dragon 11

Nuance released Dragon NaturallySpeaking 11 only a few months before the publication of this book. Although the information included here about Dragon 10 and its use for respeaking still applies to Dragon 11, it is worth noting some of the changes introduced in the new version. First of all, Dragon Standard and Preferred are now called Home and Premium respectively. The main difference between Dragon 10 and Dragon 11, however, is the multithreading ability of the latter. When users select the option BestMatchIV, as opposed to for example BestMatchIII, Dragon 11 creates two acoustic models and uses two cores (the dual core available in many computers nowadays) to increase and improve upon accuracy. The sampling rate, previously 11.025 kHz, has been increased to 22.5 kHz[4], which accounts for a significant increase in accuracy when using high-end microphones such as Samson Airline 77 and Sennheiser MD 431 II.

However, the release of Dragon 11 has also brought about a series of problems for many users.[5] Its multithreading option (BestMatchIV) is very resource-intensive and has caused Dragon to perform with too much latency in computers that do not meet the basic requirements set by Nuance and even in those that are just above these requirements. Given the importance of latency in respeaking (see section 5.2), this poses a serious problem. A possible solution in this case is to use Dragon with BestMatchIII (which does not involve multithreading) or to upgrade to a computer with at least 4 GB of RAM and a running a minimum of a Core2™ Duo 2 GHz or better.

More specific changes introduced in Dragon 11 are described in section 6.5, once the different aspects of the software have been presented, and a detailed review of this version is included in DVD > Chapter 6 > Exercises > 6.6.2.

---

[4] This applies to both BestMatchIII and BestMacthIV.
[5] For a further discussion on these problems, see http://www.knowbrainer.com/pubforum/index.cfm?page=viewForumTopic&topicId=10846 and http://www.knowbrainer.com/pubforum/index.cfm?page=viewForumTopic&topicId=10648.

5.4.5. Speaker-independent SR: Google, LLC and MIT

As well as the live version of Viascribe used in classrooms, the LLC also has an off-line speaker-independent SR application called IBM Hosted Transcription Service Engine Controller. Members of the LLC can submit the URL of an audio or video file or upload the file themselves and they will get a synchronized transcript of the soundtrack. The software also allows users to create multimedia presentations (synchronizing the video, the transcript and even PowerPoint slides) and to change custom background and colours, as illustrated in Figure 5.2:

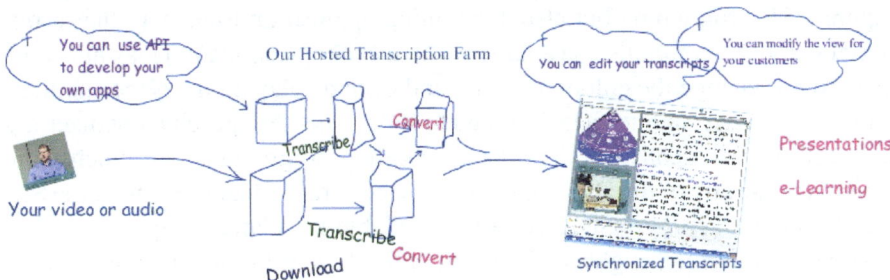

Figure 5.2: IBM Hosted Transcription Service Engine Controller

A similar service is provided by the SpokenMedia project, developed by Massachusetts Institute of Technology. The main aim of the project is to increase the effectiveness of web-based lecture media by providing users with SR-generated transcripts so that they can follow the videos and search for relevant segments. For this purpose, the SpokenMedia project resorts to its own speaker-independent SR application, developed at Massachusetts Institute of Technology.

Finally, in March 2010, and after a 4-month testing period, Google launched its **auto-captioning** and **auto-timing** services for the general public. Also known as auto-captions or auto-caps, the first feature is a combination of Google's automatic SR and the Youtube caption system to offer users the possibility of having their videos subtitled automatically. The algorithms in Google voice are used to parse words within videos and transform them into captions. Users can upload their videos (though not somebody else's) to have them subtitled. They can also download the auto-generated captions to improve them and even have the captions translated in up to 50 different languages. As is the case with most speaker-independent applications, the main challenges to achieve optimum recognition are large vocabularies, background noise, poor recordings, accent variability and distinguishing between song and speech. It is for this reason that Google auto-captioning usually requires videos with clearly spoken audio tracks and no background noise. As for the auto-timing feature, it enables users to upload their own subtitles without any timecodes. Google's speaker-independent software identifies when the words are spoken and creates captions for the video.

As has been mentioned, the main issue with regard to speaker-independent SR is accuracy, which is generally lower than that of speaker-dependent applications. An example of this is included in DVD > Chapter 5 > Discussion points and exercises > 5.6.3, where the same video is transcribed using Google's auto-captioning feature and LLC's IBM Hosted Transcription Service with 55.6% and 77.62% accuracy respectively.

5.4.6. Subtitling software to use with SR

As mentioned in Chapter 1, the production of SR-based subtitles does not only require a SR programme but also a subtitling application to display the recognized utterances as subtitles on a screen. The subtitling application may allow the respeaker to change the colour, position and even display mode of the subtitles, but it is in essence an interface designed to show what the speech recognizer has produced. Paradoxically, though, these subtitling programmes are much more expensive than any of the above-mentioned speech recognizers. Some of the SR-friendly subtitling programmes currently available are Wincaps (Sysmedia), Isis (Starfish), Protitle (Ninsight) and FAB Subtitler Live Edition, which is the only one so far to incorporate a free online demo. It remains to be seen whether free subtitling software such as Subtitle Workshop, now commonly used at universities and even subtitling companies, will be made compatible to be used with speech recognizers for live subtitling.

In any case, when training respeakers at university, for example, the use of subtitling software is not essential. Most of the practice can be done by respeaking into the SR software directly, placing the SR window underneath the video as though it was a subtitle box. What is more important for the trainer, however, is to find a way to record the students' exercises, given that, otherwise, they will all have to be assessed in real time. Screencasting software is particularly useful for this purpose.

5.4.7. Screencasting software to use with SR

A **screencast** or a video screen capture is a digital recording of computer screen output often containing audio narration. It is now a commonly used tool for software developers to show their work, for users to report bugs and especially for teachers and instructors to explain how different programmes work in online courses.

In respeaking training, screencasting software enables students to record the images of their respoken utterances as they were originally displayed on their screens as well as the sound of their voices. The video they were respeaking is not usually recorded, but this is not a problem. Once the students have recorded their screencast, the trainer can play, at the same time, the video and the screencast, thus having all the elements needed for the assessment: the original video, the respoken subtitles and the student's voice.

Some examples of screencasting software are Camtasia Studio, Captivate, HyperCam and ScreenCam. It is also possible to find screencasting freeware, such as Jing or Windows Media Encoder.

5.5. The future of SR

As has been the case for the past 70 years, the future of SR technology is largely connected to, and dependent on, the development of computing science. More powerful computers are needed to be able to cope with the latest developments in speech technology. From the point of view of speaker-independent SR, future improvements include the ability to deal with a larger number of users with different accents as well as the possibility of disregarding noise and discriminating between different speakers in instances of overlapping dialogue. For speaker-dependent SR, some of the challenges ahead are the reduction or elimination of the initial user training (which would effectively mean that the speech engine is, at least initially, speaker-independent) and the achievement, whether consistently or intermittingly, of 100% accuracy. For this to be possible, more powerful language models will be needed. Finally, a common challenge for both speaker-dependent and speaker-independent SR is the improvement of **automatic punctuation**. At present, it only works on the basis of pauses (a comma when there is a short pause, a full stop with a long pause) and some grammatical rules, but it is far from perfect (see sections 5.6.4 and 7.2.1).

In terms of research, the fields of natural language processing, machine translation and artificial intelligence are often identified as the way forward for the development of SR.

Belonging to both computer science and linguistics, natural language processing is concerned with converting information from computer databases into readable human language. Its use in SR may facilitate the analysis of the context of a word by looking at a whole sentence instead of a few words, resulting in greater accuracy. As for machine translation, projects such as DARPA's Global Autonomous Language Exploitation are already trying to combine SR technology with automatic translation, so that a foreign language can be instantly transcribed and translated without human intervention. Finally, the application of artificial intelligence may one day enable SR engines to not only decipher what a person has said but also grasp the meaning behind the words and even hold a conversation analyzing the emotional features of the human voice. Yet, for the time being, this is still very much science fiction.

5.6. Discussion points and exercises

5.6.1. Viascribe

Watch "Viascribe 1" and "Viascribe 2" in DVD > Chapter 5 > Discussion points and exercises > 5.6.1.

What are the main advantages and disadvantages of this type of SR application as compared to more "traditional" SR programmes such as ViaVoice or Dragon? What contexts or settings do you think Viascribe would be suitable for and why? What use do you think it could have for live and/or pre-recorded subtitling?

5.6.2. WSR, ViaVoice and Dragon

You can find the videos that you need for this section in DVD > Chapter 5 > Discussion points and exercises > 5.6.2.

Watch "WSR 1", "ViaVoice 1" and "Dragon 1" and describe the main differences and similarities between the three programmes, focusing, among other aspects, on the features they have (both for dictation and general control of the computer), the type of dictation they require from the user and their suitability for live subtitling.

"WSR 2" shows a somewhat unsuccessful public demonstration of WSR. What are the errors and how could they have been avoided, especially from 1:14 to 1:21?

"ViaVoice 2" and "Dragon 2" (in Spanish) contain instances of unrealistic performance by the speech recognizers, which is not uncommon in demonstrations and commercials. What are those instances and why are they unrealistic?

5.6.3. Speaker-independent SR

The document "Google vs. IBM" (DVD > Chapter 5 > Discussion points and exercises > 5.6.3) shows a comparative analysis conducted by Jan Myland, from LLC, of how the same video ("Google vs. IBM – Video") is transcribed using Google's auto-captioning feature and LLC's IBM Hosted Transcription Service.

Before watching the video, read the transcript produced by Google's SR software. To what extent would you be able to understand what the video is about if you could not hear the audio? Would you be able to understand it by reading only the transcript produced by IBM Hosted Transcription Service? Bearing in mind that the accuracy of the transcripts is 55.6% (Google) and 77.62% (IBM), what percentage do you think is necessary for a transcript to qualify as comprehensible enough? Would this percentage be valid for live subtitling too?

Check other videos in www.youtube.com to see how the auto-captioning feature performs? Do these videos offer captions in different languages? How would you rate the translations?

5.6.4. Automatic punctuation in SR

The video "Automatic Punctuation" (DVD > Chapter 5 > Discussion points and exercises > 5.6.4) shows a screencapture of Dragon adding commas and full stops automatically during dictation. What causes the error in the first paragraph? How could it have been avoided? Do you think that autopunctuation is a feasible option for live subtitling?

6. Respeaking Skills Applied before the Process II
Preparation of the Software – Respeaking with Dragon

6.0. Introduction

As mentioned in section 5.2, whereas the average user resorts to SR software for dictation, respeakers use it for the production of live subtitles. Yet, when approaching SR for the first time to create their voice profiles, respeakers may want to behave as average users. Indeed, it is particularly useful for respeakers to become skilful "dictators", knowing how to use the SR software to its full potential before moving on to the intricacies of respeaking, as the professional practice will benefit greatly from this knowledge.

The aim of this chapter is to guide the reader through some of the most important steps of the use of SR technology. Given that ViaVoice has been discontinued in some languages and that the WSR application included in Vista and Windows 7 has not yet been used for respeaking, the focus will be placed on Dragon 10 Preferred. References will be made to the Dragon End-User Workbook (included in DVD > Chapter 6 > Exercises > 6.6.1), but the description of the different steps required to prepare the software will be general enough to apply to respeakers using WSR or ViaVoice, whose user guides are also included in the DVD.

6.1. Choosing and using a microphone

6.1.1. Type of microphone

Often regarded as a minor issue, the microphone is an essential element in respeaking and overall in SR. It can make an enormous difference in terms of accuracy, which is why most experts recommend not to economize on the microphone chosen for respeaking.

There are many types of microphones available: headsets, desktop microphones, handheld microphones, USB microphones, Wireless and Bluetooth microphones, array microphones (wide set of microphones sitting on the desktop) or even in-built microphones. Of all those, the latter two don't seem to yield good results for respeaking. In the UK, respeakers have so far used desktop (IMS) and handheld microphones (RBM), whereas most other countries resort to headsets, with USB or standard audio in.

Desktop and handheld microphones, the latter being less advisable from an ergonomic point of view, resemble those traditionally used for singing. They offer respeakers the possibility of dictating within 1 metre of their computers and the freedom of not having to wear a headset. Yet, given that headphones are usually required to listen to the original soundtrack, this doesn't make much of a difference. In any case, these desktop and handheld microphones, which often have USB line in, are usually very accurate. Among those recommended by the renowned SR website Knowbrainer (http://www.knowbrainer.com/) are Sennheiser MD431 II and, as a more affordable option, Samson Q7 Microphone. The downside of this type of microphone is that, even if it does have a noise cancellation option feature, it requires a relatively quiet environment. This is not a problem if respeakers are working in booths or in soundproofed rooms, but it is not suited to, say, a classroom environment. In this case, headsets, whether or not wireless, are a better option. Wireless headsets such as Hybrid Samson Airline 77, highly recommended by Knowbrainer, are expensive but very comfortable.

A list of recommended microphones is included in DVD > Chapter 6 > Exercises > 6.6.1. It contains headsets, wireless, desktop, handheld and array microphones that have been certified by Nuance and that are expected to meet the highest performance and quality standards with different SR software. More information on microphones can be found on specialized websites such as http://www.emicrophones.com/.

6.1.2. Set up

Silly as it may seem, many of the most common recognition problems are solved by making sure the microphone is correctly adjusted. This is indeed one of those aspects respeakers should try to learn as part of their daily routine. In the case of headsets, they must be adjusted comfortably and in a stable position. The microphone should not be positioned in front of the respeaker's mouth, as it will capture breathing noises, but to either side of the mouth, at a distance of 2cm or a thumb's width. If the microphone has a foam pad, it should not be removed, since it acts as a windshield. Noise-cancelling microphones (always recommended) only listen on one side; respeakers must thus make sure that they are talking to the listening side (often marked by a dot or by the word "talk") and that the microphone is not tilted up or down. Also, some microphones have a mute switch or volume control, often an unnoticed problem when misrecognition (or non-recognition) occurs. In any case, respeakers are always advised to test the microphone before subtitling a programme, which can be done with the SR software or with Windows Start > Accessories > Sound Recorder.

6.2. Creating a user profile

The first step for a respeaker who wants to use a SR application is to create a user profile or voice model (see pages 1 to 3 in the Dragon End-User Workbook). In the case of Dragon, the first window displayed, the New User Wizard, offers three types of training: none, short and special. The no-training option (none) starts off from a speaker-independent model and learns the speech patterns of the respeaker from dictation and error correction. Although this could be useful for those who don't want to spend the necessary time training the software, the "short training" option seems more advisable for respeakers. As shown in the video "Creating a User Profile" (DVD > Chapter 6 > Exercises > 6.6.1), reading the first text, entitled "Talking to your computer [Easier Reading: Instructional]", takes only 5 minutes. The text is gradually greyed as it is read by the user and recognized by the software. If a particular word is not recognized, an arrow usually points to the word to indicate that it must be read again. In this case, and especially if the problem persists, it is often useful to resume dictation from several words back and/or to read phrases, instead of dictating only the misrecognized word time and again. During this 5-minute training, the software adjusts the profile to the unique characteristics of the speaker's voice, including pitch and volume. It is for this reason that users must try and speak just as they plan to respeak to the software later on, as this will maximize recognition accuracy.

6.3. Dictating to SR software

In his website Voice Typist (http://www.voicetypist.com/index.htm), Lamond Wood argues that "speech recognition technology has reached the point where the skill of the user has become as big a factor as the power of the software". Indeed, although after training their voice profiles, users tend to blame misrecognitions on the SR software, the responsibility is often to be shared equally between the users and the software. It is thus essential for respeakers, before delving into the production of live subtitles, to consider how they should dictate to this type of application.

First of all, new users of SR technology must try to get over two impulses that have so far proved recurrent among respeaking students: self-consciousness and a tendency to challenge the software. Very aware that they are talking to a machine (in a room full of people), some students, especially if they are shy, find it at first difficult to speak in a calm, natural manner and quickly become impatient. The sooner they get over the oddity of addressing a computer and the comic nature of its recognition mistakes, the better results they will obtain. On the other hand, bolder, more confident students often try to 'beat' the software dictating something that is bound to be misrecognized. Not much merit here – anyone can do this. Respeakers will hopefully soon understand that the SR engine is not a rival, but a colleague that will always have the final say in whatever they choose to dictate. The challenge is thus not to find flaws in the software, but to help it achieve maximum accuracy. The question is now how to help the software do this.

Most guides and experts resort to similar words when giving tips about how to dictate to a SR application. Dragon recommends to "speak clearly but naturally, using the same volume, pitch and pace you'll use day-to-day" (Dragon End-User Workbook: 3), whereas ViaVoice advises users to "speak clearly and in a normal, natural manner" (ViaVoice User Guide: 17). Yet, different users will have different ideas of what is natural and what is not, and, most importantly, there are different degrees of naturalness. A spontaneous conversation with a friend and a news item delivered by a news correspondent may both sound natural and yet they are bound to yield very different results in terms of recognition, as shown in the second part of the video "Dictation 2" (DVD > Chapter 6 > Exercises > 6.6.2).

The emphasis on naturalness may be explained by the progress made in SR technology, which no longer needs discrete, word-for-word dictation, and allows users to speak continuously. Yet, this does not mean that this technology can cope with completely spontaneous speech. The respeakers' task is thus to avoid both extremes of the continuum (robotic and completely spontaneous dictation), opting for the natural non-spontaneous dictation included in the middle column of Table 6.1:

	Robotic dictation	**Natural, non-spontaneous dictation**	**Natural, spontaneous dictation**
Enunciation	Overemphasized	Clear for every word (which is distinctively punched out) but not exaggerated	Occasionally clipped, slurred, mumbling words or leaving some words out
Pace	Very slow	Steady	Fast, uneven, abrupt
Pauses	Unnatural, after every word	As per common sense and punctuation marks	As it springs to mind
Dictation units	Words or even syllables in case of misrecognition	Logical phrases or respeaking units that have been thought in advanced	Words, phrases, fillers ("I mean"), colloquial contractions ("D'you know"), slips of the tongue – whatever springs to mind

Table 6.1: Different types of dictation

The different results produced by natural non-spontaneous and completely spontaneous dictation are clearly shown when, in yet another recurrent pattern in a respeaking class, students start making comments and observations to their neighbours when the microphone is still on. The software tries to recognize what is said but struggles to cope with the spontaneous mode used by the speaker. If this is done during the training period, it can have a very negative effect on the overall accuracy of the user. In this sense, most guides recommend users to dictate not as if they were talking to a friend, but rather to children, someone for whom

English is not the native language (ViaVoice User Guide) or "someone whom you do not quite trust to understand you, and to whom you are willing to fully display this mistrust" (Voice typist).

Perhaps the most useful tip in this sense is to try to speak as a newscast reader would, i.e. speaking naturally, in logical phrases or idea units, with a steady pace, making normal pauses that provide much-needed breathing spells and enunciating every word clearly so that it is understood by the viewers. Users will typically find it easier if they stop to think what they want to say before dictating it. Even if it is sometimes difficult, dictation should not follow the flow of ideas, which may come rushing, but a steady pace set from the onset. In the same way, respeakers are not to follow the sudden bursts of rapid dialogue delivered by the original speaker, but rather to maintain the even pace that has been set from the beginning.

The idea is thus to find a dictation mode (with its own natural but not spontaneous enunciation, pace, pauses and dictation units) that works for every respeaker and use it in a way that helps the SR engine to obtain the best possible recognition.

6.4. Improving the user profile

Once the user has finished reading the training text, the software proceeds to adapt the user files on the basis of the speech data gathered. At this stage, most SR applications offer users the possibility of adapting also to their writing style by analyzing documents they may have in their computer. As will be explained in section 6.4.5.4, it is often advisable not to do this now, at least not until the user is more familiarized with the software. What is however useful at this stage is to run through a tutorial (often suggested by the software) in order to get familiarized with the different tools available.

The following sections aim to describe some of these tools, more specifically those that can be particularly useful for respeakers to improve their user profiles and get them ready for the production of live subtitles.

6.4.1. Speed settings: faster display in Dragon

As has already been mentioned, whereas ViaVoice has a quick word-for-word display mode, Dragon requires users to pause so that the recognized text may be displayed in blocks. This is the main reason why Dragon was not the first choice for respeaking in countries such as UK and Spain. Yet, respeakers using Dragon 10 will see that this latency has significantly reduced (by 50% according to Nuance) and will be able to adjust the speed settings as follows so that words are displayed faster on the screen:

In DragonBar > Tools > Options > Miscellaneous:

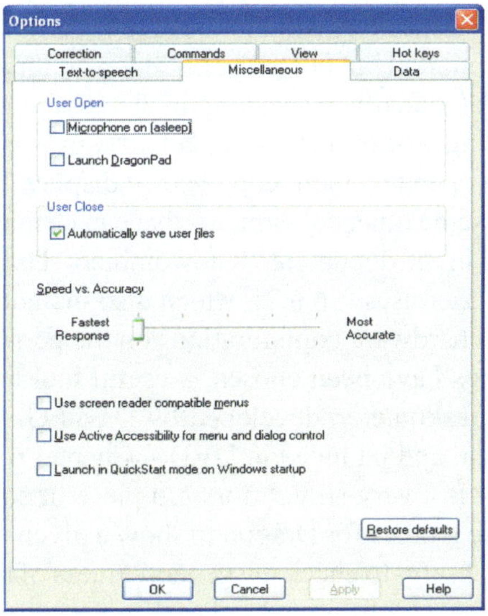

Figure 6.1: Speed settings I

In DragonBar > Tools > Options > Commands:

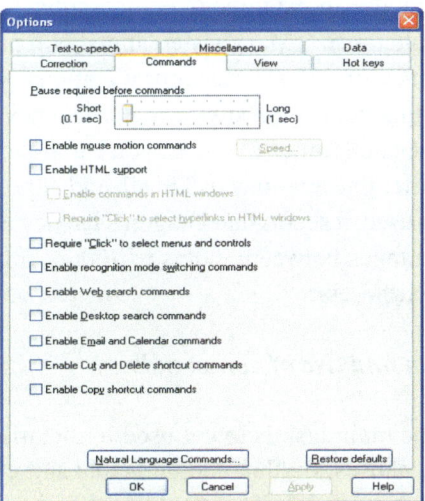

Figure 6.2: Speed settings II

Another option is to change the dictation mode in DragonBar > Words. In the normal mode, Dragon distinguishes between dictation and commands by analyzing what users say between pauses. Users are thus expected to pause before commands like "undo that" or "select all". Respeakers may want to try the dictation mode, which allows faster dictation because Dragon interprets everything as dictation and not as commands. Respeakers will thus be able to dictate more rapidly (while still using punctuation marks) but not to use common commands such as "correct that" or "scratch that". Crucially, respeaking in dictation mode means that when the live subtitler is using words such as "email", "copy" or "help" the software will not be tempted to open an email, copy text or display the help menu.

Finally, there are some other adjustments that can be made to speed up Dragon. They can be found in the document "Knowbrainer – Dragon Speed Settings" (DVD > Chapter 6 > Exercises > 6.6.2), which also includes information about the impact of different hardware configurations on the performance of Dragon.

Once these settings have been chosen, a useful tool to check the speed of Dragon is NaturallySpeakometer, developed by David G. Peters, a member of the Knowbrainer forum, and included in DVD > Chapter 6 > Exercises > 6.6.2. NaturallySpeakometer is a very straightforward piece of software that provides precise data of the time it takes for Dragon to show a given recognized utterance on the screen. It is also useful to check the general fitness of the user's installation and to compare the impact of different hardware (microphones, processors, hard drives etc.) on the SR system performance. Figure 6.3 shows the results yielded for the dictation of the phrases "Manchester United will probably win", "but it's the taking part that counts" and "at least you can travel to Italy".

The bold letters on screen show the average time (in milliseconds [ms]) it has taken Dragon to display the above three utterances after four or five dictations. The fastest is the first utterance ("Manchester United will probably win"), which shows an average latency of 453ms after four dictations. The second utterance ("but it's the thought that counts") shows a higher latency after four dictations (918 ms). Finally, the last utterance ("at least you can travel to Italy") has taken an average of 720ms after five attempts. All in all, and although it depends on the hardware and software used, it seems that Dragon's latency is nearly always under 1 second and usually ranges between 500ms to 700ms, a more than acceptable figure for respeaking purposes.

6.4.2. Initial dictation and use of commands

At this initial stage, the main task is to get used to dictation in general (to find the enunciation, pace, pauses, rhythm and units that suit every user) and to the use of commands in particular. It is important to remember little things that tend to go unnoticed such as making sure that the cursor is where the user wants to dictate (typically DragonPad in Dragon or Speakpad in ViaVoice) and that the software needs some time to "wake up". The latter should be borne in mind by respeakers, who are advised to warm up the software before going on air, as this makes a significant difference in its performance.

As far as dictation is concerned, it is advisable to start with relatively simple

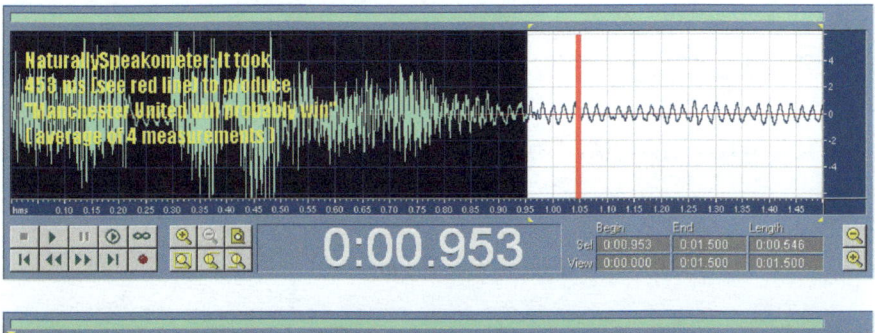

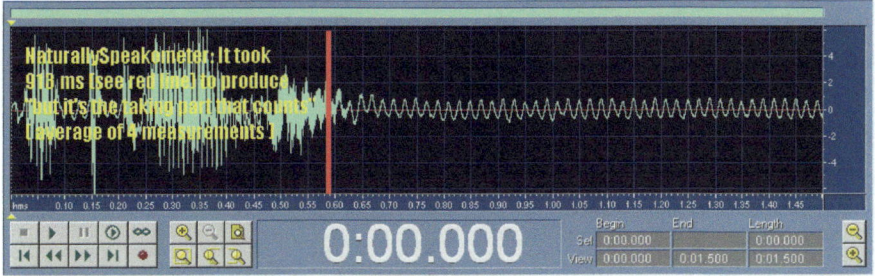

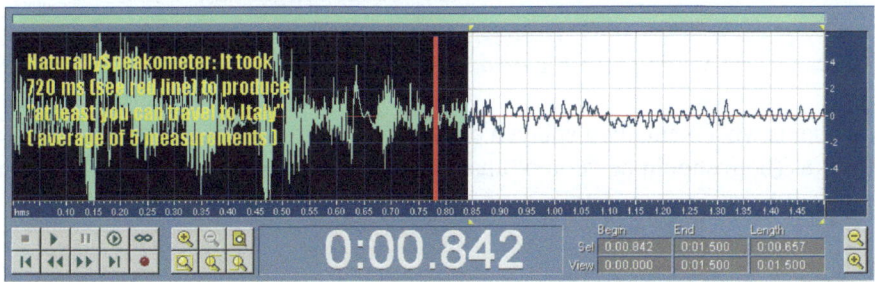

Figure 6.3: NaturallySpeakometer

texts with no specialized vocabulary in order to allow the software to achieve accurate recognition from the beginning. When errors occur, they should not be corrected straightaway, but rather when the user has finished dictating a paragraph or even a page (see section 6.4.3). In the case of Dragon, during dictation a result box appears displaying the words as they are being uttered by the user, even though nothing is displayed on the main screen. When a pause is made, the words appear in a block on the screen. Dragon uses this preliminary result box to make corrections before the final text is displayed on the screen. It could be said that, as the words are first shown on the result box, they have only gone through the acoustic model. Once they are in the result box, they are analyzed by the language model, which may change them or correct them. When the user pauses, they are finally displayed on the screen. In Figure 6.4, the respeaker says "y el portero cómo mira cómo…" (the goalkeeper looks how…). Initially, the acoustic model recognises "cómo" as "como" and thus yields "y el portero como mira como…" in the result box:

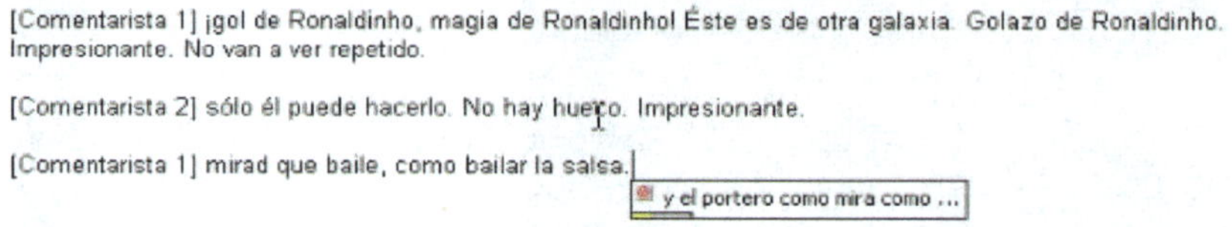

```
[Comentarista 1] ¡gol de Ronaldinho, magia de Ronaldinho! Éste es de otra galaxia. Golazo de Ronaldinho.
Impresionante. No van a ver repetido.

[Comentarista 2] sólo él puede hacerlo. No hay hueco. Impresionante.

[Comentarista 1] mirad que baile, como bailar la salsa.
                                                        y el portero como mira como ...
```

Figure 6.4: Result box I

Then, the language model comes in and corrects the second "como" into "cómo", still in the result box:

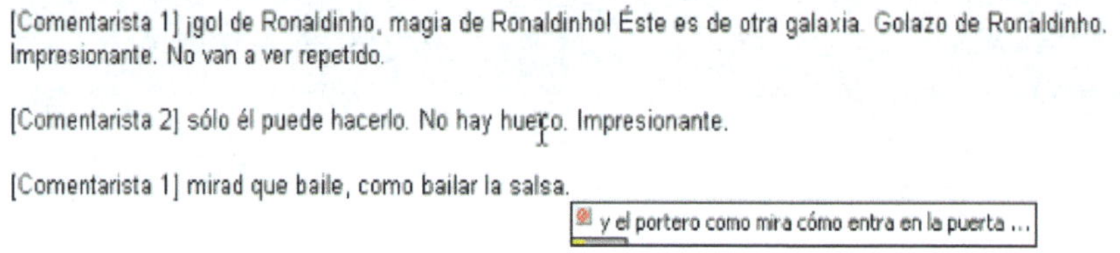

```
[Comentarista 1] ¡gol de Ronaldinho, magia de Ronaldinho! Éste es de otra galaxia. Golazo de Ronaldinho.
Impresionante. No van a ver repetido.

[Comentarista 2] sólo él puede hacerlo. No hay hueco. Impresionante.

[Comentarista 1] mirad que baile, como bailar la salsa.
                                              y el portero como mira cómo entra en la puerta ...
```

Figure 6.5: Result box II

And that is what is finally displayed on the screen. In other words, one of the two mistakes (both should be "cómo") has been corrected by the language model in the result box:

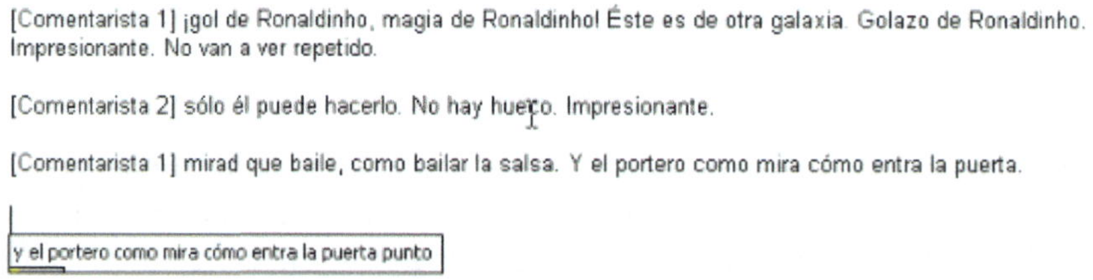

```
[Comentarista 1] ¡gol de Ronaldinho, magia de Ronaldinho! Éste es de otra galaxia. Golazo de Ronaldinho.
Impresionante. No van a ver repetido.

[Comentarista 2] sólo él puede hacerlo. No hay hueco. Impresionante.

[Comentarista 1] mirad que baile, como bailar la salsa. Y el portero como mira cómo entra la puerta.

y el portero como mira cómo entra la puerta punto
```

Figure 6.6: Result box III

Although this result box may be turned off (DragonBar > Tools > Options > Miscellaneous), respeakers may want to have it in view at the beginning to see how Dragon receives and corrects utterances.

In order to achieve accurate recognition, Dragon recommends the use of long words and long continuous utterances (Dragon End-User Workbook: 22). However, not all of this applies to respeaking.

Long words are indeed more likely to be recognized correctly than short words because they provide the software with more acoustic data and there is less homophonic competition (i.e. there are fewer words that can have the same sound). This is why, contrary to what first-time users of SR technology tend to think, "the" or "a" are usually much more problematic than say "electroencephalography". Needless to say, respeakers often have to use the same words uttered by the original speaker but, when rephrasing is needed and synonyms must be used, longer words are always preferred. Likewise, these initial dictations will be useful for respeakers to identify problematic words such as recurrent homophones (buy/by/bye, cent/scent/sent or right/write/rite/wright). If respeakers manage to dictate them as part of longer units, the language model should be able to find the right option and correct it in the result box before displaying it on the screen. Yet, this is not always possible. When tackling a string like "Peter has confirmed he'll be coming. Alison too", respeakers may be better off using a homophone-free word such as "also" than opting for the more problematic "too" (too/two/to).

As for the second recommendation included in the Dragon End-User Workbook, that of dictating in long continuous utterances, it is indeed bound to increase recognition accuracy. Longer units will allow the language model in Dragon to have more contextual data, calculating, with its quadgram model, the likelihood of occurrence of the four words before and after every word dictated. However, respeakers cannot afford to do this. If they choose to respeak in very long utterances with no pause, nothing will be shown on screen as they talk, increasing the delay with regard to the images. More importantly, when they do pause, the resulting utterance is likely to take up more space than the two lines available for subtitles and the viewers will not be able to read it. Respeakers must thus find an adequate speech-pause rhythm, a happy medium where they dictate in units that are long enough for Dragon to use the contextual information of its language model and short enough to be included in two subtitle lines and be readable for the viewers. To practise this, respeakers can reduce the window of the application in which they are dictating to fit only two lines of say 37 characters each, which will help them get used to the length required in live subtitling.

As far as the use of commands is concerned, the first thing to remember is that, to make sure that the software understands an utterance as a command instead of as a word to be transcribed, the speaker must make a brief pause before and after the command but not in the middle. The briefness of this pause can be determined in DragonBar > Tools > Options > Commands, as has been described above. Rushed as they usually are, respeakers may want to set this pause as short as possible. Indeed, whereas ordinary SR users often dictate a full stop after a given sentence has been displayed on the screen, this is not advisable in respeaking, as it would mean that viewers would see a subtitle on screen and then, some seconds later, a full stop being added at the end. Respeakers must thus try to pause briefly before punctuation marks so that they are displayed along with the utterance they modify. Also important is to become familiar with the most commonly used commands, such as comma, full stop, colon, semi-colon, new line, new paragraph, question mark, exclamation mark, open/close quote, open/close parenthesis, ellipsis, dash, hyphen and, in the case of Dragon, more general ones such as microphone off and go to sleep/go to work. If more commands are needed or some of these are not remembered, most SR applications offer thorough lists in their help guides.

In any case, respeakers should bear in mind that voice writing is not the only option and that, very often, a combination of manual (for example using shortcuts or hot keys with the keyboard) and voice commands may be the most efficient use of SR software. This is why many professional respeakers use vocal commands for punctuation marks while resorting to the keyboard to introduce new lines or turn the microphone off. A list of shortcuts or hot keys in Dragon is available in DragonBar > Tools > Options > HotKeys.

In sum, when beginning to dictate, users are advised to start off with simple texts, trying to find the enunciation, pace, speech-pause rhythm and dictation units that suit them best, as well as to become familiar with the use and dictation of commands. This is also a good opportunity to find out what words lend themselves better (longer words) or worse (homophones, short words) to SR. As for Dragon users, this initial dictation should be useful to help them find a good speech-pause rhythm to produce utterances that are long enough to be properly recognized by the software and short enough to be read as subtitles. Finally, whether or not using Dragon, users should not correct errors as they occur, but rather after dictating a paragraph or a whole text. The next section explains how to go about this.

6.4.3. How to correct errors

Correcting mistakes can be one of the most effective ways to improve the user profile. What needs to be remembered here is that whereas some correction methods allow the software to learn from its mistakes, others don't. Usually, deleting an error and typing the correct words or dictating it again does not improve the user profile, as the software does not register the error as such. Instead, SR applications often have specific tools and commands that allow the user to correct recognition errors while enabling the software to learn from these errors and fine-tune the user profile.

In Dragon, and according to both the End-User Workbook and Knowbrainer, the best correction method is to use the Spell dialog box. For this, the user can select the option "'Correct' commands bring up Spell dialog box" in DragonBar > Tools > Options:

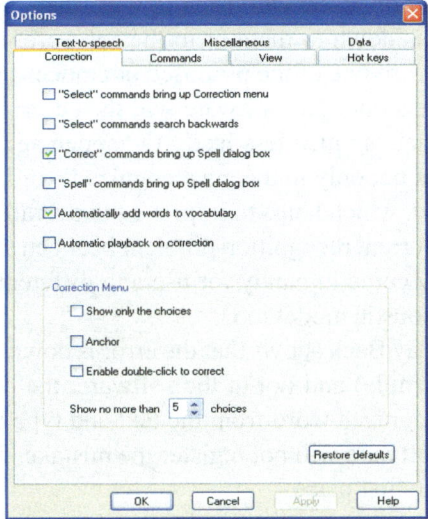

Figure 6.7: Correction I

When an error occurs, users can place the cursor before the misrecognized word and say "correct that" or press – on the keyboard (FN– if it is a laptop). Dragon will then highlight the dictated unit containing the error and will show the Spell dialog box:

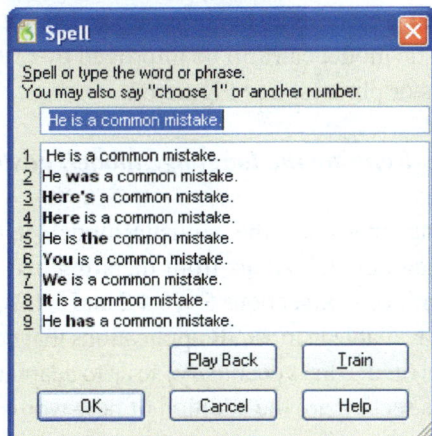

Figure 6.8: Correction II

With the Play Back option, users can listen to what they have dictated and find out whether the error is down to them or to the software. If it is a software error, they can either choose one of the proposed utterances in the list (in this case number 3) or type a new one. The software will then correct the error and learn from this mistake, which is much less likely to happen again. As the correction is made in context, and not only in the misrecognized word, the language model is also being fine-tuned, which helps to improve the overall accuracy of the user profile. If there is a recurrent recognition problem between two words or phrases, the option "train" may come in handy for users to differentiate pronunciations, thus fine-tuning the acoustic model too.

However, if the Play Back shows that the error is down to the user (incorrect pronunciation, for example) and not to the software, the best way to correct it is to delete the misrecognized word from the text and type or dictate the correct one. In this way, the software will not register the mistake, for which, after all, it was not to blame in the first place.

If there are recurrent recognition problems, it may be worth checking the troubleshooting application in DragonBar > Help > Improve my accuracy (pages 24-26 in ViaVoice user guide).

6.4.4. Refining the acoustic model

At this stage, when users are more familiar with dictation and correction, it is a good idea to perform further training, which will help to fine-tune the acoustic model and increase the overall accuracy. SR applications usually include a number of texts or stories that users can read/dictate at any given time for this purpose. In DragonBar > Tools > Accuracy Center > Perform Further Training, there are several texts ordered by difficulty and genre. Once these texts have been read, the acoustic model can still be improved by re-training the pronunciation of specific words or phrases. See Figure 6.9.

6.4.5. Refining the language model: customization of the vocabulary

Having fine-tuned the acoustic model, it is now time to follow suit with the language model. Apart from dictating and correcting in a way that maximizes recognition (see sections 6.3, 6.4.2 and 6.4.3), this can be done by using a number of tools available in most SR applications that help to add information to this language model (and to the vocabulary) so as to adapt it to the user's needs. The tools covered in this section are the addition of new words, the addition of word lists, the use of documents to improve the language model and the creation of macros.

6.4.5.1. Adding new words
One of the main sources of errors in SR is the use of words that are not included in the vocabulary of the software, the so-called out-of-vocabulary words. Most

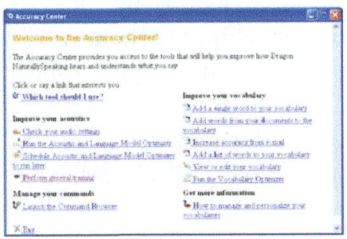

 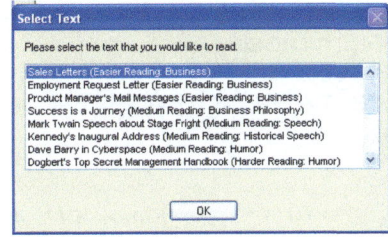

Figure 6.9: Further training

SR applications have a quick an easy way of solving this by using the "add new word" tool (in the case of Dragon, DragonBar > Words > New). If the word is still being misrecognized, most applications offer the possibility of training its pronunciation to provide the acoustic model with further data and increase the likelihood of accurate recognition.

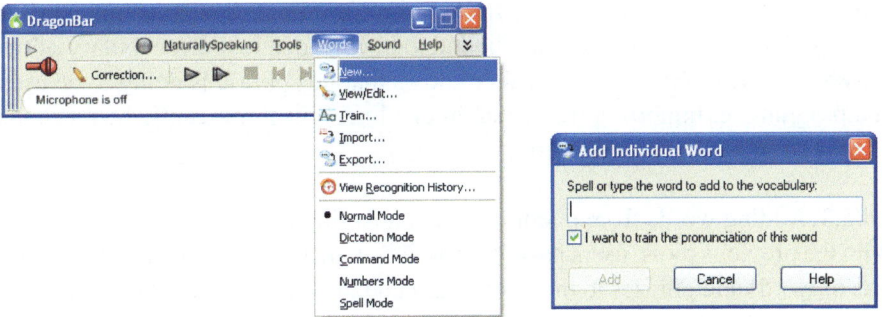

Figure 6.10: Adding new words

6.4.5.2. Adding words/phrases from lists

Although useful, the "add new word" tool is not very effective for respeakers, who are bound to deal with large amounts of out-of-vocabulary words and have little time to import them individually into the vocabulary. Luckily, most SR applications allow the introduction of whole word lists, which makes this task considerably easier. To use this in Dragon, respeakers must create their word lists in a ".txt" file (with Notepad, for example), having each word on a separate line and properly spelled, spaced and capitalized. It is also possible to include a suggested pronunciation by typing a backslash (\) after the word and the spoken form afterwards:

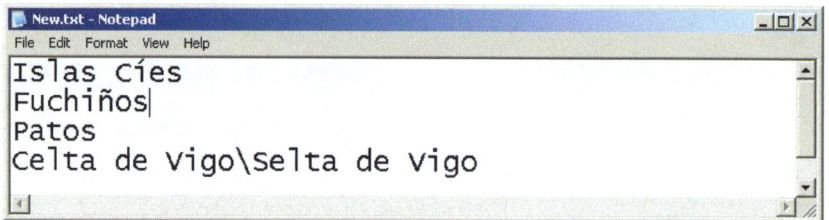

Figure 6.11: Adding words from lists

Once the list has been created and saved, respeakers will be able to import it to Dragon's vocabulary by saying "import custom words" or going to DragonBar > Words > Import (see pages 13-14 in Dragon End-User Workbook for further explanation).

As highlighted in section 6.4.2, the longer the utterances or units dictated, the easier it is for the software to recognize them. In this sense, respeakers should bear in mind that the "add word lists" tool also allows the inclusion of multi-word terms or even whole phrases. Thus, if an out-of-vocabulary name such as "Daniele Matteo Alvise Barbaro" is likely to come up in an arts programme, it is a good idea to include it in one line as a single term. Crucially, this doesn't only apply to out-of-vocabulary terms. In a phrase like "deaf, deafened and hard of hearing viewers", all the words are bound to be included in the vocabulary of the software already. Yet, if the respeaker knows that this phrase is going to be used in a programme, importing it as such, in one line, will significantly increase the likelihood of accurate recognition.

6.4.5.3. Adding words from documents and adapting to writing style
With the previous tools, users have the possibility of adding individual words and lists of words and phrases to the vocabulary and language model of the software. The next tool goes even further, allowing the introduction of whole texts, with which the software will be able to internalize not only single and multi-words but also whole sentences and longer strings. Often presented as "Analyse my documents" (ViaVoice) or "Add words from documents" (Dragon), this tool increases accuracy dramatically and is extremely useful for respeaking. The common recommendation in this case is to introduce texts that are very similar to what will be dictated (for a news programme, for instance, previous scripts with similar

vocabulary) or, if possible, the same texts (if the script is available beforehand). As for the latter option, many broadcasters and subtitling companies are able to get hold of some scripts before they are broadcast live. Some channels, such as VTM in Belgium, prefer to make these subtitles semi-live, with no SR involved. Others, like the BBC in the UK, opt for respeaking these programmes live making no use of the script. In this case, running the script through the "Analyse my documents" or "Add words from documents" tool would be very useful and would increase recognition notably.

In Dragon, users can find this application by saying "add words from documents" or going to DragonBar > Tools > Accuracy Center > Add Words from your documents (see pages 15-17 in Dragon End-User Workbook for full explanation). Dragon will ask users whether they want the software to "adapt to writing style". If selected, this option enables Dragon to learn not only new words and phrases, but also structures, strings and sentences and a great deal of word-frequency and context information in what is probably the best method to improve the language model in Dragon Preferred.

If for whatever reason (for example if the document has sentences that the user does not want Dragon to learn) the "adapt to writing style" option is not selected, Dragon will only learn new words and phrases, but it won't obtain information about word occurrence or co-occurrence. In any case, it is extremely important to make sure that the document contains no mistakes. If there are any, Dragon will reproduce them later on "thinking" they are correct. Respeakers may find it useful to select the option "Preview the list of unknown words" to be able to train (pronunciation) and/or edit the words before they are introduced in the vocabulary.

6.4.5.4. Use of macros: the vocabulary editor
One of the most effective tools used by respeakers on a daily basis are the so-called macros, vocal shortcuts or customized commands created by the user to achieve a given intended effect. Respeakers use them to "ensure that certain labels or phrases are always correctly formatted, and save a great deal of time and effort" (Marsh 2004:32). Marsh mentions the example of the subtitle "REFEREE: Foul and a miss.", very common in snooker. For this to appear on the screen, respeakers would have to say "all caps referee colon foul and a miss full stop". Alternatively, the command "miss macro" (or any other chosen by the respeaker) could trigger the exact same subtitle. Respeakers can choose or make up any command for the subtitle they want to be displayed as long as it is not an existing command. However, it is advisable not to prepare too many macros for the same programme, as it is not easy to remember them all in a live situation. It is also important to find a regular pattern to name them. Many respeakers resort to the structure "word + macro" or "mac + word" and create macros such as "cheer macro" or "maccheer" (for the subtitle CHEERING AND APPLAUSE), "whistle macro" or "macwhistle" (WHISTLE BLOWS), "mobile macro" or "macmobile" (MOBILE PHONE RINGS), etc. Macros are not only used for labels or tags but also to save

time with long phrases ("queen macro" for "Her Majesty Queen Elizabeth II"), problematic homophones ("macro hayles" for the surname "Hayles" as opposed to "hails"), and even punctuation ("ex macro" for "!" or even "poss macro" for the apostrophe "'s" if the software struggles to recognize it).

In Dragon, macros can be added in different ways, but perhaps the most useful one is through the vocabulary editor (saying "open Vocabulary Editor" or going to DragonBar > Words > View/Edit):

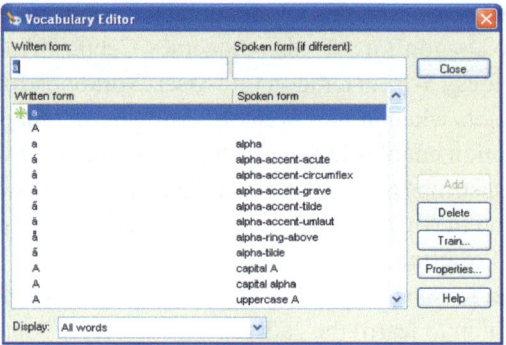

Figure 6.12: Vocabulary editor

The vocabulary editor is a key tool for the respeaker. First of all, if the display mode (at the bottom of the window) is selected as "all words", it allows users to see all the words that are included in Dragon's vocabulary. If a word is not included there, it will not be recognized by Dragon.

The buttons on the right-hand side enable users to re-train the pronunciation of these words, edit them or add new ones and their pronunciation (in "spoken form"). It is also possible to delete existing words. For example, if the word "loop" keeps coming up as "loupe" and the user considers that the latter is not necessary, deleting it from the vocabulary will solve the problem.

As for the creation of macros, it is very similar to the addition of new words. To introduce for instance "macro children" as a macro for the label "CHILDREN:", users would have to introduce "CHILDREN:" under written form and "macro children" under spoken form. Training the newly introduced macro is always advisable to make sure it has been properly processed by the software. In this particular case, though, the respeaker may want to refine this macro. If, for example, the subtitle to be respoken is "CHILDREN: We don't want to go.", saying "macro children we don't want to go full stop" will trigger "CHILDREN: we don't want to go.", with "we" in small letter. It is necessary to tell the software that, in this particular macro, capitals are needed for the first word after the colon. This can be done by double clicking on the macro in the vocabulary editor (or by selecting "Properties" on the right-hand side). The window "Word Properties" will then pop up allowing the user to format the label in several ways (in this case, the option needed is "Format the next word capitalised"):

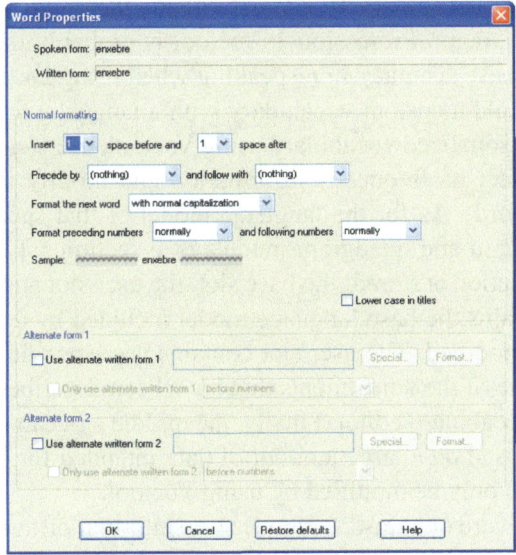

Figure 6.13: Word properties

As mentioned before, respeakers should be very familiar with the Vocabulary editor, not only for the creation of macros, but also to see the words that are included in the vocabulary and those that are not and therefore cannot be recognized unless they are manually added. Also, by selecting "Custom words only" in the display box at the bottom respeakers will be able to see all the words and macros introduced by them, regardless of whether they have been incorporated through "Add new word", "Add word list" or "Add words from documents".

All in all, SR applications offer many different tools to refine the language model and the vocabulary of the software. Very often there are several ways of performing the same action (for example, adding new words). In the case of Dragon, an effective way of handling these tools for respeakers would be to use

- the Vocabulary editor to add new individual words or phrases, to create and edit macros, to edit, delete or re-train existing words, to check what words are included in the vocabulary and what words are not, and finally to keep track of the macros that have been created;
- the "Add words from word lists" tool to import long lists of words, which will have to be created and saved in a ".txt" file;
- the "Add words from documents" tool to import whole texts or scripts so that the software can learn new words and phrases as well adapt its language model to the style of the text, thus improving significantly the likelihood of accurate recognition.

When using these tools, respeakers must make sure that the words, word lists and documents fed into Dragon have no mistakes whatsoever.

6.4.5.5. The Dragon Vocabulary Tool (Voctool) and the middle slot

Available only in Dragon Professional, Voctool is probably the most effective application to increase accuracy in respeaking when using Dragon. Basically, it enables users to build a custom vocabulary with a language model. When adding a word to a personalized vocabulary using Voctool, users can specify its text representation, affect its frequency information and modify its pronunciation (by training the word). As for the language model of that specific vocabulary, it has bigram, trigram and quadgram models (see section 5.1.2) but also three slots where information is stored: the base slot, the user slot and the middle slot. The base slot contains the base language model included by default in Dragon, which cannot be modified. The user slot contains user-specific data that can be modified with some of the adjustments that have been described in this chapter, such as with the vocabulary editor. Finally, the middle slot can contain a custom language model based on a large amount of data intended for a target group of users. This slot can only be modified by using Voctool.

If, for a given word or phrase, Dragon has no information available in the user or middle slot, it will only base its prediction on the base slot. If there are data in the user and middle slot, Dragon will combine statistical information from both to produce a result. The better a slot is over time, the more Dragon will resort to it in order to make predictions. For respeaking, the use of the Dragon Vocabulary Tool in Dragon Professional is extremely useful. Respeakers can create vocabularies and language models for specific topics (weather, football, different types of news) and introduce them in the middle slot, which is likely to increase the overall recognition. More information about Voctool can be found in "Dragon Voctool" and in pages 159-177 of "Dragon System Administrator Guide" (DVD > Chapter 6 > Exercises > 6.6.2).

6.5. Dragon 11

As explained in section 5.4.4.2, the main modification introduced in Dragon 11 with regard to Dragon 10 is the introduction of dual core multithreading, that is, the use of the dual core, available in many processors, to increase accuracy. Other changes include a new pop-up help sidebar, an improved help file including videos, a new interface and audio menu, a new tool to correct different instances of the same word, the introduction of the spoken form option in the "add word" tool and the ability to learn and improve the users' language model not only with the correct/train option, as explained in section 6.4.3, but also by simply typing the right word.[1] Of all these changes, the last two are particularly interesting for respeakers. On the negative side, Dragon 11 does not allow users to modify the middle slot by using the Voctool. However, users can still create and import/export vocabularies which, unlike word lists, comprise not only words but also all the

---

[1] A detailed review of Dragon 11 provided by KnowBrainer is included in DVD > Chapter 6 > Exercises > 6.6.2.

information included in the user profile (pronunciation, training and corrections, properties, etc.).

In any case, respeakers using Dragon 11 must make sure that these modifications, not least the multithreading option, do not cause an increase in latency, which would be very detrimental to the provision of live subtitles (see discussion in section 5.4.4.2).

6.6. Exercises

6.6.1. Creating a user profile

You can find the videos and documents that you need for this section in DVD > Chapter 6 > Exercises > 6.6.1.

To complete the exercises in this chapter, you have to create a voice model or user profile. The steps are usually similar regardless of the SR software used, although some differences may be found. If you're using ViaVoice, follow the steps described in pages 8-11 of the User Guide. In WSR, once you have set up your microphone you have the option to perform initial training ("Take speech tutorial").

If you're using Dragon, follow the steps described in section 6.2 and in pages 1-3 in the Dragon End-User Workbook. Choose the "short training" option in the New User Wizard. The way you train your profile now (tone, pitch, enunciation, speed, volume etc.) will determine the future performance of the software. To find out how to dictate to the software during this training process, watch the video "Creating a User Profile". Try to speak naturally, enunciating clearly and in phrases instead of word by word. Don't dictate punctuation marks at this stage. Make sure that you use the "pause" button if you need to speak to someone or clear your throat while the microphone is on. Dragon is learning your speech patterns and will try to match those words or sounds to the text on the screen, which may affect recognition in the future. As you can see in 0:26 in "Creating a User Profile", when you make a mistake or Dragon fails to understand what you're saying, you have to repeat the misrecognized word so that the training process can go on. If you get stuck with a word that Dragon cannot identify, resume your dictation from the previous words and avoid dictating only the misrecognized word. Once you have finished this initial training, Dragon will offer you the possibility of analyzing your documents and emails. It is usually better to skip this step, as your documents and emails may contain misspelt words, terms in other languages or information that may not be relevant to what you will be dictating/respeaking.

Once your user profile has been created and you're ready to dictate, remember to save it as explained in the video "Saving User Profile".

6.6.2. Dictating to SR software and improving the user profile

The material that you need for this section is included in DVD > Chapter 6 > Exercises > 6.6.2.

As you can see in the video "Dictation 1", the user dictates a letter with very good accuracy. How would you describe his dictation in 1:22-3:00 and 6:44-7:09 with regard to the contents of the table included in section 6.3?

Now watch "Dictation 2". How does it compare to the previous dictation mode, especially from 2:34 to 3:52? How is that reflected in the performance of the software?

Before you start dictating, make sure you adjust the speed settings as explained in section 6.4.1. To check whether this has made any difference, install NaturallySpeakometer and try it out with different phrases and sentences. What is the average latency?

You can now start practising dictation with "Dictation Practice 1" and "Dictation Practice 2". Open DragonPad (in DragonBar > Tools) and resize the window to half of the screen. Set the font to a big enough size (28 or 32, for example) so that you can read the recognized words comfortably, almost as though they were subtitles. Resize the pdf document ("Dictation Practice 1" or "Dictation Practice 2") to the other half of the screen and start dictating into DragonPad. The first document is the same text you have read for the initial training. In this case, however, you must dictate punctuation marks. Once you have finished the dictation, provide the following information:

- number of errors and error rate in relation to the total amount of dictated words;
- list and commentary of the errors.

Do the same exercise with a text of your choice but make sure that it does not contain specialized vocabulary. At this stage, you should aim at obtaining 93%-95% accuracy.

Watch the video "Editing and Correcting" to see how you can select, edit and correct texts by voice. Go back to the texts you have dictated and correct the errors using these methods and especially those described in section 6.4.3.

Find another text of your choice, slightly more specialized than the ones before. Dictate it and provide the same information (error rate, list and commentary of errors). Correct the mistakes as indicated above. If there are words that are still not recognized or are not included in the vocabulary of the SR software, add them using the "Add word" tool or through the Vocabulary Editor in the case of Dragon. The video "Vocabulary Editor" contains an explanation of how to do this.

Finally, if there is a considerable number of new words that need to be introduced in the vocabulary, add them as a list, as explained in section 6.4.5.3.

7. Respeaking Skills Applied during the Process I

7.0. Introduction

Once the respeakers have mastered the dictation skills and the use of the SR software, or even as this is happening, it is time for them to start working on the skills that they will need to apply during the respeaking process. These include, among others, the ability to split their attention and multitask, to dictate punctuation and to respeak with a particular rhythm and speed, especially in the case of Dragon.

7.1. Split attention: dealing with simultaneous but non-overlapping inputs

The respeaking training is here more live-oriented and thus closer to simultaneous interpreting, albeit the differences between the two disciplines also become more noticeable at this stage. Split attention in simultaneous interpreting involves listening, speaking and listening again, this time to yourself, so as to monitor what you say.[1] In respeaking, even though there is usually no change of language, the tasks involved may be as many as listening (to the original soundtrack), (re)speaking (the target text), listening (to yourself), watching (the images and the text on screen) and typing (corrections or even changing the position of the subtitle).[2] Furthermore, the main difficulty lies here in the fact that, even though these tasks are happening at the same time, they do not overlap completely.

7.1.1. Listening and speaking (and listening again)

Although interpreting studies encompass many different views and takes on similar subjects, the notion of split attention, divided attention or attention-sharing seems to be, as stated by Pöchhacker (2004:116), "now beyond doubt". This mental process is described by Gerver (in Arumí Ribas and Romero-Fresco 2008) as follows:

> ... interpreters receive and understand a unit of meaning, and begin to mentally translate it and verbally formulate it. At the same time, they receive and understand a new unit of meaning while still occupied in the vocalization of the previous one. Thus, they must be able to retain the second unit in their memory before beginning the interpretation; while they formulate the second unit, they receive the third unit, and so on successively.

---

[1] It is worth noting here that simultaneous interpreters also have to watch the event/conference they are working on and sometimes even follow written texts, PowerPoint presentations or check terms in the booth computers.
[2] This applies to live respeaking, but not to scripting, that is, respeaking for pre-recorded programmes, where respeakers can pause and play the original video without the need to perform the above tasks at the same time.

The focus is placed here on listening and speaking but, as Jones (1998:69) puts it, the interpreters' attention must be divided further to monitor their own voices:

> The simultaneous interpreter, while not ceasing to listen actively to the speaker, must learn to listen carefully and critically to themselves. ... If the interpreter is not monitoring their own input they can be ungrammatical, pronounce words incorrectly, forget words, such as they may even flatly contradict themselves in two successive sentences by forgetting to say the word *not* in one of them.

In respeaking, the risks of changing the meaning or producing flawed delivery if no monitoring is done also apply. As a matter of fact, the former risk is even more important in respeaking than in interpreting. A mispronunciation may still be comprehensible for an interpreting audience but is very likely to be misrecognized by SR software. Being able to monitor your own voice is thus crucial in respeaking.

There are several exercises often given to interpreting students that may be useful for respeakers who want to train their split-attention skills, such as listening to a narration while counting to a hundred or reciting a well-known poem while listening to a speech and then summing up the speech before an audience. Likewise, respeakers may be asked to improvise a speech, thus thinking about the next sentence as they are producing the current one, or to render a prepared speech while other students show cards with keywords that the respeaker must incorporate into the discourse.

However, the most useful exercise for respeakers wanting to develop split-attention skills is shadowing. As pointed out in Chapter 5, this technique has often been criticized in interpreting teaching, but this criticism may be more pertinent to interpreting than to respeaking. In interpreting, shadowing fails to provide students with skills to translate into another language and it doesn't guarantee comprehension of the source text. Respeaking does not usually involve change of language and, if students are asked to shadow with punctuation marks, comprehension may not be an issue. Indeed, the introduction of punctuation marks, when correct, will normally entail processing and, to some extent, comprehending the source text.

Starting off with the easiest exercise and gradually building up to more difficult ones, respeakers may begin shadowing in a low voice or just mentally (not hearing your own voice makes things considerably easier) with no punctuation marks, then shadowing mentally with punctuation marks, going on to shadowing out loud without punctuation marks and finally shadowing out loud with punctuation marks. Also, since they will already know how to dictate, they will be advised to shadow in "dictation mode" even though to begin with it is probably better not to start doing all these tasks into Dragon, but just into a turned off microphone. As for the types of programmes to be used for these exercises, again from easier to more difficult respeakers may want to start shadowing speeches (steady pace), then sports programmes, news and finally weather reports, interviews and chat shows, where speech rates are usually faster and the speakers' turns tend to overlap. Once this has been done (and more or less mastered), respeakers may want to try respeaking these programmes with Dragon.

7.1.2. Watching: reading and keeping the audiovisual coherence

Watching and typing are probably the most complex tasks in respeaking, which is why it is advisable to introduce them one by one and only after the listening + (re)speaking + monitoring has been mastered. Otherwise, we will be teaching respeakers how to run before they can even walk.

When respeaking for the first time, students typically tend to forget punctuation marks and are not able to pay attention to the screen (some may even close their eyes to concentrate). Once the step described in the previous section comes naturally, respeakers must make an effort to watch the screen. Not just to look at it, but to actually watch both the subtitles and the images. As for the subtitles, respeakers are expected to read them and check how the speech recognizer is transcribing their words. For this purpose, students are advised to resize the screen to make it look like a subtitle box (with two or three lines and a big enough font) already at the dictation stage, before they start respeaking. In this way, they get used to producing subtitle-like utterances and to watch the screen from the beginning. A possible exercise for this task would be to have students respeak a short programme and then ask them to recall the misrecognitions and, in general, their impressions about the performance of the software.

Furthermore, this "watching stage" also includes the visuals. Respeakers will have to pay attention to the images (while listening to the sound) and determine whether the fact that the subtitles are delayed is affecting the audiovisual coherence of the original programme.[3] Say for example that the original speaker uses deictic elements in their speech, thus referring to "this painting", "that part of the room", "here", "there", etc. If this is respoken verbatim, the usual 3-5 second delay will mean that a subtitle referring to "here" will be shown along with an image relating to "there". See Figure 7.1.

In these cases, respeakers will have to change the original text to restore the audiovisual coherence that has been lost due to the delay in the subtitles. Students may practise this skill by respeaking weather forecasts, where presenters usually refer to "this" or "that" area in the map, or live talks in which speakers describe pictures, paintings or slides that they have in front of them. Of the different strategies available to restore the audiovisual coherence lost by the delay in the subtitles, perhaps the most common one is explicitation. Respeakers will then

---

[3] For a detailed explanation of coherence in Audiovisual Translation see Chaume (2004a) and Chaume (2004b).

Figure 7.1: Deictics in respeaking I

replace utterances like "this area" by the actual name of the area the speaker is referring to, which will also apply to deictics such as "here" or "there". In similar programmes or live events in which the use of deictic forms is to be expected, respeakers may choose to prepare beforehand macros for the titles of the paintings, pictures or slides that are going to be discussed.

As well as keeping the audiovisual coherence, watching the images is also essential in at least two more instances: when respeakers need to allocate colours/labels for different speakers or sound information and when they have to move the subtitles up and down in order to avoid covering on-screen captions. In the case of Figure 7.2, it was not possible:

Figure 7.2: Moving subtitles

Finally, it is important to note that on certain occasions, far from being a constraint, the images may help the respeaker have a much-needed breather. Whenever speakers refer, often with deictics again, to charts, graphics, quotes or figures that are displayed on the screen, the respeaker can keep silent to avoid unnecessary redundancies. This is the case in figures 7.3 and 7.4, separated by 15 seconds during which the commentator reads out the list of names on screen and the respeaker adds no subtitles:

Figures 7.3 and 7.4: Deictics in respeaking II

7.1.3. Typing

Once students have managed to respeak watching what is on the screen as they listen, speak and monitor their own voices, it is time to move on to the last skill: typing. First of all, if the respeakers are not using vocal commands to introduce punctuation, identify speakers (with colours or labels) or introduce sound information (labels), then typing may entail any of these elements. Yet, more often than not, what respeakers type are corrections.

The complexity doesn't lie in typing the corrections, which can be done with a standard method such as introducing a hyphen with the corrected word after a misrecognition:

Figure 7.5: Correction

What is difficult here is that this is the only skill that cannot be multitasked with the others. You can respeak as you listen, you can monitor your voice as you listen and respeak and you can even watch images and text as you listen, respeak and monitor your voice, but you cannot respeak as you correct. As a consequence, these instances where corrections are made are very demanding for respeakers. They feature maximum *décalage* (distance between original speaker and respeaker); they require maximum concentration on the part of respeakers to keep listening to something new while they are correcting something old; and finally they require excellent editing skills to be able to catch up with the original speaker without speeding up or changing the dictation mode, so that accuracy is not affected.

Exercises to practise this last skill are straightforward. All students need to do is to respeak programmes such as the ones mentioned above introducing corrections with a previously agreed method. Then, it would be a good idea to compare the average amount of editing carried out throughout the programmes to the editing carried out after the corrections are implemented, and also to assess how much information has been lost in this editing process.

7.1.4. Dealing with simultaneous but non-overlapping inputs

Alas, the biggest difficulty involved in respeaking does not lie in the multitasking required, but in the fact that we are dealing with five actions (listening, (re)speaking, monitoring, watching and typing) that may be happening at the same time, but do not overlap fully.

The example below illustrates the simultaneous but non-overlapping nature of the tasks involved in respeaking:

```
0      1      2      3      4      5      6
```

[watch and listen]
In 1998, the financial recession brought about the loss of hundreds of jobs in Europe.

[watch, listen and respeak]
                    In 1998, the financial recession has brought about the loss ...

[watch, listen, respeak and read]
                                        In 9098, the financial recession brought

[watch, listen, read and type]
                                                            In 1998, the...

Timeline in seconds

1. The original speaker starts uttering the sentence *In 1998, the financial recession...*;
2. After 2 seconds, the respeaker starts his/her utterance (*in 1998 comma the financial recession...*);
3. In second 4, when the respeaker says "*recession*", s/he can read on the screen that *1998* has been misrecognized as *9098*.
4. Two seconds later, in second 6, s/he manages to correct the misrecognition.

By now, though, the original speaker has already finished the sentence and the respeaker must start from *brought about* and quickly catch up with the original to keep a reasonable distance. It is in step 4, when the respeaker is correcting, that maximum concentration is required to pay attention to what is being said (*brought about the loss of...*), as missing this would render the subtitle unintelligible. Effectively, respeakers are asked here to watch and correct the past as they make an effort to listen to the present in order to respeak it in the future.

Being able to work with distance from the original speaker (known as *décalage* in interpreting) and then editing are key skills to be implemented here. Whereas interpreters often speed up their delivery a little bit to catch up with the original, respeakers cannot afford to do this, as it could affect recognition accuracy. As for the *décalage* required, once again respeaking differs from interpreting, as will be discussed in section 7.3.1.

Before moving on, though, it is important to point out that although the individual presentation of the efforts involved in respeaking may give the impression that this is a nearly impossible task to perform, this is far from true. If we break down the efforts involved in a commonly performed action such as driving (listening, watching, changing gears, stepping on clutch, brake and accelerator, turning on and off the lights, etc.), it may sound just as difficult. Respeaking may be more complicated than driving, but it is a skill that can be acquired through training if the right conditions (calmness, capacity to multitask, etc.) are already there.

7.2. Punctuation

7.2.1. Automatic vs. non-automatic punctuation

Automatic punctuation or autopunctuation is, along with the development of a truly accurate speaker-independent engine, one of the biggest challenges facing SR technology. There are different applications that have attempted to tackle this issue.

IBM's Viascribe (see Chapter 5), which has been designed to be used by speakers (mainly lecturers in classrooms) as opposed to respeakers, introduces new lines and paragraph breaks when speakers make a pause in their speech. There is no need to dictate punctuation marks. Lecturers can give their class in the same way for their hearing and deaf students, who will be able to read a live transcription on a screen with an average accuracy of 70% to 85%. The problem is that, although this may be acceptable for a classroom environment, where there may not be so much need for accuracy and the format of the transcription is not essential, the situation regarding subtitles is different. Subtitle viewers are very used to watching more or less proper punctuation in most programmes and are likely to react against subtitles that are 15% less accurate and have no commas, full stops or even question marks.

Another option to save users from having to dictate punctuation marks is to have the SR introduce them automatically. Dragon has had this option available since DNS6 and it has been further developed in DNS10. Presently, it only introduces full stops and commas. This is based, as in Viascribe, on the length of the speaker's pauses and some basic grammar rules. Although it may sometimes work well, it is difficult to make an accurate use of it, especially since any long pause, be it for hesitation or not, will be transcribed as a full stop. An example of this is shown in the video "Automatic Punctuation" (DVD > Chapter 5 > Discussion points and exercises > 5.6.4). Besides, concerned as it is with full stops and commas, this tool neglects other key elements such as dashes, colons, quotation marks and especially exclamation and question marks.

Most experts still seem sceptical about automatic punctuation:

> Simply put, automatic punctuation doesn't work. You can almost get it to work if you speak in very short sentences and the concept is impressive but unfortunately, the NaturallySpeaking developers have never been able to make it work even though this feature has been around for several versions of NaturallySpeaking. In our opinion, Nuance should simply remove this crippled feature from the product. (Knowbrainer)[4]

Current research in this field points to the need to introduce neural networking/ artificial intelligence in the autopunctuation algorhythms so that this tool can be reliable. This would require the software to perform a semantic and prosodic (intonation-based) analysis of the utterances, which, for most experts in the field, is still five to ten years off.

For the time being, then, respeakers have no choice but to introduce punctuation themselves. Here, too, different options are available.

7.2.2. Punctuation in respeaking

Most respeakers dictate punctuation marks to the software along with the rest of the original text. This does not mean, however, that they cannot combine manual and vocal punctuation. They still have the keyboard in front of them if they choose to type commas, full stops and so on.

Alternatively, some companies have come up with different methods to save respeakers from having to dictate punctuation marks that, as will be explained in section 7.4, usually constitute 15% to 18% of the respoken words. In Canada, respeakers working for TVA use a Nintendo 64 joystick to introduce not only punctuation marks but also sound labels for the deaf and hard of hearing audience. In Italy, respeakers at Colby use a touch screen in front of them to insert punctuation marks, key words and other specialized vocabulary with accurate results. The problem in this case is that, when using the touch screen (yet another task), respeakers seem to take a couple of seconds more than usual to utter their words, which results in an overall 6-8-second delay in the subtitles.

In any case and whatever the method used, respeaking students must pay a great deal of attention to the norms governing the use of punctuation marks, which are among the few elements that are always going to be present in respeaking, whatever the genre or content tackled. Given the impossibility of dealing here with the norms applied in every language, the focus will be placed on the English language. In this sense, a good place to start is the set of punctuation

---

[4] https://www.knowbrainer.com/PubForum/index.cfm?page=viewForumTopic&topicId=6327&pageNo=1

conventions put forward by Díaz Cintas and Remael for pre-recorded subtitling (2007:104-124). Only a few aspects need to be added in view of the specific nature of respeaking.

Firstly, unlike subtitlers, respeakers working on live programmes cannot afford to think and doubt about the use of a given comma or a full stop. Observing punctuation norms must come as second nature. Furthermore, respeakers must make sure that a) punctuation marks are properly recognized and b) not much time is wasted in their dictation. As far as accuracy is concerned, the literal (mis)transcription of a command ("full top") may be really confusing for the viewers. As for time, a sentence like "That was great!", uttered by the original speaker in three words, may have to be respoken in five (*that was great exclamation mark*). This will cause the respeaker to lag behind the original speaker and the subtitles to be delayed on the screen.

Different strategies may be applied to improve the recognition of punctuation marks and to avoid wasting too much time dictating them. Most respeakers resort to macros for long commands such as exclamation or question marks. Shorter commands like comma and full stop may not need macros, but it may be a good idea to avoid misrecognitions ("full top", "full pop", etc.) by getting rid of homophones. In Dragon, respeakers can delete the "incorrect" options from the vocabulary or even create macros to tell the software that every time a "full top/pop" is heard, a full stop must be displayed on the screen. A further problem would arise if the respeaker ever needs to actually respeak "full stop" as a unit, for instance in the utterance "I don't like sharing, full stop". In this case, and if no macro has been prepared beforehand, the respeaker can either edit the phrase (*I don't like sharing comma that's it*) or introduce a pause between "full" and "stop" ("I don't like sharing comma full [pause] stop"), which will tell Dragon that "full stop" is not to be transcribed as a command but as an utterance.

7.2.3. The use of the comma in respeaking

Due to the particular nature of respeaking, some punctuation marks that are used in subtitling seem to be absent from respoken subtitles. Parenthesis/brackets, colons or italics are hardly ever used by respeakers, who do use however commas, full stops, exclamation and question marks, dashes, quotation marks and triple dots in a similar way to pre-recorded subtitling. Of all these signs, the comma is probably the most important one, which is why respeakers should be very aware of the rules governing its use. These are the main rules as applied by several respeaking companies in the UK:

(1) *Series*: use a comma to separate elements in a series:

Tania, Carolina, Godefroy and Scott were great to live with.

This is the most straightforward rule and usually causes no problems for respeakers. A brief mention must be made, however, to the so-called Oxford comma, that is, the comma before "and" in a series. Seeing as the standard recommendation in subtitling is to keep punctuation to a minimum (Díaz Cintas and Remael 2007) and that respeakers are likely to fall behind the original speaker, it does not seem a good idea to use it in this case.

(2) *Vocative*: use a comma to separate a vocative (the name of the person addressed) from the rest of the sentence:

> Andreas, I'm afraid
> you're not much of a footballer.

If the vocative is in the middle of the sentence, then it should be surrounded by commas:

> I'm afraid, Andreas,
> you're not much of a footballer

This use is particularly common in respeaking, for example in news programmes, where presenters often address each other or other correspondents by their names.

(3) *Adjectives*: use a comma to separate coordinate adjectives:

> Antón is a tall, distinguished,
> good-looking fellow.

This rule would not apply to cases such as "That was a nice little touch" or "They are wearing a light blue shirt". In general, if *and* or *but* can be used between the adjectives, then a comma can be used too. "That was a nice *and* little touch" or "They are wearing a light *and* blue shirt" would not make sense whereas "Daniel is a tall and distinguished fellow" would.

(4) *Parenthesis*: use commas to open and close an element which, if taken out of the sentence, would not disturb its structure:

> Luis, who still lives in Alcabre,
> is a world-renowned engineer.

An exception may be made for cases in which the element is very short or is particularly close to the previous word in the sentence. Thus in "His wife Helen decided to leave him", there is no need to use commas before and after "Helen". In any case, respeakers must be careful not to confuse this "parenthesis rule" with the following examples:

> The football legend Fer de Vega
> was invited to present the awards.

> The famous designer Emilio Bianchi
> is now based in Italy.

In these two cases, taking out "Fer de Vega" and "Emilio Bianchi" would make the sentences nonsensical, so no commas are needed.

(5) *Introduction*: use comma after introductory clauses, time/place references, yes/no and conversational interjections:

> If they can play like Celta de Vigo,
> the fans will be delighted.

> Since he didn't want to commit,
> his boss had to look for a replacement.

> Although they were ahead in the polls,
> nobody expected such a landslide.

> Three years ago(,) Paulo decided
> he wanted to make a difference.

> Over the past couple of years,
> Beatriz has changed considerably.

In the first three examples above, the comma is used after clauses that introduce a condition, a cause and a concession respectively. It can also be used after an introductory reference to time or place, as in the last two sentences. As a rule of thumb, if this reference has three or fewer words, the comma is not strictly necessary. If it is longer, then the respeaker should normally use it. Finally, respeakers will often come across utterances beginning with *yes/no* or conversational markers such as *well, oh, er, um, I mean, you know*, etc. A comma will be needed after them:

> No, I can't remember that.

> Well, what can I say?

> Oh, what a save!

(6) *Quotations*: use a comma to introduce quotations

Although quotations can sometimes be introduced with colons in written English and in pre-recorded subtitling, this punctuation mark is not common in respeaking, probably to avoid misrecognitions. Quotations are thus introduced with commas:

> Andrés said, "I'll do it".

> What Andrés said was, "I'll do it".

(7) *Tag questions*: use a comma before tag questions and conversational markers acting as such (*right, OK*, etc.). These elements are very recurrent in respeaking and also very easy to identify:

> He will be up to scratch, won't he?

> There won't be any problem, right?

> Remember what Sofi said, OK?

(8) *Joining*: use a comma to join two independent clauses that are separated by a conjunction (*but, and, while, whereas, although,* etc.):

> The exam was very difficult,
> but Uxía passed it with flying colours.

> United take on Arsenal,
> while Sunderland will play Chelsea.

Although usually included in grammar books, this comma is often left out in respeaking, unless it is needed to avoid confusion. In the case of *and*, for example, respeakers often choose to break a single sentence into two. Thus, "The defendant provided his own billing system, and he also paid for his own bookkeeping services" would normally turn into "The defendant provided his own billing system. He also paid for his own bookkeeping services".

As well as the eight cases described here, the comma may also be used for other purposes, such to express contrast ("I asked for tea, not coffee"), to avoid confusion ("To George, Harrison was a dear friend") or for typographical reasons ("He was born in Hartford, Connecticut").

With regard to exercises, as well as having students respeak a programme to provide them with feedback on their use of punctuation marks, it is sometimes useful to give them tasks on paper. In this case, they can be given an unpunctuated script to introduce different marks. As far as commas are concerned, they may be asked to indicate, beside every comma, the number of the rule it corresponds to (1-8 and perhaps 9 for "other cases"). In a live situation respeakers tend to rely on instinct, which may not always adhere to the above rules. This type of exercise should help internalize the rules so that, when it comes to respeaking a programme in real time, they come as second nature.

7.3. Rhythm: respeaking units and the salami technique

7.3.1. Décalage and units of meaning in interpreting

A commonly discussed issue in interpreting is *when to start speaking* or, put differently, the *décalage* that interpreters are supposed to maintain with regard to the original speaker. According to Jones (1998:72-80), there are at least two well-known approaches to this, both of which place the focus on the original utterance, not on the seconds that the interpreter has to wait to start speaking.

In the first approach, interpreters start speaking as soon as they have heard a **unit of meaning**, the smallest usable unit for the interpreter and defined by Jones (*ibid*:74) as "a *micro-component* of the meaning of a speech". According to this author (*ibid*), "the minimum length of a unit of meaning is determined by the shortest possible passage that may engender a clear cognitive representation in the mind of the listener". These units of meaning may vary from a single word to a shorter or longer phrase as can be seen in the following examples:

> Britain, despite the ruling of the Court of Human Rights in Strasbourg, has decided to maintain its position on the treatment of prison inmates.
> The Minister of the Interior does not intend to propose any change to the rules governing treatment of prison inmates.
> Despite the ruling in the Court of Human Rights in Strasbourg, the British prison authorities have decided to maintain their position on the treatment of inmates.

A second approach explained by Jones (1998:79) would involve "waiting until there's enough material to finish the sentence and beginning the sentence in such a way as to be sure to finish it". Although this may work in interpreting, it is more problematic in respeaking, where *décalage* is less desirable. It is true that, particularly when corrections are being made or when the speech rate of the original speaker is fast, respeakers must be able to cope with a considerable distance. In this sense, good respeakers should be able to keep a more or less constant *décalage*,[5] be flexible when they happen to lag behind and make an effort to get closer to the original speaker when the utterance is going to finish, which can be predicted by the content or the tone of the utterance. The latter aspect is important because ends of utterances are sometimes followed by quick changes of turn. If the *décalage* is too long, respeakers may struggle to convey the change of turn without too much delay in the subtitles. What must be highlighted here is that *décalage* in respeaking is often problematic. Taking into account that the

---

[5] In order to practice décalage, Van Dam (1989:170) proposes the distance exercise, made up of two phases. In the first one, the teacher pauses following every idea for the student to reformulate it; in the second phase, the teacher begins the enunciation of the next idea while the student is still in the midst of reformulating the prior one.

respeaker, with a programme such as Dragon, needs to pause for the utterance to appear on the screen (which could take up to one second) and that the emission of the subtitles can take two seconds, a 4-second *décalage* would turn into a 7-second delay on the TV screen, where viewers could struggle to relate the subtitles to the images.

It is for this reason that the first approach, speaking as soon as a unit of meaning is heard, is probably more appropriate for respeaking than waiting until there is enough information to finish the sentence. Yet, here too respeaking may slightly differ from interpreting. In the first two examples above, respeakers may start with *Britain comma* and *The Minister of the Interior*. In the third example, however, the unit *Despite the ruling in the Court of Human Rights in Strasbourg* would cause too much delay in the subtitles. Although it may be an appropriate unit of meaning for interpreting, it would not be an adequate respeaking unit.

7.3.2. Unit level: respeaking units

Respeaking units may be defined as the units of meaning used by respeakers; whenever possible, idea units that lend themselves to accurate recognition by the SR software (phrases as opposed to single words) and to comfortable reading for the viewers (around one line in a one-, two- or three-line subtitle).

Respeakers working with Dragon must try to find a good speech-to-pause rhythm, given that no subtitle will be shown until a pause is made. One line, usually five to seven words, is an ideal respeaking unit. It could also be shorter than one line or a bit longer, but when it is much longer (closer to two lines) the subtitle may take too long to appear on the screen and will be too delayed with regard to the pictures. Besides, a respeaking unit that takes longer than one line presents the problem of line segmentation. Unless the display mode is line-by-line or the software takes into account syntactic principles, scrolling or block respoken subtitles usually have no control over line segmentation, which makes these subtitles difficult to read for the viewers.

Let us consider again the examples above in the light of this definition of respeaking unit:

The Minister of the Interior does not intend to propose
any change to the rules governing treatment of prison inmates.

(Great) Britain, despite the ruling // of the Court of Human Rights
in Strasbourg, has decided to maintain its position
on the treatment of prison inmates.

Despite the ruling in the Court of Human Rights in Strasbourg,
the British prison authorities have decided to maintain their position
on the treatment of inmates.

The first sentence offers optimum respeaking units that lend themselves to accurate recognition and to convenient display in approximately one line within, for example, two-line subtitles. In the second sentence, the respeaker may choose to begin with *Britain comma*. Yet, in this case, dictating just one word means that all the accuracy will be down to the acoustic model, as the language model will have no other words to use contextual data with. A possible solution would be to use *Great Britain* as a respeaking unit, which will improve the likelihood of accurate recognition. In the third example, the respeaker has to decide whether to start with the short option (*Despite the ruling + in the Court of Human Rights*) or with the long one (*Despite the ruling in the Court of Human Rights*), which is just about as long as a respeaking unit could be. The third and longer option (*Despite the ruling in the Court of Human Rights in Strasbourg*) is usually best avoided, as it would take almost two lines and would cause too much delay on the screen.

Having described the unit level, it is now time to turn to the sentence level, where line segmentation is also an issue that may be tackled with the so-called **salami technique**.

7.3.3. Sentence level: the salami technique

Very much following Díaz Cintas and Remael's (2007:172) advice with regard to standard subtitling, respeakers should aim whenever possible to contain their sentences, including several respeaking units, within two lines. Longer sentences are difficult to read, particularly in live subtitling, where there is no perfect synchrony with the sound or the images. Also, as explained in the previous section, line-segmentation becomes an important issue here. Whereas subtitlers segment with their hands (on the keyboard) what they see (on the screen), respeakers segment with their voice (on the microphone) what they hear (on the headset). As explained in the previous section, they usually have no control (except for when there is line by line segmentation) over the segmentation of every line, which means that the longer the sentence, the more likely it is to have poor line-segmentation. An analysis of ten respoken programmes broadcast by the BBC in 2008 (live coverage of the Olympics in Beijing on 18/08/08; news clips from BBC News at One on 3/10/08 and interviews from Newsnight on 23/09/08) shows that 71.8% of the respoken subtitles for these programmes had poor segmentation. see figures 7.6 and 7.7.

This carries important implications from the point of view of reading. As pointed out by Perego (2008:35), appropriate line segmentation is critical, given that "only in this way can the cognitive process of reading the subtitles and watching the action proceed with the least effort". In Perego's view, this is particularly relevant in situations where viewers are under pressure, which may perfectly apply to live programmes such as the ones analyzed in this article. As a matter of fact, eye-tracking-based research carried out by D'Ydewalle *et al.* (1989:42) has shown that unusual line-splitting "increases considerably the time in the subtitled area" for most viewers.

Figures 7.6 and 7.7: Segmentation in respeaking

It is for this reason that respeakers must try to avoid dictating very long sentences that extend over many lines. Considering that the average number of words per line in the programmes analyzed is six, sentences should be up to 12 words and preferably not longer than 24. That is, they should not take more than four lines. Longer sentences are likely to involve many poor line-breaks and to be too long for the viewers to follow. This means that respeakers may have to "chop" original sentences, applying the "salami technique" often used in interpreting to "slice up" sentences and make them shorter and simpler than the original ones.

In the video "BBC News" (DVD > Chapter 2 > Discussion points and exercises > 2.4.5), the presenter speaks in sentences that would take, if they were subtitled verbatim (just as they are spoken) an average of 26 words, that is, 4.2 lines. The distribution of the sentences would be as follows:

- 23% would take 7 lines
- 23% would take 6 lines
- 23 % would take 5 lines
- 15% would take 3 lines
- 15% would take 2 lines
- 0% would take 1 line

Needless to say, such long sentences would be very difficult to read for the viewers. Having applied the salami technique, the respeaker has managed to reduce the average sentence length to 12 words, that is, 2 lines. The distribution in the respoken subtitles shown on the screen is as follows:

- 45% takes 2 lines
- 30% takes 3 lines
- 15% takes 1 line
- 10% takes 4 lines

This salami technique is sometimes applied in ordinary subtitling too. Ivarsson and Carroll (1998:91), for example, criticize long sentences such as:

> Welcome to the first of four programmes
> in this series that every four
> weeks will show how big money
> governs England, and how your
> money can be used
> to change society.

Instead, they recommend:

> Welcome to the first
> of four programmes in this series.
> Every four weeks we will show
> how big money governs England,
> and how your money
> can be used to change society.

Yet, respeaking seems to take this salami technique a step further than ordinary subtitling. Let's take the same clip as before. Between 0:24 and 0:40, the presenter says:

> Inside this aircraft are likely to be the clues to its fate, and so everything had to be recovered, from the 200 tonne plane itself to the bits that fell off, including part of the undercarriage.

In ordinary subtitles, this sentence could have been segmented on the screen as:

> Inside this aircraft
> are likely to be the clues to its fate.
>
> So everything had to be recovered,
> from the 200 tonne plane itself
>
> to the bits that fell off,
> including part of the undercarriage.

In contrast, instead of opting for two sentences to convey the original spoken sentence, the respeaker makes four:

> Inside this aircraft
> are likely to be the clues to its fate.[full stop]
>
> So everything had to be recovered. [full stop]
> From the 200 tonne plane itself, [comma]
>
> to the bits that fell off.[full stop]
> Including part of the undercarriage.[full stop]

The programmes analyzed show that respoken subtitles have their own specific syntax, where sentences are on average 12 words long (two lines) and usually no longer than three lines (18 words).

To sum up what has been explained in this section, whenever possible, respeakers should wait for the original speaker to have uttered an idea unit, dictate respeaking units that lend themselves to accurate recognition by the SR software (phrases as opposed to single words) and to comfortable reading for the viewers (one line in a one-, two- or three-line subtitle), and finally produce sentences that are not longer than two or three lines long.

7.4. Speed: edited vs. verbatim respeaking[6]

Among the most commonly debated topics of discussion in the subtitling literature, speed has always occupied a privileged position. This may be explained by the fact that it is the speed of subtitles that determines whether they can be verbatim or edited. Fast subtitles can convey every single word of the dialogue whereas slower subtitles typically summarize or condense what is being said. Often considered very important in "standard" subtitling (interlingual subtitling for hearing viewers), this issue becomes critical when applied to SDH, hence Ofcom's description (2005:11) of speed as "arguably the key underlying issue behind nearly every important issue" in SDH. As will be explained in the next section, speed in SDH is as much a technical matter as it is economic (broadcasters, service providers), political and ideological (deaf associations). It is also a research topic for scholars, who often try to determine the extent to which different speeds are readable for different groups of viewers.

Respeaking students, who are effectively producing live SDH, must be aware of the interests and parties involved in this issue (section 7.4.1), the usual speech rates of the programmes they have to respeak (section 7.4.2), the reading rates of their viewers (section 7.4.3), the speed at which respeakers usually speak (section 7.4.4), the extent to which they edit the original speech and finally the amount of information that is lost in the process (section 7.4.5).

7.4.1. More to speed than meets the eye: the parties involved

The speed of subtitles is a thorny issue that concerns different parties who hold different views for different reasons. Firstly, broadcasters and subtitling companies, under pressure to provide more SDH, support verbatim subtitles, as they require less effort on the part of the subtitlers and are thus more economical than edited subtitles:

> The cost of subtitling a programme relates, in part, to the amount of editing required. Unedited subtitles are faster than edited ones. Reducing the

---

[6] An extended version of this section may be found in Romero-Fresco (2009) and Romero-Fresco (2010).

amount of editing required, thereby increasing the speed of text on screen, might assist broadcast licensees to meet the new increased subtitling requirements. (Ofcom 2005:6)

Secondly, and surprisingly, most deaf viewers (or rather deaf associations) also demand verbatim, and therefore faster, subtitles. In this case, the reason is not financial, but political. There is among these viewers a great deal of sensitivity and antagonism towards the idea of editing, regarded as "a form of censorship and 'denying' deaf people full access to information available to the hearing population" (Ofcom 2005:17).

Finally, a third group is formed by scholars and researchers, the only ones who usually support edited subtitles. They often agree with Sancho-Aldridge (1996:24), who calls for the need to "disentangle the politically sensitive issue of 'access' from the practical issue of which style, in real terms, provided deaf viewers with most information". Among scholars, there seems to be consensus that verbatim subtitles are often too fast to provide full access for many deaf viewers (Neves 2008). This view is backed by several studies on reading speeds, described in 7.4.3, as well as by the second thoughts expressed on some occasions by deaf viewers when asked to reflect on this issue. A case in point is the study carried out by Sancho-Aldridge and IFF Research Ltd (1996:24):

> Initially, over half (54%) the respondents said they wanted word-for-word subtitles, while 33% opted for summarised (13% had no preference). When respondents were asked to consider the practical difficulties of reading word-for-word subtitles, however, 10% fewer chose them, resulting in an even division between the two methods – word-for-word (45%) versus summary (43%).

Yet, even though it may be true that the wider deaf audience may appreciate the benefits of editing when considered more fully, the reality is that the "official" stance of deaf associations is to push for verbatim/fast subtitles, thus forming an unlikely partnership with broadcasters. As a result, the paradox remains that whereas scholars support editing to provide full access for the deaf, the latter line up with broadcasters to push for verbatim, which may not always give them full access after all.

Respeakers must be able to differentiate between at least three different types of speed: speech rate (of the original speakers), reading rate (of the viewers) and respeaking rate (of the respeakers), all of which are influenced by numerous factors that make generalizations on this issue particularly difficult. In this sense, since speech and reading rate are typically given in wpm, this is the unit that will be used here. When necessary, however, the equivalent in characters per second (cps) will be provided, as this is commonly used to evaluate subtitling speed. This will apply mainly to the English language, where the average word is considered to have five characters (Díaz Cintas 2008:97).

7.4.2. Speech rates

As for speech rate, a further distinction is to be made between extemporaneous speech and televised speech. Early studies such as the one carried out by Kelly and Steer (1949) set spontaneous speech in English at 159 wpm. Although this figure is to be taken with some reservation given the countless factors that can affect spontaneous speech rate, it has been later confirmed by Steinfield (1999), who points to 160 wpm, and by Wingfield *et al.* (2006), who suggest between 140 and 160 wpm. Televised speech presents a different situation. As noted by Uglova and Shevchenko (2005), who compare the speed of spontaneous and televised speech in different American cities, the average speech-to-pause ratio in spontaneous speech is 3:1, that is, there is one pause every three seconds. In the news, this changes to 14:1, i.e. one pause every 14 seconds. Given this decrease in the number of pauses and a typically faster delivery, Uglova and Shevchenko (2005) set televised speech in US news programmes at 200 wpm, and even faster in weather forecasts, which is corroborated by Wingfield et al. (2006). As for the UK, recent research (Romero-Fresco 2009) carried out on programmes broadcast by the BBC in the UK points to the existence of different speeds for different genres. In sports, the speed would appear to range from 124 wpm to 182 wpm, with an average of 160 wpm. News seem to be spoken faster, between 161 and 198 wpm, with an average of 180 wpm, and interviews and weather reports even faster, between 211 wpm and 245 wpm with an average of 230 wpm. It would thus appear that televised speech is usually faster than spontaneous speech. Given the widely held notion, especially among psychologists, that an individual can usually hear and digest acoustic information more quickly than they can read it, the question now remains of whether viewers can read subtitles displayed at such speed.

7.4.3. Reading rates

As is the case when dealing with speech rate, figures on reading speed must be taken with a pinch of salt, given that an individual's reading rate may depend on a number of factors as varied as the reading level of the materials, the purpose of the reading, the conceptual context of the material and especially the accuracy or efficiency of comprehension (Carver 1974), among many others. Besides, it is also essential to take into account the different types of readers/viewers, especially when dealing with SDH:

> Even among groups of hearing subjects, one finds considerable differences in reading speeds. These differences, though, are particularly relevant within the deaf community, which is known to be very heterogeneous, with outlooks and needs so different that it is difficult to adequately meet them all together. (de Linde and Kay 1999:11)

A distinction must be made at least in terms of readers (hearing/hard of hearing and deaf adults) and material (print/subtitles). As far as hearing adults are concerned, their average reading speed of printed material seems to be about 300 wpm (Carver 1976; D'Ydewalle and de Bruycker 2007). As for subtitles, not many studies have been carried out on hearing adults' reading speed. Particularly relevant in this sense is the research conducted by D'Ydewalle *et al.* (1987), who used eye-tracking technology to test three different presentation times for subtitles: 192 wpm, 130 wpm and 96 wpm. The object of this study was to ascertain if the so-called six-second rule (a full two-line subtitle displayed on screen for 6 seconds and shorter subtitles scheduled proportionally, equivalent to 130 wpm), accepted as common practice in most subtitling countries, could be validated by empirical research on reading speed. His results leave little room for doubt, the six-second rule being confirmed as setting the appropriate reading speed for the participants. In recent years, and based on the idea that regular exposure to subtitles may have increased the viewers' reading speed (Ofcom 2005), this six-second rule has been applied to longer lines than the ones referred to by D'Ydewalle (78 characters instead of 64) which results in subtitling companies setting the recommended speed at 160 wpm and even 180 wpm. Further research is still needed to investigate the reception of such speeds on the part of hearing viewers.

As far as deaf and hard of hearing viewers are concerned, the first problem comes from the impossibility to regard them as one homogeneous group.[7] For those referred to as Deaf by Neves (2008:143), reading presents some added difficulties to those faced by hearing people, given that they have less language-specific knowledge (semantic and syntax), fewer oral skills necessary for reading (i.e. phonological processing) and poor encyclopaedic language knowledge necessary to understand texts (Torres Monreal and Santana Hernández 2005). It is for this reason that, as shown by both Conrad (1977) and Torres Monreal and Santana Hernández (2005), the reading level of deaf high school students corresponds to that of hearing students who are seven years younger.

With regard to reading subtitles, although research is scarce, the most relevant study is probably the one carried out by Jensema (1998), who tested different subtitle speeds (96-200 wpm) with 205 deaf, 110 hard of hearing and 262 hearing participants. Results indicated that, for most viewers, 145 wpm was the preferred speed and that anything over 170 wpm was generally deemed as too fast.

---

[7] As pointed out by Neves (2008:143), an important distinction is to be made between the deaf, that is, "people who are deaf but who belong to the social context of the hearing majority and relate to the oral language as their mother tongue", and the Deaf, "a social and linguistic minority, who use a sign language as their mother tongue and read the national language as a second language". Given that the focus of this article is on the subtitles and not on the audience, the term deaf will be applied to both groups and distinctions between the two groups will only be made explicit when necessary.

The question is now whether, as mentioned above regarding hearing viewers, ten years later reading speeds have increased. The subtitling industry seems to believe so, as reflected in many of the subtitling guidelines available. In the UK, the standards for subtitling laid out by the Independent Television Commission (ITC) in 1999 set the reading speed for SDH at 140 wpm, very much following Jensema's (1998) findings. Yet, this recommendation was revisited in 2005 by Ofcom, which carried out a study presenting different subtitling speeds to 21 moderately deaf, 21 severely deaf and 22 profoundly deaf people. Although, as stated in this report (2005:4), almost 40% of the participants considered 180 wpm to be too fast and "the majority of deaf viewers would like subtitle speed to stay the same", Ofcom's final recommendation ("subtitling speed should not normally exceed 180 wpm [15 cps]") effectively allows broadcasters to increase up to 40 wpm the previous recommended subtitling rate. Following this study and extensive consultation with disability organisations, broadcasters and access service providers, the set of SDH guidelines drawn by Ofcom in 2006 recommends 160-180 wpm given that it attracted "little adverse comment". Yet, important organizations such as Sense, Tag, the Royal National Institute for the Blind and the Royal National Institute for Deaf People regarded these speeds as too fast and likely to pose problems to some viewers.

In other words, 180 wpm (15 cps), the maximum SDH speed set by the UK guidelines, has been agreed upon with consensus among broadcasters, service providers and some deaf associations, but is seen as somewhat excessive by many viewers and most academics. In this sense, the research I have carried out at Roehampton University (London) with deaf, hard of hearing and hearing viewers (see Chapter 11) suggests that, as far as respeaking is concerned, 180 wpm is already a fast rate that may hinder comprehension seriously, let alone rates over 200 wpm, which have resulted in very poor understanding of the respoken programme.

Let's look now at how fast respoken subtitles are usually produced, taking the UK as an example.

7.4.4. Respeaking rates

The little research carried out so far (Eugeni 2009; Romero-Fresco 2009) seems to indicate that the respeakers' speech rate (RSR) depends largely on the speech rate of the source text (original speech rate – OSR). According to this research, respeaking speed may range from 106 wpm to 190 wpm and it is often lower than the speed of the original speaker. Indeed, respeakers lag 0-20 wpm behind original speakers who speak at up to 180 wpm and approximately 40 wpm behind speakers who speak faster. In other words, respeakers do not usually manage to produce verbatim subtitles, even though this is what they are encouraged to do. Figure 7.8 (Romero-Fresco 2010) includes a comparative analysis of the OSR in three sports programmes, three news programmes and four interviews/weather reports, indicated in the x axis, and the RSR, shown in wpm in the y axis:

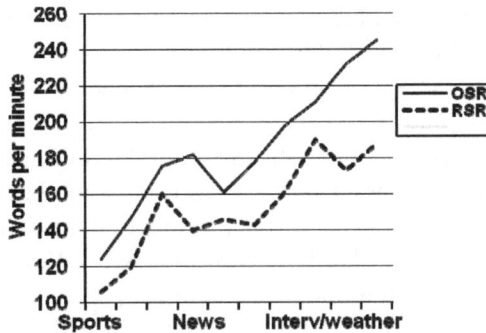

Figure 7.8: Comparison of original speech rate and respeakers' speech rate

These data beg the question of why, if respeakers are asked to produce verbatim subtitles, they don't do so in programmes where the slow source text rate makes it technically possible. The reason for this may lie in the introduction of oral punctuation by respeakers when they are dictating to their SR software. Indeed, the average number of full stops and commas introduced is very similar to the number of words respeakers lag behind original speakers. Thus, if we consider punctuation marks as words, the comparative graph of source text and target text speed changes considerably:

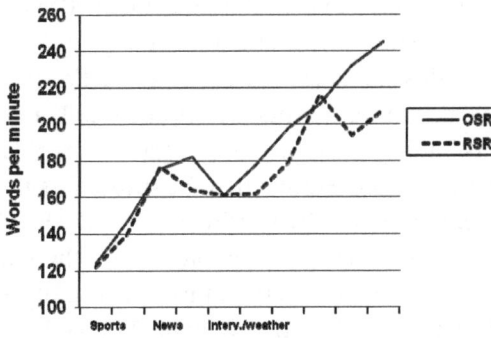

Figure 7.9: Original speech rate and respeakers' speech rate including punctuation marks

In other words, respeakers do adapt to the source text speech rate and, especially in speeds up to 180 wpm (sports and news), manage to say the same amount of wpm as the original – if we include full stops and commas in this count. This would be the reason why respoken subtitles seem to be invariably edited. In order to produce verbatim subtitles, respeakers would have to speak faster than their original speakers (uttering all the source text plus punctuation marks), which is probably against the grain in this shadowing-like type of translation.

Another issue that is worth highlighting is that of the maximum respeaking speed. As explained above, subtitling speeds of or over 180 wpm are deemed as too fast by most academics and many viewers. Despite the fact that the maximum speed usually calculated for the use of SR software such as Dragon is 160 wpm and that the respeaking world record set by Fabrizio G. Verruso in the conference Intersteno 2005 is 174 wpm, respeakers in the UK seem to reach up to 190 wpm in fast programmes. In this regard, Neves (2005) warns that subtitles displayed at 180 wpm or faster, even if they are displayed in blocks, with careful line breaks and synchrony with image, pose a great deal of difficulty for deaf (and even some hard of hearing) viewers. What about respoken subtitles, overlooked by most guidelines and displayed at speeds of up to 190 wpm, word-for-word, without careful line breaks and with no synchrony with image? The data presented in Chapter 11 on the reception of respoken subtitles displayed at 180 wpm and 220 wpm shows that both speeds hinder comprehension significantly.

From the point of view of respeaking training, the fact that respeakers usually fall behind original speakers' speech rate means that editing is an essential task.

7.4.5. Edited vs. verbatim respeaking

As pointed out above, many deaf viewers equate editing to censorship and therefore support verbatim subtitles, regardless of their speed, as the only method to provide them with full access to the original content. The analysis presented in Romero-Fresco (2009) shows that, at least in the programmes under study, verbatim respoken subtitles are not an option, given that respeakers seem to lag between 20 (sports and news) and 40 (interviews and weather) wpm behind their original speakers. This finding is consistent with the results obtained in Flanders by Luyckx *et al.* (2010:17), who explain that the respeakers taking part in their study "found it impossible to literally subtitle a live talk show".[8]

The question is now how much information is lost in this editing process and how the loss can be quantified. To ascertain this, it is useful to take up Chafe's notion of idea units (1980, 1985),[9] used also by the ITC Guidance for Real-time Subtitling (1999). These guidelines recommend subtitlers, when it comes to editing, to include a "reasonable percentage" of the words spoken and to make sure that idea units appear as a "good percentage" of the spoken message.

Using Chafe's criteria for the identification of idea units, the percentage of information lost in the editing process of the programmes mentioned above is

---

[8] Luyckx *et al.* (2010) highlight a series of factors determining text reduction in respeaking (delay, amount of source text, overall number of reductions, etc.) and find that, in some cases, respeakers prefer to omit comments rather than reducing them to a certain extent.

[9] Chafe (1985:106) defines idea units as "units of intonational and semantic closure", which can be identified because they are spoken with a single coherent intonation contour, preceded and followed by some kind of hesitation, made up of one verb phrase along with whatever noun, prepositional or adverb phrase are appropriate, usually consist of seven words and take about two seconds to produce.

consistently lower than the percentage of text reduced. Whereas the average text reduction is 17%, the average loss of idea units is half this percentage: 8.5%. In other words, on half of the occasions on which the source text is reduced, no important information (or idea units) is lost. Respeakers seem to have successfully complied with the above-mentioned ITC guidelines, relaying a more than "reasonable percentage" of the words spoken (83%) and a better than "good percentage" (91.5%) of the spoken message with a very low error rate (1.4% on average). Indeed, this illustrates the particular ability acquired by respeakers to identify and omit words without which the content of a script may still be conveyed.

Given that in most cases verbatim respeaking is not an option, students must be quick to develop good editing skills that allow them to reduce the original message without losing key information. A qualitative analysis of the respoken subtitles studied here shows that the main types of words omitted by respeakers are:

- Discourse markers: *so, well, I mean, you know*;
- Connectors: *and, but* and *though*. This means that respoken sentences are notably shorter than source text sentences, given that the absence of these conjunctions often entails the beginning of a new sentence.
- Intensifiers: *really, much more, well*.
- Repetitions and "unimportant" asides such as *you were saying* or *worth bearing in mind*.

Finally, a number of additions to the source text have also been identified. In all cases, these were contractions (*they'll, wasn't, it's*) that were expanded (*they will, was not, it is*), probably to ensure good recognition on the part of the software, which is less likely to produce an error with two words than with one.

7.4.6. Training respeaking speed

Once the respeaking students have learnt about the different views on verbatim and edited subtitles, the usual speech rates they have to deal with, the speed at which viewers can read and what can be and is usually done in professional respeaking, it is time to find out their own optimum respeaking speed.

This could also be included in the stage where respeakers are learning how to dictate to the SR software and thus before they actually start respeaking. First of all, students may be given transcripts of programmes that they have to dictate to the SR software. Their aim would be to achieve a given accuracy rate, which could be 95% to start with and 97% as the training goes on. First of all, they would be asked to dictate it more or less slowly, enunciating clearly, with no rush, making sure that they achieve the agreed accuracy rate. If they time their dictation, they will be able to determine their respeaking rate, which will presumably be low. Then, they will be asked to dictate the same text again several times at faster rates but always aiming at 95% to 97% accuracy. By the end of the exercise, and provided that they time their dictations, they should be able to know what their optimum respeaking rate is. They should also have learnt what their limit is, that is, the fastest respeaking speed over which accuracy starts dropping and where editing is required. Needless to say, these speeds will be different for different respeakers.

The second part of the training on respeaking speed involves editing and is included in the respeaking stage. In this case, students may be given programmes over their optimum respeaking rate, which will force them to reformulate and usually summarize the original speech. Then they are asked to find out their respeaking rate and especially to compare text reduction versus loss of information.

In sum, what respeakers are expected to find in this part of their training is the optimum speed at which they can dictate their respeaking units with accuracy, the maximum speed over which editing is required and finally the skills to edit the original text without losing much information.

7.5. Exercises

7.5.1. Split attention

For your first respeaking practice, it may be advisable to use speeches, particularly if they are delivered clearly and at a steady pace. Here are some recommendations:

Fictional speeches:
- *Quiz Show*: Charles Van Doren testifying before the House Committee on Interstate and Foreign Commerce, delivered at 80 wpm.
- *To Kill a Mockingbird*: Atticus Finch's closing argument in Tom Robinson's trial, delivered at 90 wpm.
- *Adam's Rib*: Amanda Bonner's closing arguments in defence of Doris Attinger, delivered at 130 wpm.
- *The Great Dictator*: Adenoid Hynkel's closing address, delivered at 170 wpm.

Real speeches:
- Martin Luther King's speech "I Have a Dream", delivered at 100 wpm.
- Barack Obama's Election Victory Speech, delivered at 140 wpm.

You can find videos of these speeches in many general websites, such as Youtube (www.youtube.com) and Yahoo! Video (http://video.yahoo.com), or more specialized ones like the online speech bank American Rhetoric (www.americanrhetoric.com). Transcripts of all the above speeches are included in DVD > Chapter 7 > Exercises > 7.5.1.

In order to develop the split-attention skills gradually, it's important to start shadowing without using the SR software. Starting from the slowest speech to those that are delivered faster, you can
- shadow the speeches mentally or at low volume with no punctuation marks;
- shadow the speeches mentally with punctuation marks;
- shadow the speeches out loud without punctuation marks;
- shadow the speeches out loud with punctuation marks.

Once you have achieved a good performance, you can practise respeaking into the SR programme. Start again from the easiest speech to the most difficult one, introducing punctuation marks from the beginning. Once you are comfortable listening + (re)speaking + listening, it is time to develop the next skill: watching. For this, respeak any of the above speeches and note down, as soon as you have finished and without looking at the screen, the errors that have been displayed and your general impression on the performance of the software. This will force you to read the subtitles as you respeak.

Finally, to develop the final skill (typing/correcting), choose any of the above speeches and introduce corrections as you respeak. Once you have finished, compare your editing rate (how much you have summarized/rephrased the original text) throughout the speech to your editing rate after corrections were introduced. Also, assess how much information has been lost in this editing process.

7.5.2. Punctuation

Read the script "BBC World News - Karin Giannone - Script" (DVD > Chapter 7 > Exercises > 7.5.2) and punctuate it. Introduce, beside every comma, a number indicating which one of the eight rules described in section 7.2.3 you are applying. Use number nine for those cases that are not included in these rules.

Do the same exercise with "Obama's Election Victory Speech 2", in the same location. Respeak this part of Obama's speech and compare the punctuation of your respoken subtitles to the punctuation you chose for the transcript on paper. How do they differ?

7.5.3. Rhythm

Break "Obama's Election Victory Speech 2" (DVD > Chapter 7 > Exercises > 7.5.2) into respeaking units and sentences applying the salami technique.

Here are two examples, the first one with shorter respeaking units than the second:

EXAMPLE A
[Sentence 1]
There will be setbacks and false starts. [respeaking unit 1]
[Sentence 2]
There are many who won't agree [respeaking unit 2]

with every decision or policy [respeaking unit 3]
I make as president. [respeaking unit 4]
[Sentence 3]
And we know the government [respeaking unit 5]
can't solve every problem.[respeaking unit 6]

EXAMPLE B
[Sentence 1]
There will be setbacks and false starts. [respeaking unit 1]
[Sentence 2]
There are many who won't agree [respeaking unit 2]
with every decision or policy I make as president. [respeaking unit 3]
[Sentence 3]
And we know the government can't solve every problem [respeaking unit 4]

What's the average length of your respeaking units? What's the average length of your respoken sentences? Compare the average length of your respoken sentences to the average length of the sentences in the transcript?

Do the same exercise with "Newsnight 2" and "BBC News 1982", whose videos and transcripts you can find in DVD > Chapter 7 > Exercises > 7.5.3.

7.5.4. *Speed*

In order to work on respeaking speed, it may be useful to start off practising fast dictation and then move on to actual respeaking. For this, you can use the transcripts "BBC News 24 - Wrong Guy - Transcript" and "Film 2008- Jonathan Ross - Transcript" (DVD > Chapter 7 > Exercises > Exercise 7.5.4).

First of all, read the transcripts slowly to your SR programme trying to achieve the highest possible accuracy. Calculate your dictation rate and your accuracy rate, which should be over 95%. Then, read the transcripts faster and calculate your dictation rate again. Try to determine what your fastest speed is while maintaining an accuracy rate over 95% and, most importantly, the speed at which you feel more comfortable.

Finally, try respeaking the videos "BBC News 24 - Wrong Guy" and "Film 2008- Jonathan Ross" (DVD > Chapter 7 > Exercises > 7.5.4), bearing in mind that they feature very high speech rates and are thus very challenging.

Alternatively, you can do this exercise with any of the other videos included in this unit.

8. Respeaking Skills Applied during the Process II
Respeaking Different Genres

8.0. Introduction

When the basic respeaking skills have been acquired or even as they are being acquired, students may want to turn their attention to the various genres at play in live subtitling on TV. Indeed, different genres require different approaches and present different degrees of difficulty. Although as legislation becomes stricter, more and more programmes are being respoken, TV live subtitling has traditionally focused on four macro-genres: sports, news programmes, interviews/debates/chat shows and special events such as concerts, speeches, funerals, weddings, etc. Let's have a look now at the specific features of each genre and the impact they have on the respeakers' daily task.

8.1. Sports

As far back, at least in terms of live media accessibility, as April 2001, the BBC chose the World Snooker Championships to test respeaking for the first time. Only several months later, Wimbledon became the second live event to be subtitled by respeaking in the UK. Gradually, respeakers started subtitling more and more live output, including coverage of BBC Parliament, regional news and finally national news on BBC News 24 (Marsh 2006). The choice of sports as the genre to first test respeaking with may be explained by the fact that its content is less important than that of the news, considering that errors were bound to crop up, but also by the general belief that sports are the easiest genre to respeak.

This belief is founded on several factors, such as the speech rate of the speakers. Unlike news presenters, who often achieve an average of 180 wpm, sports commentators usually speak at around 150 to 160 wpm, judging by the programmes analyzed in Chapter 7 and by the file size of several 15-minute sections of sports programmes facilitated by RBM. Needless to say, this is far from being an exact science. Sports such as snooker may have less density than a football match and even the latter may feature a much lower speech rate during match play than during a fast-and-furious multi-speaker halftime, which may be just as challenging to respeak as a chat show. Overall, though, sports programmes do seem to feature fewer wpm. There are often sudden bursts of dialogue that may be considerably fast, but also longer periods of silence, where the visual elements take precedence over the rest. This is perhaps the most characterizing feature of respeaking in sports and what makes it less difficult than respeaking other genres. In sporting output, the viewer is often more interested in the action on the screen than in the information contained in the soundtrack. Respeakers at RBM, for example, are expected to subtitle only the elements of the soundtrack that are not visible on the screen, and avoid blocking the action with subtitles. Because of the slight delay in the subtitles appearing on the screen, respeakers try to avoid subtitling commentators' descriptions of the actions, instead trying to focus on their analyses and on any background information about the competitors that is not visible on the screen.

Figure 8.1 from the 200m Women Series in the 2009 Olympics illustrates this point:

Figure 8.1: Sports I

In 1:40:57, the commentator says "the start list for the second heat".
Then, he proceeds to introduce the athletes, mentioning their nationalities,
the lanes they will be running on, etc.

Figure 8.2: Sports II

As shown here, it takes him 15 seconds (we're now at 1:41:11), during which the respeaker remains silent.

Likewise, in a football match there would be no need to respeak passes from one player to another, as this can already be seen by the viewers. True enough, this type of information is being conveyed by commentators to viewers who can already see it. Yet, given the usual delay in respoken subtitles, respeaking this sort of passes will mean that subtitles will provide information that is no longer relevant to what is going on in the game at a given time. What need to be respoken instead are other comments or remarks that add opinion to what is being seen ("they have never managed to win in this stadium", "they are playing beautifully", "he was sent off last week", etc.). You can even choose to respeak actions that are taking place on the pitch, such as certain passes ("that's a great cross over to Iniesta"), as long as they are not just brief mentions to the player who is giving or receiving the ball ("Iniesta", "Iniesta to Xavi", "Xavi to Messi", etc.).

In view of this, candidates applying for jobs as respeakers are often asked to start respeaking sports programmes before moving on to more difficult genres such as news or chat shows, and professional respeakers usually work up to 40 minutes in this type of programmes, as compared to 15 to 30 minutes in news.

There is, however, a number of challenging aspects respeaking students must take into account when tackling sports. As well as the sudden bursts of quick dialogue mentioned above, sports programmes often feature more than one commentator. Respeakers are expected to identify this second speaker (with a tag, a colour or a dash) and to look out for moments of overlapping dialogue, where a great deal of editing will be required. Also, helpful as it is to be able to omit comments from the commentators in say a football match, deciding what to include in the subtitles and what to leave out may be a difficult balance to strike. It may be a good idea to focus on these three issues, as well as on the research needed for every programme, when training respeakers for sports programmes.

8.2. News

The European Broadcasting Union (2005:25) defines news and information programmes as those that are

> intended primarily to inform about current facts, situations, events, theories or forecasts, or to provide explanatory background information and advice. Information programme content has to be non-durable, that is to say that one could not imagine that the same programme would be transmitted e.g. one year later without losing most of its relevance.

When tackling news programmes, respeakers must be ready to face a variety of situations. Respeaking the main news presenters when they are on screen is different from respeaking them when they are reading the headlines, in the same way that a news item presented by a correspondent demands a different approach to a weather forecast.

Given the importance of this genre, respeaking students are expected to be familiar with the different sections in a news programme and the challenges they pose in terms of respeaking.

In his article "A Strategic Analysis of Respeaking on the BBC" (2009), Carlo Eugeni examines how respeakers from RBM tackle the BBC news in the UK. Eugeni provides a thorough analysis of the different parts the news are made up of and the strategies employed by respeakers to deal with them. His study constitutes the core of this section.

Eugeni's study is based on the *BBC News programme* (BBC News 24 channel), mainly composed of pre-prepared news reports and live reports. As many other news programmes, it tends to conform, unless breaking news alters the original order, to a traditional structure made up of six moves subdivided into different steps:

- jingle, digital clock and opening images
- headlines
- news reports
- weather forecasts
- news summary
- jingle, digital clock and closing images

8.2.1. Headlines

After the jingle, the digital clock and the opening images, the newsreader notes the time, utters a standard greeting and proceeds to read the main headlines of the day. If there are two newsreaders, they can either alternate in reading the headlines or leave the headlines for one and the first news item for the other.

Typically, headlines are spoken at high speech rates of around 180 wpm over images that act only as a support. In other words, viewers need to be able to access what is being said to find out about the news item. Headlines feature a low grammatical intricacy, as they have been written and structured in advance, and a high rate of lexical density, as the contents are highly condensed to make the most of the limited time available. Sentences succeed one another without any link, usually follow the basic Subject-Verb-Object syntactic structure and are often made up of a main clause and two subordinate clauses.

Needless to say, headlines are very challenging for respeakers. While the high speech rate of the newsreaders requires editing, the high lexical density of the headlines, where no superfluous information is included, makes it difficult to omit any part of the content. Rephrasing is not easy either, given that respeakers may not be very familiar with news items that are being presented for the first time in the programme. Finally, headlines present one more added difficulty for respeakers, namely the fact that the images supporting them are often brief and fast. Given the standard 3- to 5-second delay, respoken subtitles are usually displayed along with the wrong images.

A case in point are figures 8.3, 8.4 and 8.5, which show a BBC news programme dealing with (1) the US primaries in New Hampshire, (2) starvation in

Kenya and (3) social policies in New York. Displayed with the usual delay, the subtitles were shown with images which…

…were not showing New Hampshire…

Figure 8.3: News I

…did not correspond to Kenya…

Figure 8.4: News II

…showed New York, but not Nairobi…

Figure 8.5: News III

Considering how difficult it is to edit headlines, there's not much respeakers can do about this delay with regard to the images. However, despite all these difficulties, headlines do have a positive feature – they're over soon. After the last one, an utterance explaining that full details will follow introduces the next part of the programme, and we're on to the news reports.

8.2.2. News reports

This section takes up the bulk of the news programme. First of all, the news presenter gives the floor to the live reporter by posing a series of questions, making an introduction with a formulaic expression ("there at the scene is our correspondent Scott Jarvie") or simply by clearly finishing his or her turn. Then, the reporter usually sums up what has happened and sometimes the newsreader intervenes to pose some questions. This section finishes with a formulaic expression by the reporter (e.g. "Carolyn Schmieder, BBC News, Chorley") and an expression of thanks by the newsreader, who turns their head to engage directly with the camera again.

The news report given by the correspondent may be live or pre-recorded. When it is live, it often deals with breaking news that has not been presented yet. It has not been prepared in advance as much as the headlines, and so features higher grammatical intricacy (with more features of orality), lower lexical density (the content being less condensed), a slower speech rate and often poor quality of transmission. The challenge is here to understand the source text and turn its oral nature into written subtitles. Often, live reports also contain on-the-spot interviews, press conferences and other live events which have not been edited beforehand. Different speakers may intervene, which results in a succession of question and answers (sometimes short and quick) with a variety of speech rates, sound conditions, lexical and grammatical features, etc. Bearing in mind that, having no script in advance, respeakers are relying exclusively on their research prior to the programme, it is only logical that the error rate should be higher in live reports than in any other section of the news.

Pre-recorded reports present a more manageable situation for the respeaker. They have a more structured content, fewer oral features and slower speech rates. Also, they often resort to visual information that can be omitted by the respeaker, such as the name of the journalist, the location where the story is taking place, etc.

In Figure 8.6, from a Newsnight journalist reporting on the primaries in the United States, the correspondent spends 17 seconds describing the vote percentages displayed on the screen. The respeaker only mentions the results obtained by the winner, but could have just as easily omitted them, as it is redundant information:

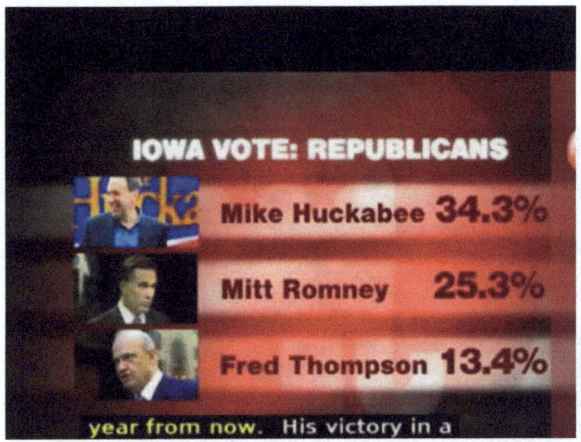

Figure 8.6: News IV

8.2.3. Weather forecasts

Following a formulaic expression by the news presenter (e.g. "Now, let's have the weather forecast with Álvaro Bruzon"), the camera focuses on the weather reporter, who thanks the newsreader and moves into the forecasts.

Here more than ever, the main challenge for respeakers is the speech rate. Put bluntly, weather reporters are a nightmare to respeak. On the BBC, they often speak as fast as 220 wpm and 230 wpm, which requires heavy editing on the part of respeakers. Given that the forecast has been prepared in advance, the information is very condensed (high lexical density) and it is difficult to omit or summarize information without losing important content.

Fortunately, weather forecasts also feature different kinds of images (graphics, maps, etc.) which can provide respeakers with much-needed breathers to pause and get their breath back:

Figure 8.7: Weather I

The flipside in this case is that, sometimes, weather reporters point to particular parts of the map without naming them. They only explain, for instance, that there is going to be rain in "that area":

Figure 8.8: Weather II

Taking into account that the subtitles will be displayed on the screen three to six seconds after the utterance, the chances are that the subtitle will be referring to an area that is different from the one that is being pointed to by the presenter. In other words, as well as trying to maintain as much essential information as possible while editing some 60 wpm, respeakers may have to include additional information: the names of the areas in the map that the presenter is pointing to.

8.2.4. News summary

Once the weather report is over, the presenter introduces the news summary ("a news summary first") to put an end to the programme. Very similar to the headlines, the news summary is written to be read, with short sentences, high lexical density, low grammatical intricacy and no visual support. Unlike headlines, though, the information is already known to the respeakers, which makes this section easier to deal with. After the last summary, a reminder that further information can be accessed via the BBC online service gives way to the jingle and signals the end of the working day for both journalists and respeakers.

8.3. Interviews, debates and chat shows

Again, this may be a difficult genre to respeak, not least because of the presence of several speakers who often overlap and improvise interventions with grammatical, syntactic and pronunciation errors. When dealing with this sort of programmes, respeakers must pay attention to two important SDH features: speaker identification and extralinguistic information.

There are four main methods to identify speakers in SDH: dashes, colours, tags and subtitle displacement. These conventions vary across countries and even across formats (DVD and TV, for example). In respeaking, identifying speakers is just as important. While, at least for Spanish speakers, there's no doubt as to who is speaking in Figure 8.9...

Figure 8.9: Debates I

...this one is far more difficult...

Figure 8.10: Debates II

Unlike in SDH, however, displacement is hardly an option in respeaking, since respeakers don't have time to allocate different positions to different speakers who may even be moving around the shot. Colours and tags (and perhaps dashes) are thus the most feasible methods.

Colours can be introduced, as in the case of RBM UK, with a small keypad featuring white, yellow, cyan and green keys. See Figure 8.11.

As for tags, they are usually not typed in respeaking, but dictated with macros. This can be seen in the video "Respeaking – South Africa" (DVD > Chapter 8 > Exercises > 8.4.1), featuring an example of a student from South Africa respeaking a video clip from the film *The Shawshank Redemption* and using the tags "MacAndy" and "MacRed" to identify the two speakers in the clip.

Finally, contextual information is also different in respeaking, where it is

Figure 8.11: Keypad

difficult to add as much extra-linguistic information as in SDH. The few tags used in respeaking provide information about laughter, cheering, booing, etc. In figures 8.12 and 8.13, the respeaker attempts to subtitle the reaction of the crowd to Barack Obama's speech, but the SR software fails to work properly:

Figures 8.12 and 8.13: Correcting errors

As in the case of tags for speaker ID, respeakers are expected to come up with a list of useful tags for extralinguistic information and prepare macros for them so that they are readily available for the different programmes.

8.4. Exercises

8.4.1. Sports

As explained in this chapter, it may be useful to start practising respeaking with sports programmes. At this initial stage, it's often better to watch the videos first and then respeak them. Once the basic respeaking skills have been acquired and you feel more confident with the technique, there should be no need to do this, as long as you have an idea of what the clips are about.

In websites like www.youtube.com, you can find sport clips that are suitable for this initial practice. For football clips, for example, type in keywords such as "goal/s", "highlights", "season review/s" plus the name of football teams or national leagues.

Another option is to type in "penalty shoot-out", which usually yields a large number of clips with football matches decided on penalties. An example would be "penalty shoot-out Manchester United Chelsea 2008", to find the clip of the last few minutes of the 2008 Champions League Final. Before attempting to respeak this clip, make sure you introduce a list in Dragon (or any other speech recognizer you may be using) with the names of the players in both the Manchester United and Chelsea squads in 2008. Think of other keywords that are likely to be mentioned in the clip (other tournaments, teams, stadiums, etc.). Respeak the clip and then note down all the keywords that have been mentioned by the commentators and you had not included in the list. Try respeaking the clip again with all the keywords introduced and trained in Dragon. You'll see that, as explained in this chapter, the speech rates in this type of clips are not very high. There are sudden bursts of dialogue but also moments where nothing is said or when what is said doesn't need to be respoken, as it is already being seen. After some attempts, once you're familiarized with the comments, you should be aiming at achieving a 95% accuracy rate, that is, not more than a 5% error rate.

You can find the videos for the following exercises in DVD > Chapter 8 > Exercises > 8.4.1.

First of all, watch "Match of the Day 1", broadcast on the BBC on 30 August 2009. Prepare a list with all the keywords that are mentioned by the commentator, train them in the software and then respeak the clip. What was your accuracy rate? How much of the original soundtrack did you have to edit in order to keep up with the commentator? For the first 30 seconds, the commentator describes the situation of the Premier League table, which is being seen on screen. Does this help at all when it comes to editing the subtitles? The following section of the clip, called "2 Good 2 Bad", contains fast-paced comments on different images. Did you manage to respeak for instance the remarks made in 0:36-0:44 without too much delay?

Respeak the next two videos ("Match of the Day 2" and "Wimbledon") without watching them first. For "Match of the Day 2" (BBC, 22 November 2008), prepare a list of the players in the Arsenal and Manchester City squads in 2008. What accuracy rate did you obtain? Between 0:42 and 0:48, the commentator mentions the name of a player which may be problematic in terms of recognition. You may have to create a macro to solve this problem.

The third video is "Wimbledon". Broadcast on the BBC on 6 July 2008, it is a quick analysis of Roger Federer's serve included in the 2008 Wimbledon final between the Swiss player and Rafael Nadal. There are no keywords here other than the names of the players but the speech rate is fast (over 190 wpm), as there are virtually no pauses. Try to take advantage of the information on screen in order to edit the original speech without losing too much information.

Very often, sports programmes feature debates and discussions involving fast turn-taking and overlapping dialogue. This is the case of "Match of the Day 3", a quick and challenging clip that will serve as a transition to the interviews. Whether or not you choose to watch the clip before respeaking it, you will have to create tags and macros (see section 6.4.5.4) for the speakers: Gary Lineker, Alan Hansen and Mark Lawrenson (although you may not have time to use this one). You can also create macros for non-verbal information, in this case "laughter".

8.4.2. News

You can find the videos and documents you need for this section in DVD > Chapter 8 > Exercises > 8.4.2.

8.4.2.1. Headlines

Watch the first news video, "BBC News - Intro and Headlines", broadcast on the BBC on 21 April 2008. Here you'll find an example of how the main headlines, in this case only three, are read by the news presenters Simon McCoy and Carrie Gracie. The video is introduced by Bill Turnbull and Sian Williams, presenters of *BBC Breakfast*. Prepare tags and macros for all the presenters as well the names of the programmes mentioned in the clip.

Did you manage to respeak the headlines without much delay? Were you able to edit without losing important information, considering that headlines are already very concise messages?

8.4.2.2. News

As far as news reports are concerned, once again in websites such as www.youtube.com you can find a large number of clips to respeak by typing keywords such as "news", "news report/s", "news item/s" plus the name of a programme or a channel.

Watch the video "BBC World News – Martine Croxall". Take a note of the key words that may have to be introduced in the vocabulary of the speech recognizer and respeak the clip.

Respeak (without watching it first) the video "BBC World News - Karin Giannone", whose script you punctuated in exercise 7.5.2. In order to do this, introduce in your speech recognizer the document "Karin Giannone – BBC

World News – Wordlist". In the case of Dragon, this is explained in section 6.4.5.2. Some of the words included in this list, such as Laura Trevelyan, Justin Webb, Sri Lankan government or Judith Morris may already be part of the vocabulary, but it's always a good idea to include them (and train them) so as to make sure that they are recognized properly. In the case of "Jamahiriya", it may be useful to add the whole name as mentioned in the news report (Libyan Arab Jamahiriya), which will increase the likelihood of correct recognition.

In the next video, "BBC News - Kasia Madera", the presenter has to deal with some breaking news for which no script has been prepared. Respeak the clip without watching it first. Just as the presenter copes with the live situation despite having no script, try to produce live subtitles without preparing any keywords.

Did you find any names that were not included in the vocabulary? If so, how did you solve this problem?

In order to respeak the last video in this section, "BBC News – Chris Lowe", you only have the following information available:

- Title of the news item: "Chris Lowe retires".
- Date of emission: 4 January 2009.
- Programme: BBC News.
- Presenters: Chris Lowe, Annita McVeigh and Matt Taylor (weather).

Do your own research on the basis of this information and then respeak the clip without watching it first.

Were the key words you found mentioned in the clip? Now that you've respoken the clip, would you have gone about your research in any other way? Were there any out-of-vocabulary terms that you hadn't prepared? How did you deal with them?

8.4.2.3. Weather

The weather is one of the most challenging genres for a respeaker, mainly due to the high speech rate of the presenters and the specialized vocabulary used. With speech rates of up to 230 wpm, the respeaker must usually try to edit the original script, which has already been trimmed to the essential information. The second challenge, the need to deal with specialized vocabulary, can be dealt with by preparing word lists with recurrent weather terms. A useful source to find these terms are written weather reviews, often available online. You can find some examples of this in the documents "Weather Reviews 1" and "Weather Reviews 2". Read these documents and build a data base of weather terminology to include as a word list in the SR software. Make sure that your data base/wordlist includes all the weather phenomena as well as the names of cities, towns and areas that are usually mentioned in the weather forecasts in your country. You'll see that many of these terms will already be included in the vocabulary. Even so, it is a good idea to include them in recurrent phrases so that the software is more familiarized with them. For instance, "snow" and "ice" will most likely be part of the vocabulary of the speech recognizer. Yet, if the phrase "snow and ice" is found to be recurrent in the weather reviews, you may want to include it as such in the word list, which will help the software to recognize it properly and avoid the temptation of producing homophones or near homophones such as "snow and nice" or "snow nice". Alternatively, if you find scripts or weather reviews that are very similar to the clips you want to respeak, you may want to include them as documents (see section 6.4.5.3) instead of as word lists.

Now that you have fine-tuned the speech recognizer to work with weather programmes, respeak the videos "Weather 1", "Weather 2" and "Weather 3". After every video, check your accuracy rate, your editing rate and the amount of information lost in editing. Also, update your word list with any new term that may have come up in the clip before you move on to the next one.

8.4.2.4. News Summary
Respeak the videos "BBC News – Summary 1" and "BBC News Summary 2".

Did you come across any out-of-vocabulary terms? How did you deal with them? What was the average delay of your subtitles with regard to the original speech? Did you manage to edit your subtitles while maintaining the key information?

8.4.3. Interviews and debates

Interviews and debates can be found on the web by typing in the relevant keywords (interview/s, debate/s, discussion/s) plus the name of programmes or presenters, such as Parkinson, Jonathan Ross or Newsnight in the case of the UK.

The four videos and the documents needed for this section can be found in DVD > Chapter 8 > Exercises > 8.4.3. Unlike in previous exercises, the videos are to be respoken without watching them first.

First of all, respeak the video "Interview with Kara Tointon", for which you have been given

(a) the following paragraph:

> EastEnder's Kara Tointon and boyfriend Joe Swash get ready for panto this Christmas. The actress talks to BBC News presenter Tasmin Lucia Khan on E24.
>
> (b) the information included in the document "Interview with Kara Tointon – Research".
>
> For the next video, "Interview with Nicola Roberts", you only have the following information:
>
> BBC news presenter Huw Edwards interviews Girls Aloud singer Nicola Roberts about fake tan on BBC News 24 (17 November 2008).
>
> Do your own research and respeak the clip.
>
> Now respeak the third video, "Interview about Regional Accents". This clip is more challenging than the previous ones, as there are more than two speakers, high speech rates and overlapping dialogue. Fortunately, though, all the keywords are included in the following explanatory paragraph:
>
> > BBC News interview with Helen Sewell, voice coach and managing director of *Simply Speaking*, and Jo Cameron, former contestant in The Apprentice.
>
> Finally, the fourth video, "Interview with Michael Howard", includes part of a famous interview conducted by the British presenter Jeremy Paxman in Newsnight on 13 May 1997. In this clip, Paxman presses his interviewee, ex Home Secretary Michael Howard, about his role in the possible dismissal of the governor of Parkhurst Prison. Paxman famously asked the same question 14 times, only to obtain evasive answers from Michael Howard. From the point of view of respeaking, the challenge lies not only in the use of out-of-vocabulary words throughout the clip but also in the way questions and answers overlap, which constitutes the highlight of the interview.

9. Respeaking Skills Applied during the Process III
Respeaking in Other Settings

9.0. Introduction

Having become consolidated as a successful technique for the provision of live subtitles on TV, respeaking is now being used in different settings such as museums, galleries, theatres, conferences, classrooms and even churches. This chapter describes some of the present applications of respeaking and points to other potential uses of this technique in these and other settings.

9.1. Respeaking in museums and other arts venues

In many big cities such as Barcelona or London, deaf and hard of hearing people can have access to theatre plays or operas by means of subtitles. Sometimes they are closed captions, that is, visible only for those who wish to make use of them and thus available on small screens behind the seats or on hand-held devices. This is the approach adopted by the British company Show Translations, whose hand-held device Airscript provides theatre captions in English as well as in 7 other languages. In contrast, open captions, as provided by Stagetext in the UK and Mark Hall Associates in the US, are visible for everyone in the audience. They are displayed on a screen that may be positioned on one side of the stage, at the bottom or even on top, which is usually known as surtitling and is very common in opera. Videos of theatre captions are included in DVD > Chapter 9 > Discussion points and exercises > 9.5.1.

What all these subtitles have in common is that they are produced semi-live. Subtitlers receive the script of the play or the opera and prepare the subtitles before the show. When the play or the opera starts, the subtitlers listen to the audio and launch the subtitles in synch. What happens, though, when deaf and hard of hearing people wish to access live events such as talks, tours or Q&A sessions, where no script is available beforehand?

So far, the access facilities thanano live events in museums, theatres and arts venues in big cities such as London are limited. They often consist of the provision of British Sign Language (BSL) interpreters, which is only useful for the signing deaf, that is, a small proportion of deaf and hard of hearing people. In view of this, Stagetext is collaborating with Roehampton University to assess whether respeaking is a viable method to provide subtitles for live events in these settings. Some of the areas identified as needing accessibility are Q&A sessions in theatres and illustrated talks in museums and galleries.

Between February and June 2009, a series of lunchtime talks were made accessible through respeaking to ten participants with different hearing abilities at the National Gallery in London. The aim of the trials was to find out the viewers' opinion and comprehension of respoken subtitles provided for talks with different speech rates (fast, steady and slow), material for the respeaker (no script or script in advance) and delay (usual delay vs. no delay at all).[1]

For those trials where subtitles were displayed with the usual delay, participants were sitting in the lecture theatre with a laptop while I was respeaking in a separate booth. Thanks to a shared desktop application, the words recognised by the SR software were displayed on the participants' laptops with a 3- to 5-second delay so that they could read them while watching the speaker:

Figures 9.1 and 9.2: Talk at the National Gallery

Figures 9.3 and 9.4: Respeaking at the National Gallery

In order to run trials with no delay in the subtitles, participants were taken to a separate room where they watched the talk on a TV screen. The video signal was delayed so that the subtitles could be displayed in synch with the audio. After every trial, participants were asked about their opinion of the subtitles (how easy it was to read them, to hear or lipread the speaker and to understand the talk) and their comprehension of the content (images, text and overall meaning):

---

[1] Thanks are due to Peter Pullan (Stagetext), who organized the trials and analyzed the results.

	Speech rate	Material for the re-speaker	Delay of the subtitles	Result
Trial 1	Fast	No script	Usual	Difficult to follow, poor comprehension
Trial 2	Fast	Full script	Usual	Easier to follow, better comprehension but still not good
Trial 3	Fast	No script	None	Difficult to determine what delay in the video signal must be set so that subtitles are in synch; OK to follow; comprehension OK
Trial 4	Fast	Full script	None	Difficult to determine what delay in the video signal must be set so that subtitles are in synch; OK to follow; comprehension OK
Trial 5	Steady	No script	Usual	Easy to follow; excellent comprehension
Trial 6	Steady	No script	None	Very easy to follow, excellent comprehension
Trial 7	Slow	No script	None	Very easy to follow, excellent comprehension

Table 9.1: Results of the respeaking trial at the National Gallery

As was expected, comprehension was better whenever there was no delay in the subtitles. Yet, this proved controversial, as half of the participants were not happy having to watch the talk on a TV screen in a separate room instead of live at the lecture theatre. Other than this, the defining factor seems to be the speech rate of the original speaker. With a fast speech rate of over 180 wpm for a 70-minute talk, only subtitles with no delay proved successful. In contrast, when the speech rate was steady or slow, whether or not there was delay in the subtitles, results were good and in some cases excellent. Finally, trials where the script was available beforehand scored generally higher than those where no material was provided. Yet, this didn't prove to be as important as speech rate, as proved by trial 5, where a steady speaker was successfully respoken without script.

Having analyzed these results (including an overall accuracy rate of 97.8%), the general conclusion drawn by the participants and the partners in the project was that, as long as speakers may be approached to deliver their talks at a normal pace and to provide a list of keywords, respeaking can be applied for the provision of accessibility in this type of talks in museums and arts venues.

However, this conclusion led to yet another challenge, namely how to provide accessibility for guided group tours that are not static, but rather take place across different rooms. The solution tested so far is the use of a PDA or hand-held device along with the respeaking technique. The respeaker will thus be sitting in a room respeaking the explanation of the guide, which will be displayed in real-time on the participants' PDAs as they follow the tour:

Figure 9.5: PDA for respeaking

Needless to say, one of the biggest challenges for respeakers here is that, unless cameras are set up in every room, they will not be able to see the speaker.

Another option that is being tested is *self-subtitling*. In this case, there would be no respeakers involved. The guides would wear a microphone and their words would be displayed with minimum delay on the participants' PDAs. Ideally, guides would be using a speaker-independent programme with no need for training or even punctuation marks. Given that the state of the art is not quite there yet, the plan is to use Dragon, for which two provisions need to be made. Firstly, guides must be trained in the use of SR software. Even though they are not going to be respeaking, they will need to train the software, fine-tune its tools and achieve a great deal of accuracy in dictation. In other words, they will have to follow the first part of the respeaking training to become good "dictators". The second provision is related to the use of punctuation, which cannot obviously be dictated by the guides. Given that automatic punctuation is not ready to be used yet, the two obvious solutions would be to add a space every time the guides make a pause (just like Viascribe) or to give the guides a small device (a remote control, for example) to introduce new lines manually whenever they pause.

Finally, the very last challenge emerging in this context is that of self-tours; in other words, how to provide accessibility to individual visitors who are not part of an organized tour. In this case, there seems to be no need for live subtitling, but the use of a PDA comes in handy. The pilot project devised by Stagetext, Roehampton University and the National Gallery consists of producing videoguides with subtitles. First of all, the National Gallery records videos of experts describing a series of well-known paintings in the gallery. Once the videos have been edited by Stagetext, they are subtitled for the deaf and hard of hearing by Roehampton University students. Visitors wishing to have access to these videos can ask for a videoguide at the reception of the gallery and point the device to any given painting. 2D recognition technology will identify the artwork the user is observing and return the appropriate explanatory talk with subtitles:

Figure 9.6: Videoguide

The idea in this case is to provide not only English SDH subtitles but also subtitles in many other languages, which will make museums accessible not only to the deaf and hard of hearing but also to foreign visitors.

9.2. Respeaking in the classroom

Another interesting setting for the use of respeaking is the classroom. In the US, Mark Hall Associates have been providing this service since 2003. So far, two methods have been tested. The first one is in-class respeaking. The respeaker sits alongside the student and uses a mask microphone so that only the teacher's words are heard. The student reads the captions as displayed on a laptop (closed captions) or as projected on a screen visible for the rest of the students (open captions). The second method is remote respeaking. In this case, respeakers usually work from home. They receive the audio from the classroom, where the teacher is using a wireless microphone, and send the respoken subtitles via the Internet to the student's laptop. As explained in the "Caption Mic" videos included in DVD > Chapter 9 > Discussion points and exercises > 9.5.2, this is done using remote meeting and desktop sharing software such as Elluminate, Go to Meeting or DimDim.

A similar approach has recently been adopted by the Australian company Access Innovation Media (Ai-Media), which was established in 2003 and started providing captions to subscription TV in 2004. In 2010, Ai-Media introduced live captioning through respeaking (or speech captioning, as they also call it) into mainstream classrooms using Dragon NaturallySpeaking. Videos and documents about the service provided by Ai-Media can be found in DVD > Chapter 9 > Discussion points and exercises > 9.5.2.

In Europe, classroom respeaking is still undergoing initial tests. A case in point is that of the research group TransMedia Catalonia, which is currently testing respeaking at the Universitat Autònoma de Barcelona for the benefit of both deaf and hard of hearing students and Erasmus students.

Also noteworthy in this regard is the initiative launched by the School of Languages at North-West University (Vaal Triangle, South Africa). Although there are 11 official languages in the country (English, Afrikaans and nine African languages, namely IsiNdebele, IsiXhosa, IsiZulu, Sepedi, Sesotho, Setswana, SiSwati, Tshivenda and Xitsonga), most universities teach in English and Afrikaans. Speakers of African languages, who may have English as a third or fourth language, are thus at a disadvantage with respect to English and Afrikaans speakers, who are taught in their first and second languages. With a view to integrating African students and facilitating their attendance to the classroom, researchers from the School of Languages at North-West University are using respeaking as an integration tool to provide live subtitles (in English) for different lectures. The respeakers are sitting at the back of the room so that the students cannot hear their voices. Their words are displayed on a screen on one side of the classroom, where students can read, in real time, what the lecturer is saying or has said, as several lines of text are displayed. Given the impossibility of respeaking into any of the above-mentioned African languages, this method provides students with a double input (audio and visual) in English to follow the lecture. Once it is over, DVDs are made available with the video of the lecture and the respoken words edited as synchronized subtitles for the benefit of any student who wishes to have an audiovisual record of the class.

9.3. Respeaking in conferences and churches

Conferences are an obvious setting for the use of respeaking, be it intralingual or interlingual. As explained by the conference respeaker Vera Arma (2009) in her presentation at the 2nd International Seminar on Real-Time Intralingual Subtitling (Universitat Autònoma de Barcelona, 19 June 2009), the set-up is very similar to what has just been described for classroom respeaking. The audience will read the respeaker's words on a screen situated on one side of the main speaker. Ideally, the respeakers will be sitting in a soundproof interpreting booth at the back of the room. If this is not possible, they may have to be in the same room as the audience. In this case, if the room is small and there is a chance that the audience may be put off by the respeakers, it is possible to wear a stenomask to cancel the noise.

The preparation needed is very similar to that for conference interpreting, although in this case it is the software that must learn the terminology likely to be used in a given presentation. Particular attention must be paid to the potential occurrence of errors with homophones and to the style of delivery of the different speakers, especially their speech rates. Finally, conference respeakers must also give some thought to their audience. A hearing audience, for example, may want a transcript of the conference but maybe not speaker identification or any extra-linguistic information. Hard of hearing viewers may require speaker identification but they may prefer the respeaker not to correct too many recognition errors. As described in Chapter 11, they tend to be annoyed by the delay caused by these corrections and can usually correct errors mentally by thinking of the sense and sound of alternatives. Deaf viewers, however, are likely to require more corrections and perhaps even some editing, especially signing deaf for whom written English is a second language.

Respeaking may also be used to subtitle the Holy Mass, as described by Carlo Eugeni (2009b) in his presentation at the 2nd International Seminar on Real-Time Intralingual Subtitling (Universitat Autònoma de Barcelona, 19 June 2009). Based on his experience respeaking at churches in Italy, Eugeni differentiates the following parts in the Holy Mass: Entrance Procession, Penitential Act, The Gloria, Liturgy of the Word, Liturgy of the Eucharist, Rite of Communion and Concluding Rite. Eugeni focuses on the Liturgy of the Word and highlights here what is really the most characteristic aspect of church respeaking: the combination of semi-live and live subtitling. Indeed, in the first part of the liturgy, the first and second readings are actually written texts usually read by the priest. Respeakers are expected to prepare these texts in advance. In the case of Italy, they are displayed slightly before they are read, verbatim, in full paragraphs and with black font on white background for the viewers to read. A similar approach is adopted for the silences, that is, the commands given by the priest ("be seated", "all stand"), for which the respeaker must prepare tags beforehand. As for prayers and hymns, they are also prepared in advance, but are displayed in synch with the audio, verbatim, in chunks and with dark red font (preceded by the symbol #) on white background, very much like karaoke. Finally, the homily as well as introductory and closing remarks by the priest are respoken live, thus with some delay, often edited to keep up with fast speech rates, in blocks (with Dragon) with capitals and with black font on white background.

In sum, church respeakers are expected to have a thorough knowledge of the different parts of the Holy Mass and to be quick to change from semi-live to live subtitling while applying the different subtitling features at play (timing, editing, font colour).

9.4. Respeaking in live webcasts and telephones

Yet another application of respeaking is in live webcasts and telephones. Live webcasts are live events broadcast on the Internet. Respeaking in this case is similar to remote classroom respeaking, although with a different technical setting. In live webcasts, as shown in the following illustration by Mark Hall Associates, the respeaker's words are inserted by a streaming appliance as closed captions in the video that is being broadcast live:

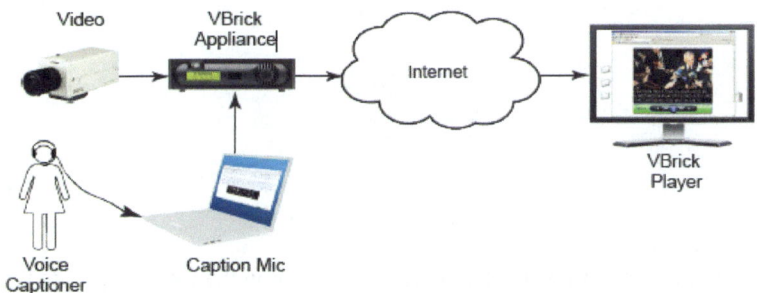

Figure 9.7: Respeaking in live webcasts

Needless to say, this application of respeaking has enormous potential, as it means that online meetings, conferences and presentations can be made accessible for deaf and hard of hearing people and even for hearing people if respeaking is carried out interlingually.

Finally, respeaking may also be used to provide accessibility in telephone conversations. In this case, it is one of several methods used for what are commonly known as relay services, text relay services or telecommunications relay services. It was Lady Pauline Ashley, a former president of the Royal National Institute for Deaf People (RNID) in the UK, and Mike Martin, pioneer of the first ever cochlear implant, who came up with the idea of the first text relay service in the 1980s. It was called RNID TypeTalk. This service, now called Text Relay and run by BT, works with textphones. When a call from a textphone is made and a voice answers, Text Relay is automatically brought into the call. The relay assistants will type the words said by the voice with a minimum typing speed of 50 to 60 wpm in a normal QWERTY keyboard. Textphone users can read the other person's words, but cannot hear their voices.

Respeaking is normally used in captioned relay services, such as the one provided by CapTel. This works with a special telephone and, unlike in Text Relay, users can choose to hear the caller and/or read their words on the screen of their telephone. The respeakers are in charge of turning the caller's message into words but the respeakers' voices are not heard in the conversation.

A modern development of this captioned telephone is Sprint CapTel. It also resorts to respeaking but in this case it is web-based and enables the user to have the captions displayed on a computer screen or even on a mobile device. The video "Sprint CapTel" (DVD > Chapter 9 > Discussion points and exercises > 9.5.3) shows how this system works. See Figure 9.8.

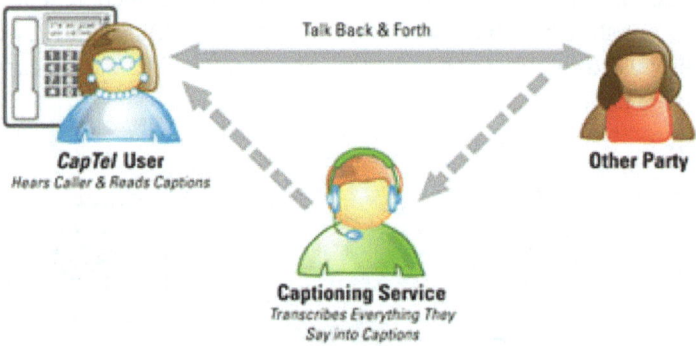

Figure 9.8: CapTel

From the point of view of the professionals doing the job, telephone respeaking poses even more challenges than live webcasts. It is done completely in the dark, as respeakers cannot even see who is speaking, and it usually involves sensitive and private information, all of which calls for further research in an area that has so far been largely overlooked.

9.5. Discussion points and exercises

9.5.1. Respeaking in museums and other arts venues

You can find the videos and documents you need for this section in DVD > Chapter 9 > Discussion points and exercises > 9.5.1.

As explained in this chapter, the London-based company Stagetext provides access for deaf and hard of hearing people to theatre performances through live captions. Watch the video "Stagetext" and answer the following questions:

- What are, according to Stagetext captioner Roz Chalmers, the main differences between theatre captioning and surtitling for the opera?
- What are the main elements to take into account with regard to the position of the caption unit?

In the United States, a similar initiative is that of Mark Hall Sales Associates with Caption Mic, as you can see in the video "Caption Mic – Theatre Captioning". What are the main differences and similarities between the service provided by Stagetext in the UK and the one provided by Mark Hall Sales Associates in the US? How do they compare in terms of setting and subtitles (particularly the non-verbal elements of the subtitles)?

Finally, a different approach to theatre captioning is that of Show Translations with a captioning device called Airscript. As you can see in the pdf file "Airscript", the idea in this case is to provide closed captions that are only displayed on the PDAs of those users who wish to have them. What are the main advantages and disadvantages of this method as compared to open captions?

Do you know of any other methods to make theatre performances accessible for deaf and hard of hearing audiences?

9.5.2. Respeaking in the classroom

You can find the videos you need for this section in DVD > Chapter 9 > Discussion points and exercises > 9.5.2.

As is the case with live theatre subtitling, the provision of live subtitles in the classroom can be approached in at least two very different ways.

The first one involves no respeaker. The lecturers speak to a microphone connected to a speech recognizer and their words are displayed on a screen for students to read in real time. This is the method used by the Liberated Learning Consortium, as you can see in the video "Viascribe 3" as well as in "Viascribe 1" and "Viascribe 2", shown in Chapter 5 (DVD > Chapter 5 > Discussion points and exercises > Discussion point 5.6.1).

The second method is based on respeaking as described in this book and thus requires a middle person between the lecturer and the students. As described in the videos "Caption Mic 1", "Caption Mic 2" and "Caption Mic 3" and in the documents "Caption Mic – Classroom" and "Captionwrap", from Mark Hall Associates, this can be done on-site or remotely. A similar approach has been adopted by Ai-Media in Australia, as you can see in the videos "Ai-Live 1", "Ai-Live 2", "Ai-Live Skills 1", "Ai-Live Skills 2", as well as in the documents "Ai Training Program", "Ai-Media Release 1", "Ai-Media Release 2" and "Ai-Radio interview".

Watch the videos and discuss the main advantages and disadvantages of this method as compared to the self-subtitling or auto-subtitling approach proposed by the Liberated Learning Consortium.

In order to practise classroom respeaking, you only have to type the key word "lecture" (or any synonym) in websites such as www.youtube.com or http://video.google.com/. Many universities are uploading lectures online. A case in point is the website of the PhD/Advanced Masters in Translation and Intercultural Studies at Universitat Rovira I Virgili (Spain), which hosts videos of several lectures given by renowned scholars on Translation Studies.

You can practise respeaking the video "Translation Lecture", where Anthony Pym, Professor at Universitat Rovira I Virgili (Spain), summarizes the different theoretical paradigms presented so far in Translation Studies. In order to prepare for this video, you can read the postscript of Pym's book *Exploring Translation Theories* (2009), on which this lecture is based.

What were the main challenges you faced when respeaking this lecture? Did you manage to respeak the (few) interventions by the students?

9.5.3. Respeaking in conferences, churches, live webcasts and telephones

You can find the videos you need for this section in DVD > Chapter 9 > Discussion points and exercises > 9.5.3.

The picture "Caption Mic – Church" shows how respeaking-based subtitles are displayed in a church. This is done with the so-called "Live Event Display Sequencer" or "church app", which allows respeakers to create a sequence of scripted and unscripted materials. The scripted materials are included as text documents within the Caption Mic computer. As the appropriate section of the service occurs, the respeaker either meters out the scripted material in time with the speaker or voices the unscripted portion.

The document "Caption Mic – Live Webcast" shows yet another application of respeaking, in this case to provide subtitles in a live streaming programme or presentation. How can the fact that subtitles are to be provided remotely affect the respeaker's task?

Finally, watch the videos "CapTel" and "Sprint CapTel" to find out how telephone respeaking works in special telephones, computers and mobile phones.

With regard to material for training, you can find videos of church services by typing key words such as "daily mass" in www.youtube.com or http://video.google.com/.

You can also practise respeaking the videos included in this section: "Roehampton 1", "Roehampton 2", "Roehampton 3", "Roehampton 4" and "Roehampton 5". In these videos, lecturers from Roehampton University, in London, talk about the subjects they teach and what they look for in applicants wanting to study their modules.

The information available for you to respeak the videos is the following:

- Video 1: Robet Dube speaks about studying Computing at Roehampton University.
- Video 2: Edward Collins speaks about studying Marketing and Management at Roehampton University.

- Video 3: Diane Bray speaks about studying Psychology at Roehampton University.
- Video 4: Sabela Melchor-Couto speaks about studying Modern Languages and Spanish at Roehampton University.
- Video 5: Keith Hicks speaks about studying Teacher Training at Roehampton University.

Respeak these videos without watching them first. You may want to visit the Roehampton University website to obtain information about the courses described in the videos.

What were the main challenges posed by these clips as far as respeaking is concerned?

Before respeaking them again, have a look at the scripts of the videos "Roehampton 1 - Script", "Roehampton 2 - Script", "Roehampton 3 - Script", "Roehampton 4 - Script" and "Roehampton 5 - Script". Read them through in case there are any typos to be corrected or changes to be made (for example with regard to capitals). Once you have done this, introduce them in Dragon or in any other speech recognizer you may be using. In the case of Dragon, this is explained in section 6.4.5.3.

Have you noticed any difference in the performance of the software?

Finally, watch the video "Interlingual Respeaking - Vigo", which includes a brief sample of live respeaking from English into Spanish during a presentation at Universidade de Vigo (Spain).

How feasible do you think it is to introduce interlingual respeaking in the professional field? What change would it entail in the training of respeakers?

10. Respeaking Skills Applied after the Process
Accuracy Rate – the NERD model

10.0. Introduction

Depending on the company, error calculation may be carried out by respeakers (marking each other's subtitles once they have respoken a programme) or by trainers. Either way, this is an essential part of respeaking, not least because it is the most common way of assessing the quality of respoken subtitles. Arguably, this quality assessment should take into account other factors, such as the viewers' opinion, perception and comprehension of these subtitles (tackled in Chapter 11), but error calculation is faster and has therefore been adopted as the yardstick to decide what constitutes good and bad respeaking. The problem is that, in the young field of respeaking, few things have proved as inconsistent across countries and subtitling companies as error calculation. Moreover, depending on the method adopted, the accuracy rate of a given set of respoken subtitles may vary greatly, some methods being much more generous than others.

Although a good starting point for this discussion is the so-called word error rate (**WER**) traditionally used in SR, its use in respeaking calls for an adaptation to the particular reality of this technique, where for instance an omission that does not lose any meaning is usually not regarded as an error. Also, it is important to consider the purpose of this calculation: are we only looking for a figure or do we want to have food for further training so that we know what needs to be improved? Are we only concerned about the statistics or do we really want to improve quality?

10.1. Basic requirements

Although it is not the aim of this chapter to be prescriptive, it may be useful to set some basic conditions for error calculation in respeaking. The model adopted must thus
(1) be functional and easy to apply. The use of multiple variables will probably help the researcher but not respeakers and trainers, who may have to calculate accuracy on a daily basis;
(2) include the basic principles of WER calculations in SR theory, which have been tested and validated for long;
(3) take into account the original spoken text, which allows identification of what has been omitted, changed, etc.;
(4) take into account the possibility of edited (summarized, expanded, etc.) and yet accurate respeaking;
(5) allow specificities of different languages while, at the same time, being applicable to all languages and account for on-air corrections;
(6) provide not only an idea of the quality in terms of accuracy but also of what must be improved (and perhaps even how).

10.2. Traditional WER methods

The quality of recognition, be it for respeaking or for the more traditional use of SR, is often expressed as a percentage. According to Dumouchel *et al* (forthcoming), the speech research community often resorts to two percentages put forward by the US National Institute of Standards and Technology: word correctness and word accuracy. The formulas used for the two percentages are based on the same idea:

$$\text{Accuracy rate} \frac{N - \text{Errors}}{N} \times 100 = \%$$

In this model, N is the total number of words spoken by the user. Yet, no distinction is made with regard to the errors, which may be very different. Dumouchel *et al* (forthcoming) illustrate this point with the sentence *where is the whole wheat flour*, recognized as *were is hole we eat flower*. In this type of evaluations, spoken sentences are usually automatically aligned to identify the errors:

Where	is	the	whole	wheat		flour
		D	S	S	I	S
Where	is		hole	we	eat	flower

As can be seen in the previous examples, at least three different types of errors can occur with the use of SR: deletion (a correct word is omitted in the recognized sentence), substitution (a correct word is replaced by an incorrect one) and insertion (an extra word is added).

Taking this into account, the measure of word correctness proposed by the US National Institute of Standards and Technology, which includes deletion and substitution errors, would apply to the above utterance as follows:

$$\text{Accuracy rate} \frac{N - D - S}{N} \times 100 = 33\%$$

The model to assess word accuracy is less lenient, as it also factors in insertion errors:

$$\text{Accuracy rate} \frac{N - D - S - I}{N} \times 100 = 16\%$$

Designed as they are for the use of SR, these models pose a significant problem when applied to respeaking, as they do not account for instances in which a respeaker edits the original text without changing or losing meaning. For instance, the omission of a relatively unimportant aside such as "you know,

I mean" in an interview, a useful strategy commonly applied by respeakers to catch their breath and keep up with the original speaker, would count in this case as four deletion errors.

10.3. The CRIM method

In order to adapt traditional WER methods to the specificity of respeaking, the Centre de Recherche Informatique de Montréal (CRIM) resorts to the word accuracy method described above, but adds a step in between. Once the spoken and the respoken text have been automatically aligned, a human operator goes through the text and decides whether or not the deletions have caused loss of information. In this way, both verbatim and edited respeaking can be accounted for.

However, a number of issues are still to be addressed. Firstly, the decision of when a deletion brings about loss of information is entirely subjective and may thus vary from person to person. This issue will be tackled in the next section. Secondly, while requirements 1 to 4 above are met, 5 and 6 are not. When looking at the results yielded by this method, although the accuracy rate may provide useful data, the deletion figure remains ambiguous. It is impossible, by looking at the formula alone, to ascertain whether the deletions have been caused by misrecognitions or by poor editing strategies on the part of the respeaker. This is very important, as it requires two different remedial actions. If the deletion errors are mostly misrecognitions, further work is needed with the software to improve the voice profile by fine-tuning the acoustic and language models. In contrast, if the deletions are actually the result of poor editing by the respeaker, the training should be based on providing the respeaker with skills to edit the original text without losing (excessive) information. Finally, this method does not seem to account for the specificities of different languages or for errors that are corrected on air by the respeaker. Indeed, whereas some companies count them as half an error, others do not regard them as mistakes, which obviously leads to better overall accuracy rates.

10.4. The NERD model

Drawing on the principles of WER in SR and on the improvements added by the CRIM method, the following model attempts to present a method that meets the requirements described in section 10.1:

$$\text{Accuracy} \quad \frac{N - E - R - D}{N} \times 100 = \text{accuracy rate}$$

CE:
SE:
Comments:

N = Number of words in the respoken text.
It is important to take N as number of words in the respoken text (or recording), including commands, as opposed to the number of words in the original text. The latter could lead to misleading conclusions. For instance, say that respeakers A and B respeak a 600-word programme in 600 and 400 words respectively with 15 mistakes each. Although respeaker B has managed to edit the original text successfully, the 15 mistakes in 400 words will be more noticeable than those made by respeaker A in 600 words. This should be indicated in the final accuracy rate. Yet, if N is taken as the number of words of the original text, the distinction is lost. It is for this reason that, in this model, N is the number of respoken words including commands. However, the original text is still used to analyze the following elements: edition errors, recognition errors and deducted items.

E = Edition errors:
These are usually caused by the strategies applied by the respeaker, in other words, they are a result of the respeaker's judgement or decision. The most common situation is that, in a given instance, and for whatever reason (for example because the original speech rate is too fast), the respeaker decides to omit something, losing an idea unit (a piece of information). It could also be that the respeaker adds idea units or paraphrases the original text losing information or introducing wrong information. Editing errors are calculated by comparing the respoken text and the original text.

R = Recognition errors
These may be insertions, deletions or substitutions. They are usually misrecognitions caused by mispronunciations or mishearing, and are calculated by comparing the respoken text and the original text.

D = Deducted marks:
These are points deducted for corrected errors (for example 0.5 as opposed to 1). Depending on the language, different issues regarded as minor may also be included here. For instance, incorrect accents in Spanish may carry a 0.5 penalty as opposed to 1.

Finally, this model accounts for two more aspects that may be of use for respeakers and trainers:

CE = Correct Editions: instances in which the respeaker's edition has not lost information, which is calculated by comparing the respoken text and the original text.
SE = Serious Errors: those that have changed the meaning significantly, often affecting key words and also calculated by comparing the respoken and the original text.

Neither of these two factors is included in the formula, as correct editions are not errors and it is difficult to assess the exact impact of a misrecognized term on a given programme.

Comments: this section includes the analysis of the results, as well as comments on different issues, such as the overall flow of the subtitles on screen, the audio-visual coherence between the original image/sound and the subtitles, whether or not too much time has been lost in the corrections, whether or not the delay in the subtitles is longer than usual, how the respeaker has coped with the original speech rate, etc.

The aim of this model is to meet all the basic requirements given in section 10.1, not least number 6, whereby the final result should provide an accuracy rate as well as clues regarding how to improve the respeaker's performance. When using this model, assessors will have to focus mainly on four pieces of information:

(1) accuracy rate: anything over 97% or 97.5% may be considered acceptable.
(2) main source of errors:
    - if it is the E (edition), the respeaker needs to be trained on editing skills.
    - if it is the R(ecognition), further work needs to be carried out with the software.
(3) correct editions: shows the respeaker's proficiency regarding editing.
(4) serious mistakes: even for a programme that has been respoken with 98% accuracy, if a key word is misrecognized six out of seven times, the result must be reconsidered.

The problem remains of how to decide when an edition is correct (does not lose information) or incorrect (loses information). Subject as it is to the judgement of the assessor, it seems difficult to find an objective method for this. A useful approach is to have, every so often, different assessors calculating the accuracy rate of the same texts and comparing the results to see whether the same criteria apply. This is done by subtitling companies such as IMS in the UK and seems to indicate that this issue looks more problematic on paper than it is in reality.

10.5. Application of the NERD model

The following is an application of the NERD model to real-life respoken programmes.

Source and respoken text are included for each programme, along with the formula and a brief discussion of the results. Highlighted in bold in the source text are those elements that have been omitted in the subtitles. In the respoken text, the elements highlighted in bold are those which have undergone some sort of change or modification. Four programmes (1, 2, 3-A and 3-B) have been analyzed. Programme 1 is a successful example of respeaking which shows how a high speech rate can be tackled by editing the original text without losing much information or overall accuracy. Programme 2 features a much lower accuracy due to poor editing on the part of the respeaker. Finally, programme 3 is presented here in two different respoken versions. In the first one (3-A), the low accuracy is due to recognition errors and thus calls for further training with the software.

In the second one (3-B), even though accuracy is very high, the overall results cannot be considered satisfactory, as there are a number of serious mistakes that alter the content of the original text significantly.

Programme 1
Source Text
- What would it mean for triathlon in Britain if a male or female British athlete were able to go to Beijing and bring back a first triathlon Olympic medal?
- **Oh, I think** it'd be, **be, be** everything **for**, for the individual, of course, **and, you know,** I'm sure, **you know**, there**'d** be loads of people, **you know, all the personal supporters but obviously, you know**, the sport as a whole would be great. **You know,** I'm sure **that** if you speak to the rest of the guys that's what everyone is **really, really** trying to do **is** get a good performance and**, you know,** try to race for a medal **and, you know**, it's the pinnacle of your career, **you know and, you know,** hopefully **and** if it's one of the younger ones, or myself **or** whoever, **you know,** it'll be a stepping stone **to, to, to,** for experience leading up to 2012.
- Inevitably, we have to touch on the three missed tests and at the fact that you were temporarily banned **by the BOA.** Do you look back on it and feel that you were maybe a victim of a system that was in its infancy at the time?
- **Uh, to a degree, yes, I think that** everyone learnt a lot from that. UK sport did, **I did**, the federation and hopefully the juniors **have. Uh, but, you know,** it happened **and, you know,** I'm not hiding behind the fact it didn't happen.

Respoken Text
- What would it mean for triathlon in Britain if a male or female British athlete were able to go to Beijing and bring back a first triathlon Olympic medal?
- It **would be** everything for the individual, of course. I'm sure **there will** be lots of people who will... The sport as a whole would be great. I'm sure if you speak to the rest of the guys, that's what everyone is trying to do. Get a good performance and try to race for a medal. **It is** the pinnacle of your career. Hopefully if it is one of the younger ones or myself, whoever, it **will be** a stepping stone for experience leading up to 2012.
- Inevitably, **be** have to touch on the three missed tests and at the fact that you were temporarily banned. Do you look back **and** it and feel that you were maybe a victim of a system that was in its infancy at the time?
- Everyone learnt a lot from that, UK sport, the federation and hopefully the juniors. It happened. I am not hiding behind the fact it didn't happen.

Results
- N: 205 (186 + 19 commands, namely commas, full stops and question marks)
- E: 3 (all the personal supporters / by the BOA / to a degree yes)
- R: 2 ("be have" instead of "we have" / "look back and it" instead "look back on it")
- D: 0

$$\text{Accuracy} \ \frac{205 - 3 - 2 - 0}{205} \times 100 = 97.6\%$$

- CE: 40 (oh / I think [x2] / be [x2] / for / and [x5] / you know [x 12], but obviously / that / really [x2] / or / to [x3] / I think that / I did / have / and / but / it would be / there will be / it is / it will be)
- SE: 0

Comments:
- Overall accuracy is good;
- Heavy editing (20.1% of the source text) due to very high speech rate (245 wpm) but, to the respeaker's credit, there are 40 instances of correct editing vs. only 3 where some information is lost. Very proficient in this regard;
- Recognition is good but attention should be paid to be/we and and/on. In any case, when respeaking with Dragon, if the respeaker manages to deliver respeaking units such as "we have to touch" or "look back on it", the algorithm in the language model is unlikely to allow mistakes such as "be have to touch" and "look back and it".
- None of the errors causes significant loss of information.

Programme 2
Source Text
Everyone agrees the economy is gonna cool down **in two years**. The question is, will it be a deep freeze or just a bracing chill? Well, if I really knew the answer to that question, I'd be in the City, not standing here talking to you. But I do know what the key questions are: the big one is **the US, and** whether it's about to slip into recession. The former head of the Federal Reserve, **Alan Greenspan,** thinks the odd on a recession this year are **fifty-fifty**. The fed has cut rates **three times** but **its governors** have been surprised **by the slowdown** and plan to do more. The same goes for President Bush, who said **yesterday** he was thinking about a stimulus package of his own **for 2009**. Now, the worse things get over there, the tougher it will be **in Britain**. Sure, people talk about all the growth **in Asia** and how the global economy can decouple from America, but Britain's credit crunch has been nearly as bad as America's. Worse, if you think Northern Rock. **And** even though Alistair Darling has announced reforms **today** that could prevent that kind of fiasco happening again **at a macro level**, it's hard to get round the fact that Britain shares many of the same big economic weaknesses as America, not least a habit of spending beyond our means.

Respoken Text
Everyone agrees the economy is gonna cool down. The question is, will it be a deep freeze or just a bracing chill? Well, if I really knew the answer to that question, I'd be in the City, not standing here talking to you. But I do know what the key questions are, the big one is whether it's about to slip into recession. The former head of the Federal Reserve thinks the odd on a recession this year are high. The Fed has cut rates but **has** been surprised and plan to do more. The same goes for President Bush, who said he was thinking about a stimulus package of his own. Now, the worse things get over there, the tougher it will be. Sure, people talk about all the growth and how the global economy can decouple from America, but Britain's credit crunch has been nearly as bad as America's. Worse, if you think Northern Rock. Even though Alistair Darling has announced reforms that could prevent that kind of fiasco happening again, it's hard to get round the fact that Britain shares many of the same big economic weaknesses as America, not least a habit of spending beyond our **mains**.

Results
- **N**: 226 (202 + 24 commands, namely commas, full stops and question marks)
- **E**: 13 (in two years / the US / Alan Greenspan / fifty-fifty / three times / its governors / by the slowdown / yesterday / for 2009 / in Britain / in Asia / today / at a macro level)
- **R**: 1 (means as mains)
- **D**: 0

$$\text{Accuracy} \ \frac{226 - 13 - 1 - 0}{226} \times 100 = 93.8\%$$

- **CE**: 1 (and [even though...])
- **SE**: 0

Comments:
- Overall accuracy is poor;
- Recognition is good. Only one error and it doesn't cause loss of information;
- The problem lies in editing, not because of the amount (only 6% edited, as opposed to over 20% in the previous programme) but because of the quality (13 instances of incorrect editing vs. 1 instance of correct editing). Facing a fairly normal speech rate in the original text (165 wpm), the respeaker has kept many "irrelevant" elements (well, but, sure, now, and) but has lost as many as 13 idea units. Many of these units are made up of only one or two words and could have easily been maintained.
- Further training is needed to improve this respeaker's editing skills.

Programme 3 -a
Source text
- In my view, it is monetary policy that needs to act, not fiscal policy. **And** what we have at the moment is interest rates which are contractionary on

the economy. **Let's not forget that** an interest rate of 15% is higher than a neutral interest rate for this economy and yet there are all these forces pushing downwards, such as **oil prices,** the credit crunch, housing, housing vulnerabilities. **In my view,** the Bank of England needs to start cutting rates and start cutting them quickly. **Now**, if it doesn't, this economy is likely to stall next year.
- So if you were still in the committee that is what you would be reckoning?
- **Basically**, I will be voting for a cut next year.
- She's absolutely right. **Look**, sure there is a risk of inflation, we're not in the Weimar Republic, we're living in Great Britain in the United States. There is pain to cutting interest rates. **I mean**, you risk a little inflation but the question is what would you rather risk, a little more inflation or a major slowdown? Given the risks, you best take a chance on inflation.
- I was just talking to some people at the White House today. It looks like we have room for fiscal policy adjustments. The president is considering increasing allowances for depreciation for instance to stimulate business investment. In this country, Gordon Brown did not leave you with that room.

Respoken text
- In my view, it is monetary **police** that needs to **and** not fiscal policy. What we have at the moment is interest rates which are **confectionery** on the economy. An interest rate of **50%** is higher than a neutral interest rate for this economy and yet there are all these forces pushing downwards, such as the **credit card**, housing, housing **and inabilities**. The Bank of England needs to start cutting rates and start cutting them quickly. If it doesn't, this economy is likely **to still** the next year.
- So if **he** were still in the committee that is what you would be reckoning?
- I will be voting for a **cup** next year.
- She's absolutely right. Sure there is a risk of inflation, **were** not in the **way my Republican**, **were** living in Great Britain in the United States. There is pain to cutting interest rates. You risk a little inflation but the question is what would you rather risk, a little more inflation or a major slowdown? Given the risks, you best take a chance on inflation.
- I was just talking to some people at the White House today. It looks like we have room for fiscal policy adjustments. The president is considering increasing allowances for **deposition** for instance to stimulate business investment. In this country, Gordon Brown did not leave you with that **run - room**.

Results
    N: 257 (230 + 27 commands, namely commas, full stops, question marks and one correction)
    E: 1 (oil prices)

R: 13 (policy as police / act as and / contractionary as confectionary / 15% as 50% / credit crunch as credit card / vulnerabilities as and inabilities / to stall as to still / you as he / cut as cup / we're as were [x2] / Weimar Republic as way my Republican / depreciation as deposition)
D: 1 (run corrected as room)

$$\text{Accuracy} \ \frac{257 - 1 - 13 - 0.5}{257} \times 100 = 94.3\%$$

CE: 7 (and / let's not forget that / in my view / now / basically / look / I mean)
SE: 7 (policy as police / act as and / contractionary as confectionary / 15% as 50% / vulnerabilities as and inabilities / Weimar Republic as way my Republican / depreciation as deposition)

Comments:
- Overall accuracy is poor;
- Editing is good: only 1 idea unit missing and 7 instances of correct edition.
- Recognition is poor. 13 recognition errors including 7 serious mistakes that distort the meaning of the original text significantly. Further training is needed to improve the voice profile. The errors occur not only with single words but also phrases and contractions. The respeaker should thus be advised not to dictate contractions in order to avoid errors such as "were" instead of "we're".

Programme 3 -b
Source text
- In my view, it is monetary policy that needs to act, not fiscal policy. **And** what we have at the moment is interest rates which are contractionary on the economy. **Let's not forget that** an interest rate of 15% is higher than a neutral interest rate for this economy and yet there are all these forces pushing downwards, such as **oil prices,** the credit crunch, housing, housing vulnerabilities. **In my view,** the Bank of England needs to start cutting rates and start cutting them quickly. **Now**, if it doesn't, this economy is likely to stall next year.
- So if you were still in the committee that is what you would be reckoning?
- **Basically**, I will be voting for a cut next year.
- She's absolutely right. **Look**, sure there is a risk of inflation, we're not in the Weimar Republic, we're living in Great Britain in the United States. There is pain to cutting interest rates. **I mean**, you risk a little inflation but the question is what would you rather risk, a little more inflation or a major slowdown? Given the risks, you best take a chance on inflation.

- I was just talking to some people at the White House today. It looks like we have room for fiscal policy adjustments. The president is considering increasing allowances for depreciation for instance to stimulate business investment. In this country, Gordon Brown did not leave you with that room.

Respoken text
- In my view, it is monetary policy that needs to act not fiscal policy. What we have at the moment is interest rates which are contractionary on the economy. An interest rate of 15% is higher than a neutral interest rate for this economy and yet there are all these forces pushing downwards, such as the credit crunch, housing, housing vulnerabilities. The Bank of England needs to start cutting rates and start cutting them quickly. If it doesn't, this economy is likely to stall the next year.
- So if you were still in the committee that is what you would be reckoning?
- I will be voting for a cut next year.
- She's absolutely right. Sure there is a risk of **information**, we're not in the Weimar Republic, we're living in Great Britain in the United States. There is pain to cutting interest rates. You risk a little **information** but the question is what would you rather risk, a little more **information** or a major slowdown? Given the risks, you best take a chance on **information**.
- I was just talking to some people at the White House today. It looks like we have room for fiscal policy adjustments. The president is considering increasing allowances for depreciation for instance to stimulate business investment. In this country, Gordon Brown did not leave you with that room.

Results
N: 253 (227 + 26 commands, namely commas, full stops and question marks)
E: 1 (oil prices)
R: 4 (inflation as information [x4])
D: 0

$$\text{Accuracy} \quad \frac{253 - 1 - 4 - 0}{253} \times 100 = 98\%$$

CE: 7 (and / let's not forget that / in my view / now / basically / look / I mean)
SE: 4 (inflation as information [x4])

Comments:
- Overall accuracy is very good;

- Editing is very good. Only 1 idea unit missing and 7 instances of correct edition.
- Recognition is very good. Only 1 word misrecognized (4 times).
- Yet, the overall result cannot be considered good. The misrecognition of the key word inflation as information distorts too much of the original content.

10.6. Exercises and discussion points

You can find further examples of how to calculate accuracy rates in the document "Application of the NERD model" (DVD > Chapter 10 > Exercises and discussion points 10.6).

Go over the respoken subtitles you have produced for the videos included in this book and compare the accuracy rate as you had calculated it and as resulting from the application of a) the CRIM method and B) the NERD model. How do the results compare using the three methods? What are the main conclusions you can draw based on the "comments" sections of the NERD model? Do you notice any difference depending on the genre of the video? Which ones yielded more recognition errors? Which ones led to more editing errors? What difference did it make in terms of accuracy rate to be able to use the full scripts in the Roehampton videos in Chapter 9?

Now that you have applied the NERD model, what are, in your view, its strong and weak points? What would you change in it to make it more useful / practical / relevant?

11. The Reception of Respeaking

11.0. Introduction

The provision of live subtitles is a service many companies and broadcasters could do without. It is expensive, it requires skilled professionals and it is bound to be flawed. Yet, the introduction of legislation on SDH means that live subtitling is no longer a privilege but a right for deaf and hard of hearing viewers, and therefore an obligation for subtitling companies and broadcasters. In many cases, this legislation sets targets of a specific number of hours that must be subtitled (live and offline) depending on the country, type of channel, means available, etc. In other words, from the beginning the emphasis was placed on quantity. As a matter of fact, until recently, subtitling surveys often identified the lack of subtitles as the viewers' main concern regarding live programmes.

Now that respeaking seems to have become consolidated as the most cost-effective method to provide live subtitles and companies and broadcasters are beginning to meet their targets, it may be time to change the focus from quantity to quality. In the UK, where the BBC already subtitles 100% of their programmes, it seems the obvious step forward. For other countries where live subtitling is still growing, it makes sense to apply quality standards now before "bad habits" are acquired.

But how do we measure quality in live subtitling and, in this case, in respeaking? Most subtitling companies limit their quality assessment to error calculation, often carried out by trainers or respeakers and included in Chapter 10 as a respeaking skill to be applied after the process. Sometimes, this is completed with views gathered from the audience, be it through consultation to target groups or setting up an email address where viewers can express their opinion about respoken subtitles. However, an in-depth analysis of quality in respeaking requires a different effort and the will to invest time and money on research. With the exception of some companies such as SWISS TXT, it is mostly scholars and research groups at university who embark upon this kind of research.

The aim of this chapter is to cast some more light on the quality of respoken subtitles by focusing on the viewers. For this purpose, this chapter includes a series of experiments about respoken subtitles in the UK that I have recently carried out at Roehampton University as part of the research group TransMedia Catalonia and in the framework of the EU-funded project DTV4ALL (http://www.psp-dtv4all.org/). Having looked at the characteristics and the accuracy of respoken subtitles, attention is directed now to the viewers and, in this case, to three different aspects: their comprehension of these subtitles, the manner in which they read/view them and their preferences.

11.1. Viewers' comprehension of respoken subtitles

Some surveys or opinion polls on subtitling include questions where participants are asked about the extent to which different types of subtitles enable comprehension.

The problem in this case is that, as noted by Tuominen (2008), it is not uncommon to find discrepancies between preference and performance in this and other areas. In other words, the viewers' opinions about say a certain subtitling convention may be conditioned by different factors, such as habit, and do not always correspond to the convention that enables better comprehension It is for this reason that the study of how much information viewers obtain through respoken subtitles needs a different experiment with a different approach. The following sections include a description of such an experiment, the results obtained and their implications with regard to how hearing, hard of hearing and deaf viewers comprehend respoken subtitles.

11.1.1. Description of the experiment

The aim of this study was to find out how much visual and verbal information hearing, hard of hearing and deaf viewers obtain from news programmes in the UK. For this purpose, four clips from the *Six O'Clock News* broadcast on 4 July 2007 by BBC1 were shown to 30 hearing viewers, 15 hard of hearing viewers and 15 deaf viewers. The hearing participants were between 20 and 45 years old, native or near native in English, proficient readers and habitual subtitle users. Half of them were postgraduate students doing an MA on Audiovisual Translation at Roehampton University and the other half was formed by lecturers and professional subtitlers. The hard of hearing participants were over 60 years old, the most common age range for viewers with this type of hearing loss, and all of them but two became hard of hearing after the age of 50. Most of them were frequent readers and subtitle users. Finally, the deaf participants were between 20 and 45 years old. Most of them were oralist (i.e. use English as their first language) and only two were signing (use BSL as their first language). All 15 were university students, frequent readers and habitual subtitle users.

As far as the methodology is concerned, participants were shown two clips with two news items each and were asked to answer questions about one of them. The clips were subtitled by respeaking at two different speeds, 180 wpm, the usual speed in the UK, and 220 wpm, so as to ascertain the impact of speed on comprehension.

In order to carry out a quantitative analysis of the amount of information retrieved by the viewers, the two news clips were notionally divided, drawing on Chafe's (1980) concept of *idea units*, into 14 semi-units: 8 verbal units and 6 visual units. In (very few) cases in which participants retrieved in their answers a semi-unit that was not included in these 14, the new unit was also factored into the analysis. For the purpose of the analysis of the findings, a simple division was made whereby any result between 0% and 25% is regarded as zero to poor information retrieval, 25%-50% goes from poor to sufficient, 50%-75% from sufficient to good and 75%-100% from very good to perfect information retrieval.

Finally, a further problem was posed by the absence of a control group with which to compare the results obtained by participants watching subtitled news. Can we indeed expect viewers under normal conditions (no subtitles) to obtain

100% of the visual and acoustic information of a news clip? In order to answer this question, a preliminary test was run with 15 other students (from the above-mentioned class at Roehampton University) who watched the same clips with sound but no subtitles and were asked the same questions.

11.1.2. Findings

Figure 11.1 and tables 11.1, 11.2 and 11.3 show the results obtained in the study, firstly with hearing participants and no subtitles and then with hearing, hard of hearing and deaf participants and subtitles at 180 wpm and 220 wpm.

No subtitles (hearing viewers)

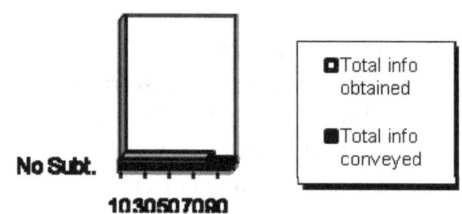

Figure 11.1: Hearing viewers with no subtitles

No subtitles Performance	
Perfect	0%
Very good	93.3%
Good	6.7%
Almost good	0%
Sufficient	0%
Less than sufficient	0%
Poor	0%
Very poor	0%

Table 11.1: Hearing viewers with no subtitles

Subtitles at 220 wpm (hearing, hard of hearing and deaf viewers)

	Hearing		Hard of Hearing		Deaf	
Good	0%		0%		0%	
Almost good	6.7 %	20%	6.7%	20%	6.6%	13.3%
Sufficient	13.3 %		13.3%		6.6%	
Less than sufficient	20%		30%		26.7%	
Poor	30%	80%	30%	80%	26.7%	86.7%
Very poor	30%		20%		33.3%	

Table 11.2: Hearing, hard of hearing and deaf viewers with subtitles at 220 wpm

Subtitles at 180 wpm (hearing, hard of hearing and deaf viewers)

	Hearing		Hard of Hearing		Deaf	
Good	3.3%	46.7%	3.3%	46.7%	0%	46.7%
Almost good	6.7%		6.7%		6.7%	
Sufficient	36.7%		36.7%		40%	
Less than sufficient	20%	53.3%	20%	53.3%	13.3%	53.3%
Poor	20%		13.3%		20%	
Very poor	13.3%		20%		20%	

Table 11.3: Hearing, hard of hearing and deaf viewers with subtitles at 180 wpm

11.1.3. Discussion

As may be expected, hearing viewers watching the news with no subtitles didn't manage to retrieve 100% of the visual and verbal information conveyed in the clips. Short term memory plays an important factor here. Yet, their results show very good comprehension (an average of 80%), particularly of the images (90.5%, as compared to 73.2% of the verbal information), which is normal considering that no subtitles were displayed.

As far as the study with subtitles is concerned, two elements are particularly striking: the poor overall average comprehension obtained and the similarity of the results across viewers regardless of the type hearing loss. The latter may be due to the fact that all participants taking part in the experiment were very used to watching subtitles on TV, be it because they study them or produce them (hearing) or because they use them as a means to access the news on a daily basis (deaf and hard of hearing). In any case, this makes the low overall score regarding comprehension even more puzzling.

As for the test with subtitles at 220 wpm, only 20% of the participants obtained sufficient information and none obtained good information. Besides, 60% could only give a poor or very poor account of the news. Although not surprising, given the high subtitle speed, these results warn against the possibility of producing verbatim subtitles for certain programmes such as debates, interviews and weather reports, which are sometimes spoken at this rate. Indeed, most viewers (76%) considered these subtitles to be too fast. Many of them also added that it caused them 'stress' and 'headache' and pointed out that the images were too fast, which, although not true (they were as fast as in the other clips), goes to show how the speed of subtitles can affect the overall perception of an audiovisual programme.

The test with subtitles displayed at 180 wpm is more significant, as respoken subtitles are often displayed at this speed in some sport programmes and many news programmes, interviews and debates. In this case, most participants (66%) were happy with the speed of the subtitles and yet more than half of them (51%)

did not obtain sufficient information. This suggests that viewers may be unaware of how much information they are losing due to the speed of respoken subtitles. Thus, although most of them regarded the speed as OK or even too slow, only 3% obtained good information and 31% got poor or very poor information. More worryingly, 1 out of 3 participants acquired incorrect information, believing, for example, to have seen the President of Nicaragua or Tony Blair, none of whom appeared on the news.

Considering that these participants were highly literate and frequent subtitle users, viewers who are not used to subtitles or signing deaf viewers, for whom English is a second language and whose reading skills are often regarded to be poorer (Torres Monreal and Santana Hernández 2005), can hardly be expected to obtain better results. Why do programmes with these respoken subtitles trigger such mediocre comprehension results? A possible answer to this question may lie in how viewers read and process these subtitles, which can be assessed by means of eye-tracking technology.

11.2. Viewers' perception of respoken subtitles

11.2.1. Eye-tracking and subtitling

Despite its obvious potential for the study of Audiovisual Translation and more specifically for that of subtitling, eye-tracking research in this area is still in its infancy. Following the initial studies by D'Ydewalle *et al.* (1987, 1991) and Jensema *et al.* (2000), it seems that an increasing number of scholars are turning their attention to this technology in order to find out how viewers read and comprehend subtitles and to assess their quality. Looking precisely at how subtitles are read, Jensema *et al.* (2000:284) found that

> When captions are present, there appears to be a general tendency to start by looking at the middle of the screen and then moving the gaze to the beginning of a caption within a fraction of a second. Viewers read the caption and then glance at the video action after they finish reading.

Yet, reading is far from being a smooth process. Rather than moving continuously across the page/screen, our eyes pause and focus on specific parts and then jump across words and images. The visual information necessary for reading is obtained during those pauses, known as **fixations**, which typically last about 200–250 ms (Liversedge and Findlay 2000). The jumps between fixations are known as **saccades**, which take as little as 100 ms and are the fastest movement the human being is capable of making (Rayner and Pollatsek 1989). During saccades, vision is suppressed and no useful information is obtained, which is known as the saccadic suppression (Wolverton and Zola 1983). But even though we cannot read during saccades, the eyes need not fixate on every word when reading a subtitle.

In figures 11.2 and 11.3, for example, reading the subtitled line in four fixations (Figure 11.2) enables the viewer to turn quickly to the image (Figure 11.3).

Figures 11.2 and 11.3: Viewing patterns in pre-recorded subtitling

There has been no need to fixate on the words "students" or "hear" because (a) they may be guessed in the context, particularly by the preceding words ("deaf" and "can't"), and (b) they can be seen with peripheral vision, given that our global perceptual span, the area from which useful information is obtained during a fixation, comprises up to 14 or 15 characters to the right of a given fixation. In this regard, Rayner (1998) explains that with the fovea (part of the eye responsible for sharp central vision) we determine the location of a fixation, the foveal area, which spans six to eight characters around the fixation point. But then, the so-called parafoveal area extends up to 15 characters to the right of fixation (Häikiö *et al.* 2009). This peripheral vision, which allows faster reading by not having to fixate on every word, applies to print and block subtitles. But what happens when we are reading subtitles that are displayed scrolling word-for-word on the screen, as is the case in respoken TV subtitles in the UK and in the above experiment on comprehension? How are these subtitles processed by the viewers?

Although not exactly applied to subtitles, the news coming from the field of psychology in this regard is discouraging. Experiments conducted by Rayner *et al.* (2006:321) demonstrate "the importance of the continued presence of the word to the right of fixation ... in order for fluent reading to occur". It would seem that when our eyes are fixated on the foveal word (n), we have enough preview benefit of the next word, the parafoveal word (n+1), to pre-process it, which is crucial to maintaining normal patterns of reading behaviour. Needless to say, in scrolling subtitles, this word to the right of fixation, the n+1 word, is often unavailable for viewers, as words are displayed one at a time. In Rayner *et al.*'s study (2006), the absence of this word causes regressions (the eye moves back to previous words already read) and considerable disruption to reading, slowing down reading speed significantly. The aim of the following experiment is precisely to look at how viewers process respoken subtitles displayed in scrolling mode (as opposed to respoken subtitles displayed in blocks) and to determine whether this may have any effect on the poor results obtained in the comprehension tests.

11.2.2. Description of the experiment

Conceived as an initial application of eye-tracking to research in respeaking, the present experiment was conducted with 30 of the 60 participants who took part in the comprehension tests described above: 10 hearing, 10 hard of hearing and 10 deaf viewers. Participants were shown two news clips from *Six O'Clock News* (4 July 2004) subtitled by respeaking. The first clip was subtitled in scrolling mode (word-by-word); the second, in blocks. Eye movements were monitored via a non-intrusive tracker, which was used to determine a) the number of fixations per subtitled line and b) the amount of time spent on images as opposed to the time spent on subtitles. The equipment used was Tobii X120 series eye tracker. The clips were presented on a 17" monitor at a viewing distance of 60 cm. The computer kept a complete record of the duration, sequence, and location of each eye fixation, as well as a video recording of the participants. Tobii Studio was used to analyze all data recorded.

11.2.3. Findings

Tables 11.4 and 11.5 show the results obtained in the study, namely the number of fixations per (full) subtitled line and the time spent on both block subtitles and scrolling subtitles.

Number of fixations

	Blocks	Scrolling
Hearing	3.75	6
Hard of Hearing	3.75	6.5
Deaf	3.9	6.5

Table 11.4: Fixations with subtitles in blocks and scrolling

Time spent on images

	Blocks	Scrolling
Hearing	33.3%	11.7%
Hard of Hearing	33.2%	11.4%
Deaf	31.7%	14.3%

Table 11.5: Time spent on images with subtitles in blocks and scrolling

11.2.4. Discussion

In line with what was described regarding the comprehension test, the results are fairly consistent across hearing, hard of hearing and deaf viewers. Scrolling subtitles cause almost twice as many fixations as block subtitles. The number of fixations per full subtitled line in scrolling mode ranges from 3 to 10, with an average of 6 for hearing viewers and 6.5 for hard of hearing and deaf viewers. Given that the average number of words per line in the clips analyzed is 6, it would seem that hearing viewers fixate on every word of every scrolling subtitle and deaf and hard of hearing viewers feature even more fixations than words. In contrast, the number of fixations in block subtitles ranges from 2 to 6, with an average of 3.75 fixations for hearing and hard of hearing viewers and 3.9 for deaf viewers. In other words, viewers skip almost every other word of the subtitle when reading it. Needless to say, this has a direct impact on the time viewers spend looking at the subtitles and the time they devote to the images. As shown above, viewers of the scrolling mode spend most of their time reading the subtitles (an average of 87.5% vs. 12.5% spent on the images), whereas viewers of block subtitles have more time to focus on the images (an average of 67.3% on the subtitles and 32.7% on the images).

The analysis of the reading patterns of each participant reveals another interesting element. Rather than differentiating the participants into hearing, deaf and hard of hearing, the results seem to establish a distinction between fast and slow readers. Besides, there seem to be two phenomena, astray fixations and regressions, that may explain the viewers' difficulty reading scrolling subtitles and perhaps the poor comprehension results obtained in the previous experiment. As for fast readers, they often get ahead of the subtitles and cast their eyes on gaps where no word has been displayed yet, which results in astray fixations. Instead of finding solid ground (a word or a whole line), the viewers' gaze falls on a sort of quicksand, which causes them to lose precious time in their reading process. In figures 11.4, 11.5, 11.6 and 11.7, this "quicksand effect" occurs in four out of five attempts of the viewer to read the line 'at least one is in the operating room'. The viewer ends up wasting a whole second (0.250 ms per each of the four astray fixations) when reading this line.

On average, these fast readers incur in two astray fixations per subtitled line. Half of the times this happens, they go back and re-read at least one word, which means they incur in one regression per subtitled line. The other half of the times, they decide to go on reading the subtitle.

In contrast, slow readers do not get ahead of the subtitles (they usually lag behind them) and therefore their patterns do not feature astray fixations and the quicksand effect. However, their eyes often "land" on words in the middle of a subtitle which are not meaningful enough to make sense of what is being said. In order to go on reading, they have to go back and re-read previous words, which has happened 1.5 times per line in the subjects analyzed.

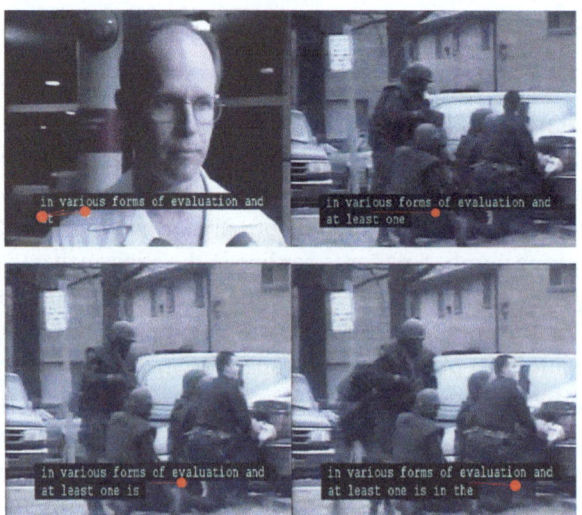

Figures 11.4, 11.5, 11.6 and 11.7: The quicksand effect

In figures 11.8 and 11.9, the viewer, who has been looking at the images, casts his or her eyes on the word "patients". Not being able to retrieve the information of the subtitled line by reading this word, he or she goes back to the previous one ("several") and yet one more time (to "we've got"), which finally provides enough information to go on reading after "patients". By then, though, the viewer has spent over a second reading a subtitle backwards:

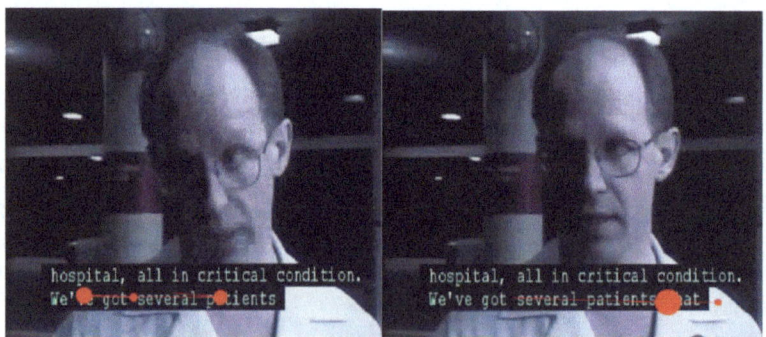

Figures 11.8 and 11.9: Regressions

In contrast with the chaotic patterns shown in scrolling subtitles, the reading pattern of block subtitles seems faster and more organized. Corroborating Jensema *et al.*'s observations (2000), viewers' gaze turns quickly to the subtitles, where this time they find firm ground on which to cast their eyes before looking up to the images. Thus, the same line as before ("we've got several patients that are") displayed in a block is read by this viewer in only four fixations (on "we've", "several", "patients" and "that"). There is no need to read all words and considerably less time is spent on the subtitle, which allows more time to focus on the image:

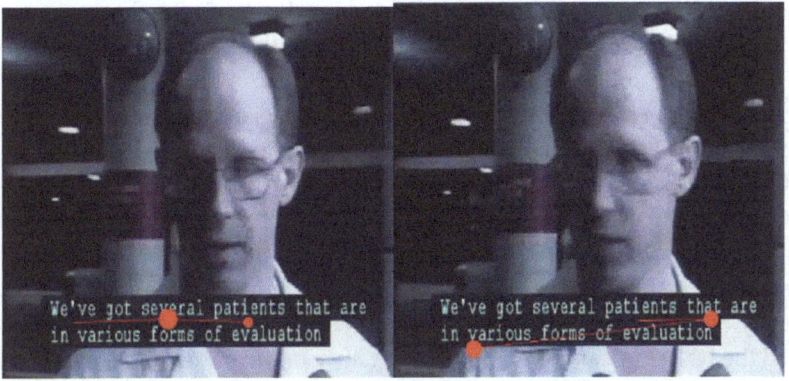

Figures 11.10 and 11.11: Viewing pattern with block subtitles

In other words, as anticipated in the literature on psycholinguistics and corroborated by the experiments included here, it would seem that scrolling word-for-word subtitles cause very chaotic reading patterns. Fast readers get ahead of the subtitles and cast their eyes on gaps without words (astray fixations), whereas slow readers lag behind and constantly go back to re-read words (regressions). Either way, they all waste precious time chasing subtitles which seem to be playing hide-and-seek with them and which prevent them from looking at the images.

Needless to say, this chaotic reading pattern and the almost non-existent time left to look at the images may go some way towards explaining the poor comprehension results obtained by these participants in the comprehension test described in this chapter. What remains to be seen now is what viewers think about this and other types of respoken subtitles. Are they happy with them? Do they realize that this display mode may be hindering their comprehension of live programmes?

11.3. Viewers' opinion about respoken subtitles

11.3.1. Introduction

Very often, the decisions adopted by broadcasters regarding subtitling features are based on the viewers' preferences. This sounds logical and certainly preferable to adopting decisions without consulting the audience, but there are still some aspects to be taken into consideration. On the one hand, it may be useful to conduct comprehension studies and perhaps even eye-tracking studies, such as the ones included in this chapter, to ascertain whether (and how) viewers understand subtitled programmes. On the other hand, viewers' preferences are not set in stone, which means that surveys need to be conducted periodically.

To give but one example, the choice of scrolling versus block subtitles in the UK has traditionally been based on two arguments, namely that scrolling subtitles have less delay than block subtitles and that viewers prefer them over the latter for live programmes. As explained in Chapter 3, the first argument can now be refuted, as respoken subtitles produced with Dragon may have a similar delay to scrolling subtitles produced with ViaVoice. As for the second argument, it is necessary to revisit viewers' preferences, especially considering the lack of reception studies on live subtitling.

One of the most recent surveys is the one carried out in early 2009 by the Royal National Institute for Deaf People (RNID) in the UK (http://www.rnid.org. uk/howyoucanhelp/join_rnid/_member_community/volunteering_campaigning/ volunteering_campaigning_news/tvaccessresults.htm). Although it was focused generally on TV access, participants identified subtitling as the main issue they wanted the RNID to campaign on. Almost 80% of the participants had had problems with subtitles and more than half had to stop watching a programme as a result. The two main problems were the delay of subtitles with regard to the audio (25%) and their inaccuracy (17%), identified as more important factors than having no subtitles available (7%). In other words, viewers seem to prioritize now quality over quantity and, judging by their main concerns (delay and accuracy), it is the quality of live subtitling they are particularly worried about.

In view of the lack of data regarding viewers' preferences about live subtitling, we decided to conduct a survey which was disseminated through the RNID website.[1] The following section includes a description of the participants and a discussion of the results, thus completing the last part of this chapter on the quality of respoken subtitles.

11.3.2. Description of the survey

Out of a total of 434 viewers who participated in the survey, 259 were hard of hearing and 164 were deaf, of whom 27 were BSL users. Only 11 viewers were hearing, so the results included here will focus mainly on the first two groups. More than half of the participants (58.7%) were over 60 years old, 33% were between 35 and 59 and 8.3% were between 17 and 34. This reflects the reality of the UK, where the largest group of SDH viewers are hard of hearing over 60. As for education, most participants in the survey (72.6%) attended university or a technical college. Finally, with regard to subtitle use, 70% of the participants use subtitles all the time, while 20% watch them some of the time, 6.5% only occasionally and 2.5% never. Deaf viewers proved more likely to use subtitles as the only way to access the audio of the programmes, whereas in the case of hard of hearing viewers, the results were more evenly split among those who use them to understand the original soundtrack better and those who rely on them completely.

Participants were asked 14 questions regarding live subtitling. The first three questions covered general aspects, namely how live subtitles are produced (questions 1 and 2) and the viewers' opinion on their quality (3). The next six questions (4-9)

---

[1] The complete survey can be found in https://rnid.wufoo.com/forms/what-are-your-views-on-tv-subtitling/.

asked for the viewers' opinion of live subtitling in the main UK channels: BBC, ITV, Channel 4, Channel 5 and Sky. Finally, the last 5 questions (10-14) dealt with specific respeaking issues such as mistakes, delay and display mode.

11.3.3. Results of the survey

Awareness of how live subtitles are produced (questions 1 and 2)
The survey shows that most participants don't know how live subtitles are produced. Out of the few (26.7%) who claim to know, only 13.3% identify current live subtitling methods. In this sense, there seems to be a general belief that live subtitles are produced by automatic SR, with little or mostly no human intervention. In other words, viewers' expectations of current SR technology are unrealistic, which may go some way towards explaining some frequent complaints about live subtitles not being error-free or in perfect synch with the original soundtrack. As for respeaking, only 3.5% of the participants knew this method. Overall, deaf participants proved more knowledgeable about live subtitling methods than the hard of hearing, and so did frequent subtitle users. According to this, the more viewers rely on subtitles, the more likely they are to know about them and perhaps to take an interest in how they are produced. In any case, the very low figures regarding knowledge about live subtitling in general and respeaking in particular send a worrying message about the visibility of this activity.

General opinion of live subtitles in the UK (question 3)
There is overall dissatisfaction with live subtitles in the UK. Most participants (55%) think they could be better, many (30.6%) find them unsatisfactory and only 11.2% consider them satisfactory. Deaf viewers seem to have a more favourable opinion than hard of hearing viewers, and so do frequent subtitle users as compared to occasional users, 50% of whom find live subtitles unsatisfactory. In other words, it would seem that the more viewers watch, or rely on, live subtitles, the happier they are with them. However, it must be noted that this difference is only reflected in more viewers choosing the "could be better" option rather than the "unsatisfactory" option. The percentage of viewers regarding live subtitles satisfactory remains worryingly low at 12%.

Opinion on subtitles as shown in the BBC, ITV, Channel 4, Channel 5 and Sky (questions 4-9)
As shown in this survey, BBC live subtitles are rated slightly more favourably than those shown on other UK channels, 28% of the participants considering them satisfactory. Yet, in line with what was explained in the previous section, most participants (52.2%) think they could be better and 19.7% find them unsatisfactory. In general, participants seem to be very familiar with live subtitles on the BBC and deaf viewers have a higher opinion of them than hard of hearing viewers.

As for live subtitles on ITV, the general opinion is slightly worse than that of BBC subtitles. Although there is a similar result regarding those who think they could be better (56%), fewer viewers find them satisfactory (18.6%) and more find them unsatisfactory (25.3%).

As for live subtitles on Channel 4, Channel 5 and Sky, participants do not seem to be very familiarized with them. 25.5% chose the "I don't know" option for Channel 4, 38% for Channel 5 and as many as 62.9% for Sky. In general, viewers seem to have a better opinion of live subtitles on Channel 4 than those on ITV, whereas Channel 5 and Sky obtain the lowest scores (with a dissatisfaction rate of 32.3% and 38.5% respectively).

More specific comments made by some participants show criticism of the subtitles provided in some sports events, many regional news programmes (where subtitles seem to disappear or to be very poor) and especially talk shows. In this sense, programmes such as *Question Time*, *Have I Got News for You*, *Mock the Week* and *The One Show* are singled out as particularly problematic. Of all the issues identified, the main concern seems to be the delay of the subtitles followed by the number of mistakes, which seems particularly noticeable in regional news. Other complaints refer to not being able to see the speakers' faces to lip read what they say, excessive editing, volume of commercials being too loud, unnecessary on-air corrections and failure to indicate in the subtitles that a new topic is being introduced.

In sum, participants are no longer placing the emphasis on quantity but on quality, which seems very much subject to improvement.

Extent to which errors affect comprehension of respoken subtitles (question 10)
The results obtained for this question show that participants are split between those who think that it is often possible (45%) to understand the original meaning when there is a mistake in live subtitles and those who think it is only sometimes possible (45.5%). A noticeable difference is found here between deaf and hard of hearing viewers. Whereas the former struggle to restore the original meaning more than half of the times, the latter tend to find it easier. This makes sense considering that many hard of hearing viewers can mentally correct a misrecognized word by thinking of the similar-sounding word that was meant to be in its place. Many deaf viewers, particularly the pre-lingually deaf, who have no recollection of sounds, may not be able to do so.

General opinion on delay, considering that it is currently impossible to eliminate (questions 11, 12 and 13)
Most participants (49.6%) find the current delay of respoken subtitles on UK TV channels unsatisfactory. Although a significant percentage (35.5%) find it satisfactory, there are more who consider it very unsatisfactory (10.2%) than very satisfactory (2%).

When asked whether it is possible to relate the subtitles to the images despite the delay, results are worse than in the question about mistakes and a similar distinction between deaf and hard of hearing may be found. Whereas hard of hearing participants are evenly split between those who can often relate images and subtitles and those who can only do it sometimes, most deaf participants choose the latter option. In any case, it seems that most people find more difficult to relate the subtitles to the images than to mentally correct mistakes. This may explain why, in question 13, when asked whether it is more important to reduce the delay or to reduce the mistakes in respoken subtitles, two out of three participants chose delay over mistakes, with very similar results among deaf and hard of hearing viewers.

General opinion on the display mode of live subtitles (question 14)
As noted above, the viewers' preference for word-for-word subtitles is often posited as one of the main reasons why live subtitles in the UK are not displayed in blocks. Yet, the results obtained in this survey question this assumption. Far from showing a clear preference for scrolling subtitles, the results are very even and, if anything, more favourable to block subtitles (45.6% versus 44.8%). A more thorough analysis reveals that word-for-word display is mostly preferred by deaf viewers, particularly those who use BSL or who have lost their hearing at birth or in the first years of their lives. Many of them cannot hear the original soundtrack but they understand how people speak and they know language is not spoken in blocks, but word for word. Some of these viewers specified in the survey that subtitles displayed in blocks look manipulated, edited or tampered with, whereas scrolling subtitles look like the real thing, giving them the impression that they are listening with their eyes in real time. Yet, this doesn't apply to all deaf viewers and certainly not to hard of hearing viewers, who seem to be more favourable towards blocks. In this sense, the strongest preference for blocks is registered among those participants who may be described as "most different" from the above-mentioned deaf viewers, that is, hard of hearing viewers who are not BSL users, who resort to lip-reading and who have lost their hearing after the age of 50.

In any case, what is interesting here is that, contrary to what has been held for a long time now, there is no overall preference for word-for-word subtitles over subtitles in blocks. Taking into account the potential negative effect that scrolling subtitles may have in terms of comprehension, their choice for live subtitles no longer seems justified.

11.4. Discussion points and exercises

11.4.1. Processing subtitles: eye-tracking

You can find the videos that you need for this section in DVD > Chapter 11 > Discussion points and exercises > 11.4.1.

Watch the video "Eye-Tracker 1", which shows how a hard of hearing person views a news programme with live respoken subtitles. As you can see, the news clip is repeated three times with three sets of subtitles. What is the difference between them? Does this have any effect on the eye-movements of the viewer? How do the three parts of the clip differ in terms of:

- time devoted to images vs. time devoted to subtitles?
- number of fixations per subtitle?
- number of regressions per subtitle?

Watch the video "Eye-Tracker 2", which shows how a hard of hearing person views a clip with pre-recorded subtitles. How does it compare to the previous clip in terms of:

- time devoted to images vs. time devoted to subtitles?
- number of fixations per subtitle?
- number of regressions per subtitle?

On the basis of these two videos, how would you describe the viewing patterns of the human eye when watching subtitles?

11.4.2. The viewers' opinions

You can find the documents that you need for this section in DVD > Chapter 11 > Discussion points and exercises > 11.4.2.

Read "RNID - Live subtitles – Leaflet" and "Complaints about Live Subtitling". These documents contain some of the most common complaints expressed by the viewers about live subtitles in the UK. What would you say are their main concerns? In your view, are they justified? In the second document, the complaints are grouped as received by deaf and hard of hearing viewers? Is there any noticeable difference between them?

Read "SDH in the UK – The Viewers' Preferences", which features a thorough study on the viewers' preferences regarding pre-recorded SDH in the UK. Do their views on the different SDH conventions correspond to current SDH practice in the UK? What is the main difference between deaf and hard of hearing viewers as indicated in this report? How do the viewers' opinions on pre-recorded subtitles compare to those on live subtitles?

In view of the constraints of live subtitling, it seems difficult to produce error-free synchronized subtitles that can be completely satisfactory for the viewers. Yet, this is what has been achieved in the Netherlands in the case of interlingual subtitles for live programmes. The video "The Netherlands – Interlingual subtitling 1" shows a first unsuccessful attempt, whereas "The Netherlands – Interlingual subtitling 2" achieves this purpose. How do they manage to overcome the issue of delay and errors?

12. Final Thoughts

A common problem in publications about Audiovisual Translation is that any attempt to capture the present state of affairs is bound to become obsolete soon. This is certainly the case in live subtitling, where the rapid evolution of the technology involved turns the present even more quickly into the past.

Yet, the ever-changing nature of live subtitling in general and respeaking in particular doesn't justify the absence of publications in this area. Software changes and practices evolve, true, but respeakers still have to learn how to respeak, trainers still need guidance on how to train and researchers can do with ideas to conduct their research. The aim of this book has been to present respeaking as one of many approaches to live subtitling or real-time transcription, and to provide students with the necessary skills to respeak professionally. It is now time to look ahead and focus on what role respeakers will be playing in the future of live subtitling and real-time transcription.

First of all, respeaking may be expected to be introduced in countries where it hasn't been tested (South Africa), to become consolidated in countries where it has only recently been introduced (Spain, France, Germany) and to extend to different settings in countries where it has already been consolidated for some time (UK, USA). But it must be remembered that respeaking is a means to an end: to subtitle or transcribe in real time. It is thus necessary to look at the bigger picture and see what role it will play among other methods and approaches. For the time being, it looks like SR is here to stay and that it will very much determine the future of this field.

Two outcomes may be expected here: the improvement of the respeaking technique and, eventually, its disappearance. Firstly, the new improvements in SR technology and the use of more powerful computers may lead to shorter training periods, more refined acoustic and language models and better recognition, approaching the coveted 100% accuracy rate. It is important at this stage to keep pushing for the improvement of both the quantity and quality of live subtitles. New legislation is needed in those countries where the provision of live subtitles is still not a legal requirement. As far as quality is concerned, there are still many issues to be tackled by broadcasters, subtitling companies and researchers, such as the refinement and harmonization of methods to calculate accuracy in respeaking or reception studies to assess the viewers' perceptions, comprehension and opinions of respoken subtitles. Other important issues are recognition errors (how to deal with them, when to correct them) and, most importantly, the delay, often singled out as the number one concern for the viewers. If, as seems to be the case, Dragon is to replace other types of software in live subtitling, a different approach to dictation in respeaking will be needed to keep delay to a minimum. The use of respeaking units, as has been explained in this book, may suit this purpose, while helping (a) respeakers to make sense of the original text, (b) the software to increase accuracy by focusing on phrases rather than individual words and (c) viewers to read commonsensical blocks instead of individual words scrolling across the bottom of the screen.

A more long-term solution to solving the lack of synchrony of images, sound and subtitles is to establish a video delay that can allow respeakers to prepare their subtitles and launch them a few seconds later. This is how some Dutch channels have managed to produce error-free real-time synchronized interlingual subtitles for events such as Obama's inauguration speech. Needless to say, this approach raises issues of competition among channels and even censorship, but this could be solved if the decision to have or not have the signal delayed was taken at the viewers' end. Be that as it may, partnership between enterprise and academia, which has so far not been very successful in this field, is a key element to make research viable and ultimately successful. A good example of this partnership is shown in the video "BBC Item on Respeaking" (DVD > Chapter 11 > Discussion points and exercises > 11.4.3), which sums up many of the contents included in this book.

Finally, as has been mentioned, the evolution of SR technology and particularly of speaker-independent SR may reach a stage where no respeakers are needed, where the speakers' words will be directly transcribed into subtitles. Viewers will have to decide whether this is desirable, as it will involve verbatim subtitles which may reach very high speeds. For the time being, it doesn't seem possible. There are still no solutions for issues such as punctuation, speaker identification and the transcription of overlapping dialogue, which means that the reality that Kubrick and Clarke envisaged for their computer HAL in *2001: A Space Odyssey* still belongs, in 2010, to the realm of science fiction.

Thus, for the foreseeable future, it looks like respeakers will still be asked to write with their voices so that deaf and hard of hearing viewers can listen with their eyes.

Glossary

Acoustic model: a collection of speech data located in the speech engine of an SR programme. It comprises (a) a large amount of audio material, (b) its exact proofed and corrected transcription, and (c) the digital representation of that audio material in the way of waveforms of individual sounds; in other words, what this audio material looks like mathematically.

As-live programmes: those which feature a broadcast delay, also known as tape delay, to prevent undesirable material from making it to air, namely technical malfunctions, coughing or more serious problems to do with profanity.

Auto-caps: see *auto-captioning*.

Auto-captioning: also known as *auto-captions* or *auto-caps*, this is a service resulting from the combination of Google's automatic *SR* and the Youtube caption system that offers users the possibility of having their videos subtitled automatically. The algorithms in Google voice are used to parse words within videos and transform them into captions.

Auto-captions: see *auto-captioning*.

Automatic punctuation: automatic introduction of punctuation marks by a *SR* programme.

Auto-punctuation: see *automatic punctuation*.

Auto-timing: application developed by Google for Youtube which enables users to upload their own subtitles without any timecodes. Google's speaker-independent *SR* software identifies when the words are spoken and creates captions for the video.

Caption: term used to refer to a subtitle aimed at deaf and hard of hearing viewers, usually in the US.

Captioning: term used to refer to subtitling for the deaf and hard of hearing (SDH), especially in the US.

CART: abbreviation for Communication Access Realtime Translation, in other words, speech-to-text transcription in counselling sessions, meetings, teleconferences, seminars, classrooms, etc.

Closed captions: see *closed subtitles*.

Closed subtitles: subtitles that are encoded in the video signal but are not visible unless they are activated with a decoder. They can be found in many DVDs and on teletext and are not an integral part of the audiovisual programme.

Correcteur: member of a respeaking team who is in charge of correcting misrecognitions and validating the subtitles so that they can go on air. See *technique du perroquet*.

Cue(ing): also known as *timing* or *spotting*, this is the process whereby the in- and out-times of individual subtitles are found.

Dual keyboard: also known as *tandem*, this is a *live subtitling* technique in which two operators take turns to transcribe alternate utterances, for instance subtitling a sentence each or even completing each other's sentences.

Fixation: the maintaining of the visual gaze on a single location for a given period of time, during which visual information is obtained. See also *saccade*.

Interlingual subtitles: subtitles that involve the translation from a source language into a target language.

Intralingual subtitles: subtitles in the same language as the dialogue of the audiovisual programme. They are usually aimed at deaf and hard of hearing viewers, but they can also be used for karaoke as well as for teaching and even therapeutic purposes.

Language model: a probabilistic mechanism included in a *SR* programme. It calculates the likelihood of occurrence of a word string. In other words, it analyzes the word recognized by the *acoustic model* and calculates how likely it is to have occurred after the previous words and before the next words in the speaker's utterance.

Latency: the time that elapses between the moment in which the respeaker utters a *respeaking unit* and the moment in which the recognised utterance is displayed on the screen.

Live-ondertiteling: term used in Flanders to refer to *live subtitling* and/or *respeaking*.

Live subtitling: subtitling produced during the broadcasting of a live programme.

Macro: a vocal shortcut or customized command created by the user of a *SR* programme to achieve a given intended affect. Respeakers use macros to save time and to make sure that certain phrases or labels are recognised correctly.

N-gram models: probabilistic models that provide the *SR* software with statistical information that helps to improve recognition accuracy.

Offline subtitling: see *pre-recorded subtitling*.

Online subtitling: see *live subtitling*.

Open subtitles: subtitles that are not encoded in the video signal and are always on the screen.

Perroquet: term used in France to refer to a respeaker who applies the *technique du perroquet*. See also *correcteur*, *souffleur* and *technique du perroquet*.

Pre-prepared subtitling: see *pre-recorded subtitling*.

Pre-recorded subtitling: subtitling that is done before the broadcasting of a programme. Also known as *offline subtitling* and *pre-prepared subtitling*.

Realtime subtitling: synonym of *live subtitling*, often used in the US.

Realtime subtitling via speech recognition: synonym *of respeaking*.

Realtime voice writing: term used in the US to refer to *respeaking*.

Rédacteur oral: term used in France to refer to a respeaker.

Rehablado: term used in Spain to refer to *respeaking*.

Respeaking: technique in which a subtitler listens to the original sound of a live programme or event and respeaks it, including punctuation marks and some specific features for the deaf and hard of hearing audience, to a speech recognition software, which turns the recognized utterances into subtitles displayed on the screen with the shortest possible delay.

Respeaking unit: the units of meaning used by respeakers; whenever possible, idea units that lend themselves to accurate recognition by the *SR* software (phrases as opposed to single words) and to comfortable reading for the viewers (around one line in a one-, two- or three-line subtitle).

Revoicing: synonym of *respeaking*, common in the US.

Saccade: jump between fixations in which no useful visual information is obtained. See also *fixation*.

Salami technique: a technique in which long or complex sentences are cut into short and more comprehensible sentences to help interpreters and, in this case, respeakers.

Screencast: a digital recording of computer screen output often containing audio narration. It is now a commonly used tool for software developers to show their work, for users to report bugs and especially for teachers and instructors to explain how different programmes work in online courses.
SDH: abbreviation for Subtitles for the Deaf and Hard of Hearing.
Semi-live subtitling: subtitling that is produced in advance but is launched manually during transmission or projection of a programme, theatre play, opera, etc. See *surtitles*.
Shadow speaking: term used in Canada to refer to *respeaking*.
Souffleur: member of a respeaking team who is in charge of (a) checking what is being said by the respeaker against what is being displayed on the screen and (b) warning the corrector should a sentence need to be modified. See *correcteur*, *perroquet* and *technique du perroquet*.
Sous-titrage vocal: term used in France to refer to *respeaking*.
Speaker-dependent SR: type of *SR* that requires users to train the software so that it learns about their pronunciation, speech patterns, etc. This technology allows for the use of very large vocabularies with high recognition (98% to 99%) and is the one chosen for respeaking so far.
Speaker-independent SR: type of *SR* that can recognise different speakers without any training. In order to achieve optimum accuracy, it is often used with small vocabularies, such as telephone menus.
Speech-based live subtitling: synonym of *respeaking*.
Speech captioning: synonym of *respeaking*.
Speech recognition: a process whereby a computer speech engine recognizes speech and converts it into text or executes verbal commands. See *voice recognition*.
Speech recognition-based subtitling: synonym of *respeaking*.
Spotting: see *cue(ing)*.
SR: abbreviation for *Speech Recognition*.
Steno: short for *Stenotype*.
Stenotype: a chording system used for *live subtitling*. The operator can press multiple keys simultaneously to spell out whole syllables, words and phrases with a single hand motion.
Surtitles: subtitles produced in *semi-live* mode for operas and theatre performances.
Tandem: see *dual keyboard*.
Technique du perroquet: term used in France as a synonym of *respeaking*. It often refers to a two- or three-people team. First of all, a respeaker (*perroquet*) listens to the original soundtrack of a programme and respeaks it in the "traditional" sense. A whisperer (*souffleur*), sitting next to the respeaker, checks what is being said by the respeaker against what is being displayed on the screen and, should a sentence need to be modified, warns the corrector about it. Finally, the corrector (*correcteur*), sitting beside the whisperer, is mainly in charge of correcting misrecognitions and validating the subtitles so that they can go on air. In some cases, the whisperer is not included in this process.
Timing: see *cue(ing)*.
Velotype: a syllabic chord keyboard used for *live subtitling* which allows the user to press

several keys simultaneously, producing syllables and words rather than letters.

Voice recognition: a form of biometrics mainly used for security purposes to identify a specific individual on the basis of the unique characteristics of his or her voice. See *Speech Recognition*.

Voice writing: term used in the US to refer to *respeaking*. When a distinction is made between *realtime voice writing* and *voice writing*, the latter refers to the technique invented by Horace Webb in the 40s: the repetition of the original speech into a microphone using a stenomask for later transcription. In this case, it does not involve speech recognition or realtime transcription.

WER: abbreviation for Word Error Rate.

WPM: abbreviation for Word per Minute.

References

Arumí Ribas, Marta and Pablo Romero-Fresco (2008) 'A Practical Proposal for the Training of Respeakers', *Journal of Specialised Translation* 10: 106-127. Available online at http://www.jostrans.org/issue10/art_arumi.php (last accessed 2 April 2010).

Boulianne, Gilles, Jean-François Beaumont, Maryse Boisvert, Julie Brousseau, Patrick Cardinal, Claude Chapdelaine, Michel Comeau, Pierre Ouellet, Fréderic Osterrath and Pierre Dumouchel (2009) 'Shadow Speaking for Real-time Closed-captioning of TV Broadcasts in French', in Anna Matamala and Pilar Orero (eds) *Listening to Subtitles. Subtitles for the Deaf and Hard of Hearing*, Bern: Peter Lang: 191-207.

Carver, Ronald P. (1974) 'Improving Reading Comprehension: Measuring Readability', *American Institute for Research, Final Report*, R742.

------ (1976) 'Word Length, Prose Difficulty, and Reading Rates', *Journal of Reading Behavior* 8: 193-203.

Conrad, R. (1977) 'The Reading Ability of Deaf School-leavers', *British Journal of Education Psychology* 47: 138-48.

Chafe, Wallace L. (1980) 'The Deployment of Consciousness in the Production of a Narrative', in Wallace L. Chafe (ed.) *The Pear Stories: Cognitive, Cultural and Linguistic Aspects of Narrative Production*, Norwood, N. J.: Ablex Publishing Corp, 9-50.

------ (1985) 'Linguistic Differences Produced by Differences between Speaking and Writing', in David Olson, Nancy Torrance and Angela Hildyard (eds) *Literacy, Language, and Learning: The Nature and Consequences of Reading and Writing*, Cambridge: Cambridge University Press, 105-23.

Chaume, Frederic (2004a) 'Film Studies and Translation Studies: Two Disciplines at Stake in Audiovisual Translation', *Meta* 49(1): 12-24.

------ (2004b) *Cine y traducción*, Madrid: Cátedra.

Damper, Robert, Andrew Lambourne and David Guy (1985) 'Speech Input as an Adjunct to Keyboard Entry in Television Subtitling', in Brian Shackel (ed.) *Proceedings Human-Computer Interaction—INTERACT'84*, Amsterdam: North Holland, 203–208.

De Linde, Zoe and Neil Kay (1999) *The Semiotics of Subtitling*, Manchester: St. Jerome.

Díaz Cintas, Jorge (2008) 'Teaching and Learning to Subtitle in an Academic Environment', in Jorge Díaz Cintas (ed.) *The Didactics of Audiovisual Translation*, Amsterdam & Philadelphia: John Benjamins, 89-103.

------ and Aline Remael (2007) *Audiovisual Translation: Subtitling*, Manchester: St. Jerome.

Dumouchel, Pierre, Gilles Boulianne and Julie Brousseau (forthcoming) 'Measures for Quality of Closed Captioning', in Adriana Serban, Anna Matamala and Jean-Marc Lavaur (eds) *Audiovisual Translation in Close-up: Practical and Theoretical Approaches*, Bern: Peter Lang.

D'Ydewalle, Gery, Johan van Rensbergen and Joris Pollet (1987) 'Reading a Message When the Same Message is Available Auditorily in Another Language: The Case of Subtitling', in John Kevin O'Reagan and Ariane Lévy-Schoen (eds) *Eye Movements: From Physiology to Cognition*, Amsterdam & New York: Elsevier Science Publishers, 313-21.

------, Luc Warlop and Johan van Rensbergen (1989) 'Differences between Young and Older Adults in the Division of Attention over Different Sources of TV Information', *Medienpsychologie* 1: 42-57.

------, Caroline Praet, Karl Verfaillie and Johan Van Rensbergen (1991) 'Watching Subtitled Television: Automatic Reading Behaviour', *Communication Research* 18(5): 650-66.

------, Gery and Wim de Bruycker (2007) 'Eye Movements of Children and Adults While Reading Television Subtitles', *European Psychologist* 12(3): 196-205.

Encyclopaedia Britannica Online (2010). Available online at http://www.britannica.com/ (last accessed 2 May 2010).

Eugeni, Carlo (2006) 'Introduzione al rispeakeraggio televisivo', in Carlo Eugeni and Gabriele Mack (eds) *Intralinea, Special Issue on Respeaking*. Available at http://www.intralinea.it/specials/respeaking/eng_more.php?id=484_0_41_0_M (last accessed 26 March 2010).

------ (2008) 'A Sociolinguistic Approach to Real-time Subtitling: Respeaking vs. Shadowing and Simultaneous Interpreting', in Cynthia J. Kellett Bidoli and Elana Ochse (eds) *English in International Deaf Communication*, Bern: Peter Lang, 357-82.

------ (2009) 'Respeaking the BBC News. A Strategic Analysis of Respeaking on the BBC', *The Sign Language Translator and Interpreter (SLTI)* 3(1): 29-68.

European Broadcasting Union (EBU) (2004) *EBU Report on Access Services*, EBU Technical-Information, 144-2004.

------ (2005) *EBU Tech 3295: The EBU Metadata Exchange Scheme*, Version 1.2 Publication Release.

Gerver, David (1971) *Aspects of Simultaneous Interpretation and Human Information Processing*, Unpublished MA Thesis, Oxford: Oxford University.

Grabianowski, E. (2010) 'How Speech Recognition Works', in HowStuffWorks, available at http://electronics.howstuffworks.com/gadgets/high-tech-gadgets/speech-recognition.htm (last accessed 11 April 2010).

Häikiö, Tuomo, Raymond Bertram, Jukka Hyönä and Pekka Niemi (2009) 'Development of the Letter Identity Span in Reading: Evidence from the Eye Movement Moving Window Paradigm', *Journal of Experimental Child Psychology* 102: 167-81.

IBM (2010) 'History of Speech Recognition', *IBM Journal of Research and Development*, available at http://researchweb.watson.ibm.com/hlt/html/body_history.html (last accessed 11 April 2010).

Imhauser, Corinne (2007) '*Sous-titrage et formation en 2006'*, in Maria Teresa Musacchio and Geneviève Henrot Sostero (eds) *Tradurre: formazione e professione*, Padova: CLEUP, 237-42.

ITC (1999) *ITC Guidance on Standards for Subtitling*, London: Independent Television Commission.

Ivarsson, Jan and Mary Carroll (1998) *Subtitling*, Simrisham: TransEdit HB.
Jensema, Carl (1998) 'Viewer Reaction to Different Television Captioning Speeds', *American Annals of the Deaf* 143(4): 318-24.
------, Sameh El Sharkawy, Ramalinga S.Danturthi, Robert Burch and David Hsu (2000) 'Eye Movement Patterns of Captioned Television Viewers', *American Annals of the Deaf* 145(3): 275-85.
Jones, Roderick (1998) *Conference Interpreting Explained*, Manchester: St. Jerome.
Juang, Biing-Hwang and Lawrence R. Rabiner (2005) 'Automatic Speech Recognition – A Brief History of the Technology Development', in Keith Brown (ed.) *Encyclopedia of Language and Linguistics*, Amsterdam: Elsevier.
Kelly, James and Mack Steer (1949) 'Revised Concept of Rate', *Journal of Speech and Hearing Disorders* 14: 222-26.
Keyes, Bettye (2005) *Voice Writing Method*, VoiceCAT Corp., presented at the Intersteno Congress in Prague in July 2007.
------ (2007) 'Realtime by Voice: Just What You Need to Know', paper presented at the Intersteno Congress in Prague in July 2007.
Kurz, Ingrid (1992) "Shadowing' Exercises in Interpreter Training', in Cay Dollerup and Anne Loddegaard (eds) *Teaching Translation and Interpreting. Training, Talent and Experience*, Amsterdam & Philadelphia: John Benjamins, 245-50.
Kurzweil, Raymond (1996) 'When Will HAL Understand What We Are Saying? Computer Speech Recognition and Understanding', in David G. Stork (ed.) *HAL's Legacy: 2001's Computer as Dream and Reality*, Cambridge Massachussetts: MIT Press: 131-171.
Lambert, Sylvie (1992) 'Shadowing', *Meta* 37(2): 263-73.
------ (1993) 'The Effect of Ear of Information Reception on the Proficiency of Simultaneous Interpretation', *The Interpreters' Newsletter* 5: 22-34.
Lambourne Andrew, Jill Hewitt, Caroline Lyon and Sandra Warren (2004) 'Speech-Based Real-Time Subtitling Services', *International Journal of Speech Technology* 7(4): 269–79.
------ (2006) 'Subtitle Respeaking', in Carlo Eugeni and Gabriele Mack (eds) *Intralinea, Special Issue on Respeaking*. Available at http://www.intralinea.it/specials/respeaking/eng_more.php?id=484_0_41_0_M (last accessed 26 March 2010).
------ (2007) 'Real-time Subtitling: Extreme Audiovisual Translation', paper presented at *LSP Translation Scenarios* in Vienna in May 2007.
Liversedge, Simon P. and John M. Findlay (2000) 'Saccadic Eye Movements and Cognition', *Trends in Cognitive Science* 4: 6-14.
Luyckx, Bieke, Tijs Delbeke, Luuk Van Waes, Mariëlle Leijten and Aline Remael (2010) *'Live Subtitling with Speech Recognition: Causes and Consequences of Text Reduction',* Antwerp: Artesis Working Papers in Translation Studies 2010-1. Available at http://www.artesis.be/vertalertolk/upload/docs/onderzoek/Artesis_VT_working_paper_2010-1_Luyckx_et_alii.pdf (last accessed 26 September 2010).
Marsh, Alison (2004) *Simultaneous Interpreting and Respeaking: A Comparison*, Unpublished MA Thesis, London: University of Westminster.

Marsh, Alison (2006) 'Respeaking for the BBC', in Carlo Eugeni and Gabriele Mack (eds) *Intralinea, Special Issue on Respeaking*. Available at http://www.intralinea.it/specials/respeaking/eng_more.php?id=484_0_41_0_M (last accessed 26 March 2010).

Merriam-Webster's Online Dictionary (2010). Available online at http://www.merriam-webster.com/ (last accessed 2 May 2010).

Moussadek, Marion (2008) 'Sous-titreur pour sourds à la TV, un nouveau métier en Suisse', *Intermittent'Sign* 140: 15.

Muller, Tia (2009) *A Study on Televised Subtitling for Deaf and Hard-of-Hearing. The French Case*, Unpublished MA Thesis, London: Roehampton University.

Muzii, Luigi (2006) 'Respeaking e localizzazione', in Carlo Eugeni and Gabriele Mack (eds) *Intralinea, Special Issue on Respeaking*. Available at http://www.intralinea.it/specials/respeaking/eng_more.php?id=449_0_41_0_M (last accessed 26 March 2010).

NCRA (2008) *Realtime Broadcast Captioning: Recommended Style and Format Guidelines For U.S. Programming*, Virginia: NCRA Captioning Community of Interest.

Neves, Joselia (2005) *Audiovisual Translation: Subtitling for the Deaf an Hard-of-Hearing*, Unpublished PhD Thesis, London: University of Surrey-Roehampton.

------ (2008) '10 Fallacies about Subtitling for the d/Deaf and the Hard of Hearing', *The Journal of Specialised Translation* 10: 128-43.

National Verbatim Reporters Association (NVRA) (2008) 'Horace Web Story'. Available at http://www.nvra.org/displaycommon.cfm?an=1&subarticlenbr=10 (last accessed 26 March 2010).

OFCOM (2005) *Subtitling – An Issue of Speed?*, London: Office of Communications.

------ (2006) *Provision of Access Services*, London: Office of Communications.

Orero, Pilar (2006) 'Real-time Subtitling in Spain', in Carlo Eugeni and Gabriele Mack (eds) *Intralinea, Special Issue on Respeaking*. Available on http://www.intralinea.it/specials/respeaking/eng_more.php?id=449_0_41_0_M (last accessed 26 March 2010).

Perego, Elisa (2008) 'What Would We Read Best?'. *The Sign Language Translator and Interpreter (SLTI)* 2(1): 35-63.

Pöchhacker, Franz (2004) *Introducing Interpreting Studies*, London: Routledge.

Porteiro-Fresco, Minia (2009) 'Therapeutic Subtitling. The Use of Subtitles to Treat Speech-Language Disorders', paper presented at the 3rd International Conference 'Media for All': Quality made to measure, Antwerp, October.

Pym, Anthony (2009) *Exploring Translation Theories*, London: Routledge.

Rayner, Keith and Alexander Pollatsek (1989) *The Psychology of Reading*, Broadway (US): Lawrence Erlbaum Associates.

------, Simon P. Liversedge and Sarah J. White (2006) 'Eye Movements When Reading Disappearing Text: The Importance of the Word to the Right of Fixation', *Vision Research* 46: 310-23.

------ (1998) 'Eye Movements in Reading and Information Processing: 20 Years of Research', *Psychological Bulletin* 124: 372-422.

Remael, Aline (2007) 'Sampling Subtitling for the Deaf and the Hard-of-Hearing in

Europe', in Jorge Díaz Cintas, Aline Remael and Pilar Orero (eds) *Media for All*, Amsterdam: Rodopi, 23-52.

Remael, Aline and Bart van der Veer (2006) 'Real-time Subtitling in Flanders: Needs and Teaching', in Carlo Eugeni and Gabriele Mack (eds) *Intralinea, Special Issue on Respeaking*. Available at http://www.intralinea.it/specials/respeaking/eng_more.php?id=492_0_41_0_M (last accessed 26 March 2010).

------ (2007) 'Teaching Live-subtitling with Speech Recognition Technology: What Are the Challenges?', paper presented at *LSP Translation Scenarios* in Vienna in May 2007.

Romero-Fresco, Pablo (2008) 'La subtitulación rehablada: palabras que no se lleva el viento', in Álvaro Pérez-Ugena and Ricardo Vizcaíno-Laorga (eds) *ULISES: Hacia el desarrollo de tecnologías comunicativas para la igualdad de Oportunidades*, Madrid: Observatorio de las Realidades Sociales y de la Comunicación, 49-73.

------ (2009) 'More Haste Less Speed: Edited vs. Verbatim Respeaking', *Vigo International Journal of Applied Linguistics* (VIAL) VI: 109-33.

------ (2010) "Standing on Quicksand: Viewers' Comprehension and Reading Patterns of Respoken Subtitles for the News", in Jorge Díaz Cintas, Anna Matamala and Joselia Neves (eds.) New Insights into Audiovisual Translation and Media Accessibility. Media for All 2. Amsterdam: Rodopi: 175-195.

Sancho-Aldridge, Jane and IFF Research Ltd (1996) *Good News for Deaf People: Subtitling of National News Programmes*, London: Independent Television Commission.

Schweda Nicholson, Nancy (1990) 'The Role of Shadowing in Interpreter Training', *The Interpreters' Newsletter* 3: 33-37.

Seleskovitch, Danika and Miriam Lederer (1989) *Pédagogie raisonnée de l'interprétation*, Bruxelles-Luxembourg: Didier érudition Opoce.

Steinfield, Aaron (1999) *The Benefit to the Deaf of Real-time Captions in a Mainstream Classroom Environment*, Unpublished PhD Thesis. Michigan: The University of Michigan.

Torres Monreal, Santiago and Rafael Santana Hernández (2005) 'Reading Levels of Spanish Deaf Students', *American Annals of the Deaf* 150(4): 379-87.

Tuominen, Tiina (2008) 'Reception or Resistance? Some Observations on the Reception of Subtitled Films', paper presented at *Multidisciplinary Approaches*, University of Montpellier 3, on 19 June 2008.

Uglova, Natalia and Tatiana Shevchenko (2005) 'Not So Fast Please: Temporal Features in TV Speech', paper presented at the meeting of the Acoustical Society of America, Vancouver, BC in May 2005.

Van Dam, Ine-Marie (1989) 'Strategies of Simultaneous Interpretation', in Laura Gran and John Dodds (eds) *The Theoretical and Practical Aspects of Teaching Conference Interpretation*, Udine: Campanotto Editore, 167-76.

van der Veer Bart (2007) 'De tolk als respeaker: een kwestie van training', *Linguistica Antverpiensia* LA NS6: 315-28.

Vincent, Keith (2007) 'A Brief Presentation to Intersteno Participants', paper presented at the Intersteno Congress in Prague in July 2007.

Wingfield, Arthur, Sandra L. McCoy, Jonathan E. Peelle, Patricia A. Tun and Clarke

Cox (2006) 'Effects of Adult aging and Hearing Loss on Comprehension of Rapid Speech Varying in Syntactic Complexity', *Journal of the American Academy of Audiology* 17: 487-97.

Wolverton, Gary S. and David Zola (1983) 'The Temporal Characteristics of Visual Information Extraction during Reading', in Keith Rayner (ed.) *Eye Movements in Reading: Perceptual and Language Processes*, New York: Academic Press, 41-52.

Index

A

Access Innovation Media (Ai-Media) 143, 147
Accessibility 2, 10, 11, 23, 41, 123, 138, 140, 141, 145
Accuracy 15, 17, 19, 20, 27, 28, 30, 32, 34, 35, 36, 38, 39, 40, 42, 53, 54, 56, 57, 59, 60, 62, 64, 65, 66, 67, 68, 70, 71, 72, 74, 76, 77, 83, 86, 88, 89, 92, 94, 99, 101, 103, 109, 114, 119, 120, 122, 133, 136, 140, 141, 150, 151, 152, 153, 154, 155, 156, 157, 159, 160, 161, 162, 172, 177, 180, 181
Acoustic model 57, 58, 59, 60, 61, 67, 8, 81, 86, 87, 109, 179, 180
Artesis University College 10, 41
Arts venues 138, 140, 146
Arumí Ribas, Marta 45, 95
As-live programmes 12, 17, 179
Auto-caps 69, 179
Auto-captioning 69, 72, 179
Auto-captions 69, 179
Automatic punctuation 71, 73, 101, 102, 141, 179
Auto-punctuation 179
Auto-timing 69, 179

B

BBC 6, 8, 10, 15, 17, 20, 21, 22, 23, 24, 25, 43, 89, 109, 110, 114, 121, 122, 123, 126, 128, 129, 130, 133, 134, 135, 136, 137, 162, 163, 173, 178
Boulianne, Gilles 2

C

Captel 145, 146, 148
Caption / Captioning 6, 7, 9, 19, 39, 42, 69, 72, 98, 142, 143, 145, 147, 166, 179
 Closed 6, 9, 37, 138, 142, 145, 147
 Open 6, 138, 142, 147
 Realtime / Live 7, 15, 19, 21, 39, 40, 42, 143, 146
 Semi-live 39
 Theatre 138, 146, 147
Caption Mic 39, 40, 142, 146, 147, 148
Carroll, Mary 110
CART 38, 39, 42, 179
Carver, Ronald P. 114, 115
Chafe, Wallace L. 118, 163
Chaume, Frederic 97
Churches 2, 138, 143, 144, 148
Classroom 7, 9, 38, 44, 69, 75, 101, 138, 142, 143, 145, 147, 179
Colby 8, 36, 44, 55, 67, 102
Comma 33, 71, 73, 84, 100, 10, 102, 103, 104, 105, 106, 108, 109, 111, 117, 121, 156, 157, 158, 160
Commands 27, 49, 56, 63, 64, 67, 79, 80, 83, 84, 89, 99, 103, 144, 153, 156, 157, 158, 160, 180, 181
Conferences 2, 6, 19, 38, 39, 46, 56, 95, 118, 128, 138, 143, 144, 145, 148, 179
Conrad, R. 115
Convention 19, 22, 35, 38, 40, 103, 131, 163, 176
Correcteur 3, 35, 179, 180, 181
Correction 3, 16, 17, 20, 33, 34, 35, 37, 38, 40, 46, 48, 49, 53, 75, 81, 85, 86, 93, 95, 99, 100, 107, 121, 144, 150, 154, 158, 174
 Method 2, 16, 84
 Parallel 16
 Self- 16, 17, 25, 28, 32, 35, 40
CRIM 37, 38, 71, 152, 161
Cue(ing) 13, 23, 26, 179, 181

D

Damper, Robert 8
De Bruycker, Wim 115
De Linde, Zoe 114

Debate 4, 13, 15, 25, 123, 130, 131, 134, 136, 165
Décalage 53, 99, 101, 107, 108
Deictics 97, 98, 99
Delay 1, 2, 12, 13, 15, 16, 17, 19, 20, 26, 28, 29, 30, 32, 33, 35, 36, 37, 38, 40, 43, 44, 50, 60, 64, 65, 66, 83, 97, 102, 103, 107, 108, 109, 118, 124, 125, 126, 127, 128, 133, 134, 136, 139, 140, 141, 144, 154, 171, 172, 173, 174, 175, 176, 177, 178, 179, 180
Díaz Cintas, Jorge 12, 103, 104, 109, 113
Dictation 7, 27, 42, 49, 60, 61, 62, 63, 64, 65, 66, 67, 68, 72, 73, 74, 75, 76, 77, 78, 79, 80, 81, 83, 84, 86, 93, 94, 95, 96, 97, 99, 103, 119, 120, 122, 141, 177
Dragon (NaturallySpeaking) 2, 7, 17, 24, 25, 26, 28, 29, 30, 31, 34, 36, 40, 41, 42, 44, 49, 50, 57, 59, 61, 62, 63, 64, 65, 66, 67, 68, 72, 73, 74, 75, 76, 78, 79, 80, 81, 82, 83, 84, 85, 88, 89, 90, 91, 92, 93, 94, 95, 96, 97, 101, 103, 108, 118, 133, 135, 141, 143, 144, 149, 156, 172, 177
Dragon Vocabulary Tool (Voctool) 92
DTV4ALL 162
Dual keyboard 13, 14, 34, 179, 181
Dumouchel, Pierre 151
D'Ydewalle, Gery 109, 115, 166

E

EclipseVox 40, 44
Editing 16, 25, 26, 28, 34, 47, 94, 99, 100, 101, 112, 113, 118, 119, 120, 121, 125, 126, 129, 130, 133, 136, 144, 152, 153, 154, 156, 157, 159, 161, 174
Error/s 13, 15, 16, 19, 20, 21, 27, 29, 30, 32, 33, 35, 36, 38, 39, 40, 43, 46, 49, 51, 54, 59, 72, 73, 75, 81, 84, 85, 86, 94, 119, 121, 123, 128, 130, 132, 133, 144, 150, 151, 152, 153, 154, 156, 157, 159, 161, 162, 173, 174, 176, 177, 178, 182
Eugeni, Carlo 2, 3, 6, 116, 126, 144
Eye-tracker / Eye-tracking 109, 115, 166, 168, 171, 175, 176

F

Findlay, John M. 166
Five-way keyboard 14
Fixation 166, 167, 168, 169, 170, 171, 176, 179, 180
FR3 36, 44

G

Genre 15, 25, 32, 35, 41, 52, 86, 102, 114, 123, 125, 130, 135, 161
Gerver, David 95
Google 56, 69, 70, 72, 147, 148, 179
Grabianowski, E. 61

H

Häikiö, Tuomo 167

I

IBM Hosted Transcription Service 69, 70, 72
Imhauser, Corinne 2
Independent Media Support (IMS) 5, 22, 23, 24, 25, 26, 27, 30, 43, 55, 65, 74, 154
Interpreting 4, 5, 31, 36, 40, 41, 42, 45, 46, 47, 48, 50, 51, 52, 53, 54, 55, 95, 96, 101, 107, 108, 110, 143, 144
Intersteno 19, 118
Interview 12, 15, 24, 25, 28, 29, 31, 32, 36, 97, 109, 114, 116, 118, 123, 128, 130, 134, 136, 137, 147, 152, 165
Italics 103
ITC 116, 118, 119
Ivarsson, Jan 110

J

Jensema, Carl 115, 116, 166, 170
Jones, Roderick 96, 107
Juang, Biing-Hwang 61

K

Kay, Neil 114
Kelly, James 114

Keyes, Bettye 2, 42, 48, 49
Knowbrainer 61, 68, 75, 80, 84, 92, 102
Kurz, Ingrid 47
Kurzweil, Raymond 61

L

Lambert, Sylvie 47
Lambourne, Andrew 2, 11, 13, 14, 15
Language model 57, 58, 59, 60, 61, 62, 66, 67, 71, 81, 82, 83, 86, 88, 89, 91, 92, 109, 152, 156, 177, 180
Latency 60, 64, 65, 68, 78, 80, 93, 94, 180
Lederer, Miriam 47
Legislation 6, 9, 10, 18, 34, 123, 162, 177
Liberated Learning Consortium (LLC) 63, 69, 70, 72, 147
Live-ondertiteling 3, 28, 180
Liversedge, Simon P. 166
Luyckx, Bieke 118

M

Macro 27, 49, 51, 65, 66, 86, 89, 90, 91, 98, 103, 131, 132, 133, 134, 180
Mark Hall Associates (MHA) 7, 39, 40, 138, 142, 145, 147,
Marsh, Alison 2, 14, 25, 45, 46, 49, 89, 123
Microphone 7, 24, 28, 30, 31, 37, 46, 58, 61, 63, 65, 66, 68, 74, 75, 77, 80, 84, 93, 96, 109, 141, 142, 147, 182
Moussadek, Marion 2
Muller, Tia 6, 11
Mundovisión 9, 27, 28
Museums 2, 138, 140, 142, 146
Muzii, Luigi 2

N

N-gram models 59, 62, 180
National Gallery 138, 139, 140, 141, 142
National Verbatim Reporters Association (NVRA) 7, 38, 39, 42
NaturallySpeakometer 80, 81, 94
NCRA 19, 40
NERD model 150, 152, 154, 161
Neves, Joselia 6, 17, 113, 115, 118
News 6, 7, 8, 9, 10, 12, 17, 20, 21, 22, 23, 24, 25, 26, 27, 28, 29, 30, 31, 32, 34, 35, 37, 41, 43, 46, 57, 59, 60, 77, 88, 92, 97, 104, 109, 110, 114, 116, 117, 118, 121, 122, 123, 125, 126, 127, 128, 129, 134, 135, 137, 163, 164, 165, 166, 168, 174, 175, 176
  Headlines 13, 125, 126, 128, 130, 134
  Reports 126, 128, 134, 135
  Summary 126, 130, 136
North-West University 143

O

Ofcom 10, 11, 18, 19, 112, 113, 115, 116
Orero, Pilar 6, 9

P

Perego, Elisa 109
Perroquet 3, 35, 179, 180, 181
Pöchhacker, Franz 95
Pollatsek, Alexander 166
Porteiro-Fresco, Minia 47
Punctuation 1, 14, 25, 32, 36, 37, 44, 45, 47, 48, 49, 53, 63, 64, 77, 80, 83, 84, 90, 93, 94, 95, 96, 97, 99, 101, 102, 103, 104, 105, 106, 117, 121, 141, 178, 179, 180
  Automatic 71, 73, 101, 102, 141, 179
Pym, Anthony 148

Q

Quick-sand effect 169, 170
QWERTY 7, 9, 13, 15, 22, 23, 27, 145

R

Rabiner, Lawrence R. 61
Rayner, Keith 166, 167
Reading
  Rate 112, 113, 114
  Speed 50, 54, 113, 114, 115, 116, 167
Realtime
  Subtitling via speech recognition 2, 3, 180
  Voice writing 2, 7, 38, 180, 182
Red Bee Media (RBM) 1, 3, 9, 17, 22,

23, 24, 25, 26, 27, 28, 30, 31, 36, 43, 55, 65, 74, 123, 126, 131
Rédacteur oral 3, 180
Regression 167, 169,
Rehablado 3, 4, 27, 180
Remael, Aline 6, 9, 12, 46, 48, 49, 50, 103, 104, 109
Respeaker / Respeaking
   Interlingual 1, 12, 13, 26, 30, 35, 41, 45, 46, 143, 145, 149, 176, 178
   Intralingual 1, 12, 17, 25, 26, 28, 30, 31, 32, 35, 38, 40, 45, 46, 143, 144
   Rate 113, 116, 119, 120
   Recruitment 22, 24, 31, 34, 36
   Rhythm 25, 80, 83, 84, 95, 107, 108, 121
   Skills 25, 28, 31, 34, 36, 39, 41, 42, 43, 45, 47, 48, 49, 50, 51, 52, 53, 54, 55, 56, 74, 95, 96, 99, 101, 119, 120, 121, 123, 132, 138, 150, 152, 154, 157, 177
   Speed 116, 117, 119, 120, 122
   Terminology 2, 3, 5, 39, 45
   Training 10, 15, 22, 24, 25, 27, 28, 29, 31, 32, 34, 38, 39, 40, 41, 42, 47, 49, 55, 65, 70, 95, 101, 118, 119, 120, 125, 141, 148, 149, 150, 152, 157, 177, 181
   Unit 53, 68, 77, 107, 108, 109, 112, 120, 121, 122, 156, 177, 180
   Working conditions 22, 23, 24
Revoicing 2, 180
Roehampton University 41, 116, 138, 141, 142, 148, 162, 163, 164
Romero-Fresco, Pablo 2, 3, 4, 16, 45, 95, 112, 114, 116, 118
Royal National Institute for Deaf People (RNID) 116, 145, 172, 176

S

Saccade 166, 179, 180
Salami technique 107, 109, 110, 111, 121, 180
Sancho-Aldridge, Jane 113
Santana Hernández, Rafael 115, 166
Schweda Nicholson, Nancy 47
Screencast/ing 70, 71, 181
SDH (Subtitling / subtitles for the deaf and hard of hearing) 6, 7, 9, 10, 11, 16, 17, 19, 20, 26, 27, 30, 35, 38, 40, 41, 43, 45, 47, 51, 52, 53, 54, 112, 114, 116, 130, 131, 132, 142, 162, 172, 176, 179, 181
Segmentation 54, 68, 108, 109, 110
Seleskovitch, Danika 47
Shadow speaking 2, 181
Shevchenko, Tatiana 114
Six-second rule 115
Sky 20, 21, 22, 23, 26, 27, 173, 174
Souffleur 3, 35, 180, 181
Soundtrack 1, 16, 17, 25, 26, 29, 35, 39, 69, 74, 95, 123, 133, 172, 173, 175, 181
Sous-titrage vocal 3, 181
Speech
   -based live subtitling 2, 4, 181
   Captioning 2, 143, 181
   -pause rhythm 83, 84, 108
   Rate 1, 8, 13, 16, 20, 21, 25, 26, 97, 107, 112, 113, 114, 116, 117, 118, 119, 122, 123, 126, 128, 129, 133, 134, 135, 137, 139, 140, 144, 153, 154, 156, 157
Speech recognition (SR)
   Software 1, 7, 9, 17, 22, 25, 29, 31, 32, 33, 34, 37, 38, 39, 40, 41, 42, 46, 47, 48, 49, 50, 51, 53, 57, 48, 60, 61, 62, 63, 64, 65, 68, 69, 70, 72, 74, 75, 76, 77, 78, 80, 81, 82, 83, 84, 86, 88, 89, 90, 91, 93, 94, 95, 96, 97, 102, 103, 108, 112, 117, 118, 119, 121, 132, 133, 136, 139, 141, 144, 149, 152, 154, 177, 179, 180, 181
   Speaker-dependent 48, 57, 62, 63, 70, 71, 181
   Speaker-independent 57, 61, 62, 69, 70, 71, 72, 75, 101, 141, 178, 179, 181
Split attention 34, 45, 95, 96, 120, 121
Sports 6, 7, 8, 12, 22, 23, 24, 25, 26, 28, 30, 32, 41, 44, 57, 97, 114, 116, 117, 118, 123, 124, 125, 132, 134, 174
Spotting 50, 52, 179, 181
Sprint Captel 145, 148
Stagetext 138, 139, 141, 142, 146
Steer, Mack 114
Steinfield, Aaron 114
Steno/type 7, 8, 10, 11, 13, 14, 15, 16, 19, 23, 27, 38, 39, 181

Stenography 13, 14, 39, 45
Stenomask 7, 143, 182
Subtitle / subtitling
  As-live 12
  (in) Blocks 17, 25, 26, 28, 29, 30, 32, 44, 64, 67, 78, 108, 118, 144, 167, 168, 169, 170, 171, 175, 178
  Character ID 17, 25, 26, 28, 32, 35, 38, 40
  Colour 8, 17, 21, 24, 25, 26, 28, 30, 32, 35, 47, 49, 53, 69, 70, 98, 99, 125, 131, 144
  Company/ies 2, 3, 9, 16, 17, 22, 23, 24, 25, 26, 27, 28, 34, 37, 39, 55, 60, 65, 67, 70, 89, 102, 103, 112, 115, 138, 143, 146, 150, 152, 154, 162, 177
  Conventions 19, 22, 35, 40, 103, 131, 163, 176
  Display Mode 17, 19, 32, 33, 34, 40, 44, 50, 64, 70, 78, 108, 171, 173, 175
  Edited 13, 16, 28, 30, 112, 113, 117, 118, 119, 144, 150, 152, 175
  Guidelines 18, 19, 40, 116, 118, 119
  Live 2, 4, 5, 6, 7, 8, 9, 10, 11, 12, 13, 15, 16, 17, 19, 20, 21, 22, 23, 24, 25, 26, 27, 28, 29, 30, 31, 32, 34, 36, 37, 38, 39, 41, 43, 44, 45, 55, 57, 60, 64, 70, 72, 73, 74, 76, 78, 80, 83, 93, 109, 123, 135, 138, 141, 143, 144, 147, 162, 172, 173, 174, 175, 176, 177, 179, 180, 181
  Near-verbatim 17, 25, 35, 38, 40
  Offline 38, 48, 162, 180
  Open 30, 180
  Position 8, 17, 24, 26, 28, 32, 35, 46, 49, 53, 70, 95, 131
  Pre-prepared 12, 180
  Pre-recorded 1, 2, 12, 17, 19, 23, 26, 27, 28, 31, 37, 40, 47, 72, 103, 105, 167, 176, 180
  Real-time 2, 3, 6, 13, 118
  Respoken 8, 17, 22, 25, 26, 27, 28, 30, 32, 35, 36, 38, 40, 44, 54, 66, 70, 103, 108, 109, 110, 112, 116, 117, 118, 119, 121, 125, 126, 138, 142, 150, 161, 162, 163, 165, 166, 168, 171, 172, 174, 175, 177
  Scrolling 17, 25, 26, 28, 29, 35, 38, 40, 44, 66, 67, 108, 167, 168, 169, 170, 171, 172, 175, 178
  Semi-live 8, 12, 24, 26, 28, 29, 31, 32, 35, 36, 38, 39, 40, 89, 138, 144, 181
  Software 1, 2, 17, 22, 24, 31, 34, 37, 39, 40, 51, 70
  Sound information 17, 20, 25, 26, 28, 30, 32, 37, 38, 40, 98, 99
  Speed 16, 113, 115, 116, 117, 165
  Verbatim 1, 8, 16, 17, 30, 35, 38, 61, 97, 110, 112, 113, 116, 117, 118, 119, 144, 152, 165, 178
Surtitling 138, 146
SWISS TXT 30, 31, 32, 33, 34, 44, 162
Synchrony   109, 118, 178

T

Tandem 7, 8, 13, 179, 181
Technique du perroquet 3, 179, 180, 181
Teletext 6, 10, 21, 180
TF1 2, 3, 8, 16, 35, 36, 44
Torres Monreal, Santiago 115, 166
Transcription 2, 7, 9, 13, 15, 19, 23, 38, 57, 69, 70, 72, 101, 103, 177, 178, 179, 182
Translation 2, 4, 22, 26, 31, 38, 40, 41, 44, 45, 46, 48, 56, 71, 72, 97, 117, 138, 147, 148, 163, 166, 177, 179
TransMedia Catalonia 143, 162
Tuominen, Tiina 163
TV2 13, 34, 35
TVA 40, 41

U

Uglova, Natalia 114
Universidade de Vigo 149
Universitat Autònoma de Barcelona (UAB) 40, 44, 143, 144
User profile 25, 41, 49, 75, 76, 78, 84, 86, 93, 94

V

Van Dam, Ine-Marie 107
Van der Veer, Bart 2, 3, 46, 48, 49

Velotype 7, 8, 11, 13, 14, 15, 28, 181
Viascribe 63, 64, 69, 71, 72, 101, 141, 147
Viavoice 2, 17, 24, 25, 26, 28, 30, 31, 34, 39, 41, 50, 59, 61, 63, 64, 65, 66, 67, 68, 72, 76, 78, 80, 86, 88, 93, 172
Videoguide 141, 142
Vincent, Keith 2
Voice recognition 56, 181, 182
Voice writing 2, 7, 38, 39, 40, 42, 84, 182
VTA 38, 44
VTM 1, 8, 13, 16, 28, 29, 30, 32, 38, 43, 89

W

Weather 6, 20, 21, 26, 35, 92, 97, 114, 116, 118, 125, 126, 129, 130, 135, 136, 165
Webcasts 39, 42, 144, 145, 146, 148
Windows Speech Recognition (WSR) 2, 64, 65, 68, 72, 74, 93
Wingfield, Arthur 114
Wolverton, Gary S. 166
Words per Minute (WPM) 7, 8, 13, 15, 16, 20, 39, 40, 42, 113, 114, 115, 116, 117, 118, 120, 123, 126, 129, 130, 134, 135, 140, 145, 156, 157, 163, 164, 165, 182

Z

Zola, David 166

TRANSLATION PRACTICES EXPLAINED

Available Titles in the Series

Volume 1: *Introduction to Court Interpreting*, by Holly Mikkelson

Volume 2: *Electronic Tools for Translators*, by Frank Austermühl

Volume 3: *Revising and Editing for Translators*, by Brian Mossop

Volume 4: *Legal Translation Explained*, by Enrique Alcaraz and Brian Hughes

Volume 5: *Translating for the European Union Institutions*, by Emma Wagner, Svend Bech and Jesús M. Martínez

Volume 6: *Conference Interpreting Explained*, by Roderick Jones

Volume 7: *Translating Official Documents*, by Roberto Mayoral Asensio

Volume 8: *Note-taking for Consecutive Interpreting – A Short Course*, by Andrew Gillies

Volume 9: *Medical Translation Step by Step – Learning by Drafting*, by Vicent Montalt and Maria Gonzalez Davis

Volume 10: *A Handbook for Translator Trainers*, by Dorothy Kelly

Volume 11: *Audiovisual Translation: Subtitling*, by Jorge Díaz Cintas and Aline Remael

Volume 12: *Translating Promotional and Advertising Texts*, by Ira Torresi